# THE
# HISTORY OF
# VIETNAM

ADVISORY BOARD

# THE
# HISTORY OF
# VIETNAM

## Justin Corfield

The Greenwood Histories of the Modern Nations
*Frank W. Thackeray and John E. Findling, Series Editors*

**Greenwood Press**
Westport, Connecticut • London

**Library of Congress Cataloging-in-Publication Data**

Corfield, Justin J.
   The history of Vietnam / Justin Corfield.
      p. cm. — (The Greenwood histories of the modern nations, ISSN 1096–2905)
   Includes bibliographical references and index.
   ISBN-13: 978–0–313–34193–9 (alk. paper)
   1. Vietnam—History.   I. Title.
   DS556.5.C67   2008
   959.7—dc22         2007049596

British Library Cataloguing in Publication Data is available.

Library of Congress Catalog Card Number: 2007049596
ISBN: 978–0–313–34193–9
ISSN: 1096–2905

First published in 2008

Greenwood Press, 88 Post Road West, Westport, CT 06881
An imprint of Greenwood Publishing Group, Inc.
www.greenwood.com

Printed in the United States of America

The paper used in this book complies with the
Permanent Paper Standard issued by the National
Information Standards Organization (Z39.48–1984).

10 9 8 7 6 5 4 3 2 1

# Contents

Series Foreword
    *Frank W. Thackeray and John E. Findling*               vii

Preface           ix

Abbreviations           xiii

Timeline of Historical Events           xv

1      Vietnam until the Tay Son Rebellion           1

2      The Nguyen Dynasty (1780–1887)           15

3      The French Protectorate (1887–1945)           25

4      From 1945 until the Geneva Agreements
      (1945–1954)           39

5      From Geneva Agreements to the Start of War
      (1954–1960)           57

6   From the Formation of Vietcong to U.S. Soldiers
    (1960–1965)                                                65

7   From U.S. Involvement to Tet Offensive
    and Death of Ho Chi Minh (1965–1969)                        77

8   From the Death of Ho Chi Minh to
    Reunification (1969–1976)                                   93

9   From Reunification until the Withdrawal
    from Cambodia (1976–1989)                                  103

10  Vietnam Today (1989–Present)                               115

Notable People in Vietnam since 1945                          127

Selected Bibliography                                         139

Index                                                        143

# Series Foreword

The *Greenwood Histories of the Modern Nations* series is intended to provide students and interested laypeople with up-to-date, concise, and analytical histories of many of the nations of the contemporary world. Not since the 1960s has there been a systematic attempt to publish a series of national histories, and, as editors, we believe that this series will prove to be a valuable contribution to our understanding of other countries in our increasingly interdependent world.

Over thirty years ago, at the end of the 1960s, the Cold War was an accepted reality of global politics, the process of decolonization was still in progress, the idea of a unified Europe with a single currency was unheard of, the United States was mired in a war in Vietnam, and the economic boom of Asia was still years in the future. Richard Nixon was president of the United States, Mao Tse-tung (not yet Mao Zedong) ruled China, Leonid Brezhnev guided the Soviet Union, and Harold Wilson was prime minister of the United Kingdom. Authoritarian dictators still ruled most of Latin America, the Middle East was reeling in the wake of the Six-Day War, and Shah Reza Pahlavi was at the height of his power in Iran. Clearly, the past 30 years have been witness to a great deal of historical change, and it is to this change that this series is primarily addressed.

With the help of a distinguished advisory board, we have selected nations whose political, economic, and social affairs mark them as among the most important in the waning years of the twentieth century, and for each nation we have found an author who is recognized as a specialist in the history of that nation. These authors have worked most cooperatively with us and with Greenwood Press to produce volumes that reflect current research on their nations and that are interesting and informative to their prospective readers.

The importance of a series such as this cannot be underestimated. As a superpower whose influence is felt all over the world, the United States can claim a "special" relationship with almost every other nation. Yet many Americans know very little about the histories of the nations with which the United States relates. How did they get to be the way they are? What kind of political systems have evolved there? What kind of influence do they have in their own region? What are the dominant political, religious, and cultural forces that move their leaders? These and many other questions are answered in the volumes of this series.

The authors who have contributed to this series have written comprehensive histories of their nations, dating back to prehistoric times in some cases. Each of them, however, has devoted a significant portion of the book to events of the last thirty years, because the modern era has contributed the most to contemporary issues that have an impact on U.S. policy. Authors have made an effort to be as up-to-date as possible so that readers can benefit from the most recent scholarship and a narrative that includes very recent events.

In addition to the historical narrative, each volume in this series contains an introductory overview of the country's geography, political institutions, economic structure, and cultural attributes. This is designed to give readers a picture of the nation as it exists in the contemporary world. Each volume also contains additional chapters that add interesting and useful detail to the historical narrative. One chapter is a thorough chronology of important historical events, making it easy for readers to follow the flow of a particular nation's history. Another chapter features biographical sketches of the nation's most important figures in order to humanize some of the individuals who have contributed to the historical development of their nation. Each volume also contains a comprehensive bibliography, so that those readers whose interest has been sparked may find out more about the nation and its history. Finally, there is a carefully prepared topic and person index.

Readers of these volumes will find them fascinating to read and useful in understanding the contemporary world and the nations that comprise it. As series editors, it is our hope that this series will contribute to a heightened sense of global understanding as we embark on a new century.

*Frank W. Thackeray and John E. Findling*
*Indiana University Southeast*

# Preface

Many books have been written about aspects of Vietnamese history, especially ists recent history; and there is intense historical, and indeed political, debate over a large number of areas. For many people outside the country, Vietnam's history is immutably tied to the Vietnam War because of its portrayal in countless films and documentaries. The views of these people, and also of many writers and commentators, vary considerably with the experiences of their own country in the war. In the United States, the period of the war largely covers the period of the major U.S. involvement, from 1957 until 1975, with many Americans either having fought in the war themselves or knowing somebody who has. For Americans, Khe Sanh, the Tet Offensive, and the Cu Chi Tunnels represent different examples of the U.S. experience in the war. For Australians, discussions of the war concern both the fighting at Long Tan and other places, and also the vast antiwar movement that was mobilized in the early 1970s in Australia, as well as the writing of Denis Warner and Morris West. The French focus on the war is largely the period of French colonial power, culminating in their defeat at Dien Bien Phu, or the war as depicted in the novels of Jean Hougron. In Malaysia, Singapore, Thailand, and the Philippines—the latter two countries supplying soldiers for the war effort—the governments of these four U.S. allies in the region saw the defeat of the United States in Vietnam as the continuation of the "Domino Theory," by which they, too, could have become communist countries. Even in many parts of French Africa, there were politicians and soldiers who served in the Vietnam War, and by the time the war was over, there were few countries in the world that did not have Vietnam War veterans or a Vietnamese expatriate community.

For the Vietnamese, even though the Vietnam War and the earlier Indochina War against the French overshadow the recent history of the country, the wars came as the culmination of many centuries of occupation—ten centuries of occupation by the Chinese, followed by attacks and occupation by Mongols, Chinese, French, and Japanese. The U.S. presence in the country remains controversial, as the United States never planned to occupy the country, as previous powers had. U.S. intervention, and also that of their allies, was in response to a request from the South Vietnamese government, although detractors challenge the legitimacy of that government. This leads to the most contentious aspect of Vietnam's history, which focuses on the status of the pro-French governments of Vietnam from 1945 until 1954, and the government of the Republic of Vietnam from 1955 until 1975.

This book details the history of the war and highlights the inadequacies of both the South Vietnamese and North Vietnamese governments to deal with major issues in the 1950s, leading to the Vietnam War during the 1960s and early 1970s, which left the country devastated. I have drawn heavily from many of the books on Vietnam, but my understanding of Vietnam is greatly influenced by Stanley Karnow's *Vietnam*, and his 13-episode *Vietnam: A Television History*. The work of William Duiker, Arnold R. Isaacs, David Marr, Ralph Smith, and Denis Warner, has also been important, as have dozens of other books listed in the bibliography and articles too numerous to list. I have only the vaguest recollections of seeing the fall of Saigon on the television news when it took place, but as a teenager I remember well going to various libraries in London to search out more information on the war, and indeed as a 15-year-old, knocking on the door of Nguyen Van Thieu's house just outside London in the hope of interviewing him.

At the University of Hull, my supervisor, David Bassett, inspired me in my fascination with Southeast Asian history, as he had done for my mother so many years before. Clive Christie took me through Vietnamese history, involving me in constant discussions and debates with my colleagues, especially Jake Glanville and Paul Schoen. Although we never agreed on certain aspects of the war, their views have been important. At Monash University, I completed my doctoral thesis on Cambodia from 1970 until 1975, and my view of Vietnam during this period draws heavily from my research in the Cambodian and French press. Discussions with Anne Blair, David Chandler, John Leary, Jefferson Lee, and many others were fruitful and interesting. At Geelong Grammar School, I have enjoyed discussions with countless students over the years about aspects of the Vietnam War, and many have contributed to my knowledge. Three I must mention are Panu Wongcha-Um who provided me important information on the Thai contribution to the Vietnam War, and Simon and James Stanistreet who told me much about the Australian Medical Corps during the war, in which their grandfather had served. The questions of many others have inspired me to read more deeply about the country, in the hope of being able to answer more points, but often only raising further questions. I must also thank Pat Burke who was a great help as a guide to me in Hanoi. I have also gained much from discussions with Lee Allen about her many visits to Vietnam and deep love of the country, as well as information provided by Bill Ward-Moss. Finally, this book could not have been written without the support and encouragement of my father.

All the research could never make up for visiting Vietnam, which I have been fortunate to have done on two occasions. This has allowed me to visit many of the sites connected with the war, using Ho Chi Minh City, Hue, and Hanoi as bases. There is little that can prepare one for the devastation in areas that have been bombed and/or defoliated, the sadness of the destruction of so much of the Imperial City in Hue, the isolation of the base at Khe Sanh, the beauty of the old city at Hanoi, or the emotional impact of wandering through the Presidential Palace in Ho Chi Minh City and visiting the Church of St François Xavier where Ngo Dinh Diem and Ngo Dinh Nhu attended their last mass before they were murdered.

# Abbreviations

ARVN    Army of the Republic of (South) Vietnam
ASEAN   Association of Southeast Asian Nations
CIA     (United States) Central Intelligence Agency
COSVN   Central Office of (Communist) South Vietnam
CPV     Communist Party of Vietnam
DRV     Democratic Republic of (North) Vietnam
ICP     Indochina Communist Party
NFL     National Front for the Liberation of South Vietnam
PAVN    People's Army of Vietnam
PLAF    People's Liberation Armed Forces
PRG     Provisional Revolutionary Government of the Republic of South
        Vietnam
RVN     Republic of (South) Vietnam
SRV     Socialist Republic of Vietnam
SVN     (Associated) State of Vietnam
VNQDD   Vietnam Quoc Dan Dang (Vietnamese Nationalist Party)
VWP     Vietnam Workers' Party

# Timeline of Historical Events

| | |
|---|---|
| 9000–7000 B.C.E. | Hoa Bin Culture |
| 3000 | End of the Bac Son Culture |
| 2500–1500 | Phung Nguyen Culture |
| 111 | Han Dynasty of China conquers Vietnam |
| 39–43 C.E. | Revolt of the Trung Sisters against Chinese rule |
| 248 | Revolt led by lady Trieu against the Chinese |
| 939 | After the battle of Bach Dang, Ngo Quyen proclaimed king of Vietnam |
| 982 | Fall of the Cham capital Indrapura to the Vietnamese |
| 1009 | Emperor Ly Cong Uan founds the Ly Dynasty |
| 1010 | Vietnamese move capital to Thang Long (now Hanoi) |
| 1070 | The Temple of Literature in Hanoi built |
| 1125 | Tran Thu Do founds the Tran Dynasty |
| 1257 | Mongols attack Vietnam for the first time |

| | |
|---|---|
| 1284 | Mongols attack Vietnam for the second time |
| 1400 | Ho Quy Ly founds the short-lived Ho Dynasty |
| 1418 | Le Loi launches the Lam Son Rebellion against the Chinese |
| 1428 | Le Loi founds the Le Dynasty |
| 1527 | Foundation of the Mac Dynasty |
| 1592 | Restored Le Dynasty in Hanoi |
| 1627 | Alexandre de Rhodes arrives in Hanoi at the start of a civil war between the Trinh and the Nguyen |
| 1692 | Vietnamese annex Champa |
| 1698 | Traditional date for the foundation of Saigon (now Ho Chi Minh City) |
| 1771 | Start of the Tay Son Rebellion |
| 1786 | Forces of the Tay Son capture Hanoi |
| 1787 | Ngugen Anh reaches an agreement with the French with the Treaty of Versailles |
| 1788 | Start of rule of the Tay Son, which ends in 1802 |
| 1802 | Final defeat of the Tay Son rebels; Nguyen Anh founds the Nguyen Dynasty and becomes the Emperor Gia Long |
| 1807 | Vietnamese establish a protectorate over much of Cambodia |
| 1820 | Death of Emperor Gia Long; proclamation of his son as the Emperor Minh Mang |
| 1841 | Death of the Emperor Minh Mang; proclamation of his son as the Emperor Thieu Tri |
| 1848 | Death of Emperor Thieu Tri; proclamation of his son as Emperor Tu Duc |
| 1858 | French and Spanish ships attack Danang |
| 1859 | French start taking control of territory in the Mekong Delta |

| | |
|---|---|
| 1861 | French troops defeat the Vietnamese at the battle of Ky Hoa near Saigon (modern-day Ho Chi Minh City) |
| 1862 | Vietnamese Emperor cedes three provinces in South Vietnam to the French in the Treaty of Saigon |
| 1867 | French take over the whole of southern Vietnam (Cochinchina) |
| 1883 | Death of Emperor Tu Duc; proclamation of his nephew and adopted son as Emperor Duc Duc, who signs the Harmand Treaty acknowledging the French protectorate over Annam and Tonkin, and is overthrown and killed soon afterward; his uncle becomes the Emperor Hiep Hoa but is murdered and is succeeded by his nephew who becomes the Emperor Kien Phuc |
| 1884 | Death of Emperor Kien Phuc who is succeeded by his brother who becomes Emperor Ham Nghi |
| 1885 | Emperor Ham Nghi deposed by the French and flees to northern Vietnam to lead the Can Vuong Movement; his brother becomes Emperor Dong Khanh |
| 1887 | French establish the Indochinese Union, formed from Vietnam, Cambodia, and Laos |
| 1889 | Death of Emperor Dong Khanh; his cousin becomes Emperor Thanh Thai |
| 1907 | Death of Emperor Thanh Thai; his son becomes Emperor Duy Tan |
| 1912 | Nationalist Phan Boi Chau forms the Modernization Movement |
| 1916 | Death of Emperor Duy Tan; his cousin becomes Emperor Khai Dinh |
| 1917 | Thai Nguyen Rebellion in northern Vietnam |
| 1919 | Ho Chi Minh petitions the Versailles Peace Conference for independence for Vietnam |
| 1925 | Phan Boi Chau arrested by the French in Shanghai and deported to Vietnam where he is placed under house arrest; death of Emperor Khai Dinh; his son becomes Emperor Bao Dai |

| | |
|---|---|
| 1927 | Nguyen Thai Hoc forms the Vietnamese Nationalist Party (VNQDD) in Saigon with support from the Chinese Nationalist Party |
| 1929 | Vietnamese Communist exiles in Hong Kong hold the National Congress of the Revolutionary Youth League (precursor to the Indochina Communist Party) |
| 1930 | Establishment, in Hong Kong, of the Communist Party of Vietnam (CPV); Vietnamese Nationalist Party involved in the Yen Bay Revolt against the French; CPV renamed the Indochina Communist Party (ICP) |
| 1931 | French manage to arrest some of the ICP leadership; Ho Chi Minh is arrested in Hong Kong |
| 1932 | Emperor Bao Dai returns to Vietnam from France and assumes the imperial powers |
| 1933 | Ho Chi Minh is released from prison in Hong Kong and goes to the Soviet Union |
| 1935 | ICP hold sits first national congress at Macau |
| 1936 | French elections result in the formation of a Popular Front Government and the release from detention in Vietnam of many of the Communists held at Poulo Condore and other places |
| 1938 | Ho Chi Minh moves from the Soviet Union to China |
| 1939 | The Hoa Hao religious sect is established; World War II begins |
| 1940 | Fall of France to the Germans; Japanese start moving soldiers into Vietnam |
| 1941 | Start of the Pacific War |
| 1943 | Ho Chi Minh, arrested in South China in the previous year, is released from prison and starts organizing the communists in Vietnam |
| 1945 | Japanese end French administration; Emperor Bao Dai proclaims Vietnamese independence; famine in central Vietnam; Japan surrenders; communists take control of northern Vietnam; Emperor Bao Dai abdicates; British |

|            | forces arrive in Saigon to help restore French colonial rule; fighting begins |
|------------|---|
| 1946       | Vietnamese communists go to France for negotiations; French ships bombard the port of Haiphong, precipitating war |
| 1947–1948  | French try to persuade Bao Dai to become the figurehead leader of pro-French government in Vietnam |
| 1949       | Elysée Agreement forms the Associated State of Vietnam with some measure of independence; Bao Dai becomes head of state of the new entity; Chinese Communists win the Chinese Civil War |
| 1950       | Communist China and the Soviet Union proclaim their support for the Communist-led Democratic Republic of Vietnam; start of the Korean War; United States provides military aid to the French in Vietnam 1951 Viet Minh is defeated by the French |
| 1952       | French forced to evacuate the northern border region, allowing the Viet Minh to bring supplies from China |
| 1953       | French adopt the Navarre Plan to win the war; establish base at Dien Bien Phu |
| 1954       | French forces at Dien Bien Phu forced to surrender; Great Powers at Geneva, Switzerland, agree on the partition of Vietnam; Ngo Dinh Diem becomes prime minister of the Associated State of Vietnam |
| 1955       | Ngo Dinh Diem establishes the Republic of Vietnam (South Vietnam) after winning referendum by which Bao Dai is deposed |
| 1956       | Turmoil in North Vietnam during its attempt to implement land reform program; Communist Party General Secretary Truong Chinh is demoted |
| 1957       | Rising discontent in South Vietnam over the Ngo Dinh Diem government |
| 1960       | Failed coup attempt against Ngo Dinh Diem; formation of the National Front for the Liberation of South Vietnam |

1961            U.S. government declares its continued support for South
                Vietnam, with Vice President Lyndon Johnson visiting
                Saigon

1963            Buddhist crisis in South Vietnam leads to the self-
                immolation of monks; military coup d'état leads to the
                overthrow of Ngo Dinh Diem, who is killed

1964            Political instability in South Vietnam during the entire
                year; Tonkin Gulf "incidents"; U.S. Congress passes
                Tonkin Gulf Resolution; Lyndon Johnson wins U.S.
                presidential elections

1965            First U.S. combat soldiers arrive in Vietnam; Nguyen
                Van Thieu and Nguyen Cao Ky seize power in Saigon;
                U.S. forces defeat North Vietnamese at the Battle of the
                Ia Drang Valley

1967            Elected Constituent Assembly in South Vietnam intro-
                duces new national constitution; Nguyen Van Thieu
                wins presidential elections

1968            Tet Offensive launched by the Communists in Saigon,
                Hue, and elsewhere; Richard Nixon wins U.S. presidential
                elections

1969            U.S. government begin secret peace talks with North Vi-
                etnam in Paris; South Vietnamese Communists form the
                Provisional Government of the Republic of South Viet-
                nam (PRG)

1970            In an attempt to destroy the Ho Chi Minh Trail, U.S. and
                South Vietnamese forces enter Cambodia; students shot
                dead during demonstrations at Kent State University,
                Ohio

1971            Presidential elections in South Vietnam see Nguyen Van
                Thieu reelected unopposed

1972            U.S. presidential election campaign while North Viet-
                nam stalls at the Peace Talks in Paris; Richard Nixon ree-
                lected; Nixon orders the "Christmas Bombing" of North
                Vietnam

1973            Paris Peace Accord signed, with the United States with-
                drawing their forces from Vietnam

| | |
|---|---|
| 1974 | Ceasefire agreements break down with fighting between North Vietnamese and South Vietnamese |
| 1975 | Communists launch a massive offensive against the South Vietnamese army, leading to their capture of Danang; South Vietnamese President Nguyen Van Thieu resigns as president; his successor, Tran Van Huong, also resigns a week later; Duong Van Minh sworn in as president and surrenders to the North Vietnamese |
| 1976 | Elections held in all parts of Vietnam; creation of the Socialist Republic of Vietnam; the Vietnamese Communists change the name of their party to the Communist Party of Vietnam |
| 1978 | Vietnamese government nationalizes many privately held assets throughout the country; refugees flee Vietnam, many by boat; SRV signs Treaty of Friendship and Cooperation with the Soviet Union; Communist Cambodia attacks Vietnam; Vietnamese soldiers invade Cambodia |
| 1979 | Vietnamese army captures most of Cambodia and installs pro-Vietnamese People's Republic of Kampuchea; China invades northern Vietnam and withdraws |
| 1980 | The SRV institutes its new constitution; Phan Tuan becomes the first Vietnamese to go into space |
| 1982 | Anti-Vietnamese rebels in Cambodia form the Coalition Government of Democratic Kampuchea to fight the Vietnamese |
| 1986 | Le Duan, general secretary of the Communist Party of Vietnam, dies and is replaced by Truong Chinh who is later replaced by Nguyen Van Linh |
| 1987 | Some of the old guard, including Truong Chinh and Pham Van Dong, resign; Vo Chi Cong and Pham Hung appointed to be chief of state and prime minister, respectively |
| 1988 | Death of Truong Chinh and Pham Hung |
| 1989 | Vietnam withdraws its soldiers from Cambodia |
| 1990 | Death of Le Duc Tho; Vietnam embarks on major economic reforms |

1991          End of the Soviet Union; Paris Peace Agreement ends war in Cambodia; Do Muoi takes over as general secretary of the Communist Party of Vietnam from Nguyen Van Linh

1992          Vietnamese government revises the constitution, lessening the importance of Marxism-Leninism

1994          United States ends its trade embargo with Vietnam

1995          United States and Vietnam agree to establish diplomatic relations; Vietnam joins the Association of Southeast Asian Nations (ASEAN)

1996          Eight Party Congress of the Communist Party of Vietnam; reelection of Le Duc Anh, Do Muoi, and Vo Van Kiet

1997          Vietnam undertakes two devaluations of its currency, and large numbers of tourists start visiting the country; Tran Duc Luong becomes president; and Phan Van Khai becomes prime minister; Le Kha Phieu becomes general secretary of the CPV

1998          Vietnam hosts its first ASEAN summit

1999          CPV embarks on a policy of self-criticism; Vietnam and United States draw up Bilateral Trade Agreement (BTA)

2000          BTA signed; Ho Chi Minh Stock Exchange opens; U.S. President Bill Clinton visits Vietnam, the first visit from a serving U.S. President

2001          Nong Duc Manh becomes general secretary of the CPV; Russian leader Vladimir Putin visits Vietnam, the first by a Russian leader since the collapse of the Soviet Union

2002          Massive Nam Cam scandal leads to trial of those involved; large increase in tourism to Vietnam

2003          U.S. frigate visits Vietnam, the first U.S. warship since 1975; Vietnam hosts South East Asian Games

2004          International Monetary Fund terminates main aid program to Vietnam after it is not allowed to audit the foreign exchange reserves of the state bank

2005                    Hanoi Stock Exchange opens; Premier Phan Van Khai vis-
                       its the United States

2006                    Vietnam hosts the APEC Annual Summit and was admit-
                       ted to the World Trade Organization; Nguyen Minh Triet
                       becomes president of Vietnam and Nguyen Tan Dung be-
                       comes prime minister

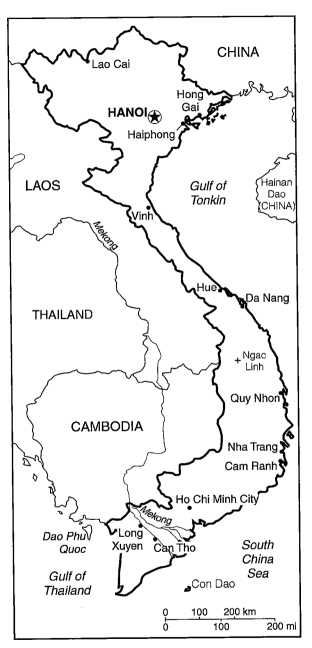

Vietnam today. Cartography courtesy of BookComp, Inc.

# 1

# Vietnam until the Tay Son Rebellion

## THE ORIGINS OF VIETNAM

The ancient history of Vietnam was recorded by the Chinese and later by the French—the latter being heavily involved in archaeological work throughout the country during the century of their occupation. Intense curiosity during that period about anthropology and archaeology has been renewed in recent years.

Archaeologists working in Vietnam have found remains of humans from as far back as the Paleolithic era (c.10,000 B.C.E.), but little else is known for certain about this period. Some anthropologists have linked the cultural traits of the Vietnamese to the people whom archaeologists have found living along the coast of southern China, from the Yangtze River to the border of modern-day Vietnam during the first millennium B.C.E. Others see them as coming from south central China, migrating to the Red River Delta at a later stage. Ethnographers see links between several customs of the Vietnamese and other Southeast Asians, tending to suggest that if they did come from China, their migration could have been the result of a failure to assimilate with the Han Chinese. Certainly there are links between these early tribes and the Muong, the hill tribes of modern-day Vietnam, with the differences between most Vietnamese and the Muong explained by the myths that surround the legendary figures Lac Long Quang and Au Co, and their separation, although these are clearly representations to explain differences which arose long before recorded history.

Linguists tend to agree with the premise that the Vietnamese and the Muong have a common ancestry, as the Vietnamese language has been shown to be a fusion of the languages of the region, with some words from the monotonic Mon-Khmer, basic words adapted from Tai (Thai), and the tones and grammar from Chinese. Certainly most of the literary, political, philosophical, and technical vocabulary is drawn from the Chinese language. Analysis of these latter terms has taken place only recently, however, and the influence of Chinese rule over the country for nearly 1,000 years would go a long way to explain the latter.

In about 9000–7000 B.C.E., a culture flourished close to the modern-day city of Hoa Binh, in the remote northwest of present-day Vietnam. Discovered in 1927, it has become known as the Hoa Binh culture, distinguishable because of the chipping of large numbers of stones to make implements for hunting, for preparing foods and skins, and also for agriculture. There is some evidence of the cultivation of plants and the making of pottery, but much of the latter is identified with the later "Bac Son culture" (or "late Hoa Binhian culture"), which flourished in the same region. These people used stones to fashion into axes. This culture lasted until 3000 B.C.E.

The Phung Nguyen culture thrived in the mountains north of the Red River Delta from 2500–1500 B.C.E., and it definitely involved the use of slash-and-burn agriculture, the domestication of animals, and houses made from wood and bamboo and raised on stilts. Decorated pottery also exists that was made with the use of some bronze implements, thus marking the start of the Bronze Age in Vietnam. That culture developed into the Dong Son period, which started about 600 B.C.E., and is noted for the manufacture of large bronze drums. Initially, it was thought that the drums had been imported from either China, or even Europe, but it is now clear that they were only one element in the Vietnamese Bronze Age, which included the manufacture of agricultural implements such as ploughs and weapons.

It was from these cultures that the semi-legendary Hung kings of Vietnam came. Vietnamese tradition traces the origins to their country to King De Minh who descended from a divine Chinese ruler called Chen Nong, well known in China as the "father of Chinese agriculture." It was said that De Minh met an immortal woman who lived in the nearby mountains. They married and their son, Loc Duc (or Kinh Duong), became the ruler of Xich-Quy, the "land of the red devils." Loc Duc married the daughter of the Dragon Lord of the Sea, and their son, Lac Long Quang, became the Dragon Lord. The Chinese were nervous about the marriage, and so Lac Long Quang married Au Co, an immortal daughter of the Chinese emperor. She laid 100 eggs, from which were born

100 sons. From them descend the Vietnamese people who were known, in old poetry, as the "grandchildren of Lac." The couple did not remain together, however, as he was a dragon and she was a fairy. They decided to divide their sons. Au Co took 50 of them into the mountains, and Lac continued ruling the lowlands with the other 50. Lac's eldest son then founded the Hung Bang dynasty, which is said to have ruled Van Lang, "land of the tattooed men," from 2879 B.C.E. to 258 B.C.E.

When the Hung dynasty was overthrown in 258 C.E., the Kingdom of Au Lac was established in its stead by the warlord Thuc Phan. He united the land previously ruled by the Hungs with his own territory. It is not certain who Thuc Phan actually was; some suggest that he might have been the ruler of a kingdom set in the hills of northern Vietnam called Au Viet. Certainly when he defeated the Hung dynasty, he declared himself King An Duong and built a new capital at Coa Loa, set in the lowlands about 20 miles north of modern-day Hanoi. The citadel of Coa Loa was protected by three walls and guarded by many watchtowers.

An Duong relied on the support of the aristocrats known as the Lac Lords, but his kingdom did not last long. During the reign of the Chinese Emperor Chin Shih Huang Di, a Chinese commander called Trieu Da was sent by the emperor to subjugate the semi-independent kingdoms in the south of China. In 207 B.C.E., Trieu Da invaded Au Viet, and in the following year, when the Chinese Emperor died, Trieu Da decided to break away from China and form a new kingdom of his own, which he called Nam Viet ("Southern Viet"), with the capital at Guangzhou (formerly Canton). He established good relations with the new Han Dynasty in China, and most of the people in the kingdom were ethnic Vietnamese who had moved south of the Yangtze as the Chinese population expanded. Trieu Da and his descendants were involved in diplomatic brinkman-ship, and sometimes war, for the next hundred years. Nam Viet maintained its independence until 111 B.C.E. when the Han Emperor Wu Ti decided to invade.

## CHINESE RULE AND THE TRUNG SISTERS

The Chinese managed to conquer the Vietnamese people in what is now southern China and northern Vietnam with relative ease. Many of the Vietnamese villages were isolated so that the people were unable to form any cohesive military force capable of resisting the Chinese. As the Chinese people gradually moved south, so did the Vietnamese people, which meant that when the Han Chinese conquered them, the Vietnamese were living in what is now northern Vietnam.

Initially the Chinese ruled the Vietnamese through the existing landowners and military chiefs. Gradually, however, most of these rulers were steadily replaced by court-appointed functionaries who ruled the area that was divided into three provinces, which together contained 56 districts. According to a surviving Chinese document, the population was 981,375, a precise figure showing the semblance of an intrusive system of ruling. Tribute had to be paid to the Han imperial court, with taxes and labor duties required by the local administrators.

Altogether Chinese rule lasted nearly a thousand years, but during that time the Vietnamese managed to retain a significant degree of national identity. Their use of Chinese agricultural practices and other elements of Chinese civilization made the Vietnamese some of the most intensive cultivators of the region. This period saw the introduction of buffalo to help plough and till the fields, as well as to pull carts. The Vietnamese may have had two annual rice crops before the Chinese. Certainly during the Chinese occupation, they were able to manage this production rate.

Before the Chinese occupation, the Vietnamese had followed animist religious beliefs, with supernatural spirits often found within dangerous wild animals. This gradually gave way to Chinese Confucian practices such as ancestor worship and filial piety, combined with Taoism and later Buddhism. In addition, Chinese weaponry allowed for greater success in hunting and fishing. Bronze arrowheads were often treated with poison to make them more effective against animals such as elephants, whose ivory was traded with China in exchange for iron.

The position of most people during Chinese rule, however, had hardly changed. The hereditary Vietnamese lords were gradually replaced by Chinese lords, with the vast majority of the population remaining poor farmers, who were kept in a state of near serfdom. Many were also often called on to give their labor to make roads, build canals, and fashion harbors to improve communication and trade. This led to greater sinicizing of Vietnam through an increase in access to Chinese culture and customs. The Chinese greatly wanted access to the resources of Vietnam—ivory, pearls from the sea, and precious metals from small mines in the hills. They also saw ports in Vietnam as a convenient place for their ships to shelter from storms while traveling to and from the East Indies. Together with all of this, the taxes paid by the Vietnamese not only maintained the local bureaucracy but also provided wealth for the Chinese court. Although many of the Vietnamese aristocracy resented Chinese rule, it was not necessarily harsh.

In the first century C.E., there was a major change in the Chinese style of governing Vietnam. A local governor realized that the local Vietnamese nobility were eager to retain control of much of the area. His plan was to replace many of the local Vietnamese administrators with Chinese rulers. The Chinese prefect Su Ting introduced many other changes. No longer were Chinese customs and rites encouraged—they were now enforced and Taoism and Confucianism became obligatory. In addition, Chinese became the official language of the region. These changes seriously upset the nobility, but they clearly did not affect many of the peasants. The surviving documents of the period are in Chinese, but it seems likely that the educated Vietnamese administrative class would have to speak to the peasants in Vietnamese in the same way that European colonial powers were later to introduce their changes on the elite while the majority of the population continued with their own customs.

In 39 C.E., a nobleman, Thi Sach, complained about the demands made on the Vietnamese by the Chinese administration headed by Su Ting. Thi Sach was then arrested and executed, causing great consternation among the other Vietnamese lords. His wife, Trung Trac, the daughter of one of the "Lac Lords," along with her younger sister Trung Nhi, then raised the flag of rebellion. They gathered together local chieftains who supported them. The rebels then proclaimed Trung Trac as Queen of an independent Vietnamese kingdom and rallied together many nobles and peasants, forcing Su Ting to flee to China. After three years of Trung Trac's rule, a massive expeditionary force sent by the Chinese emperor arrived in Vietnam. It was commander by Ma Yuan, one of the best Chinese generals of the period who had the title "Tamer of Waters." Trung Trac was abandoned by many of her supporters, and she and her sister were both defeated in battle by the Chinese. They were both captured and executed, with stories from folklore often having them dying bravely in battle or committing suicide. Although the rebellion ended in failure and led to Chinese repression, it became recognized by later historians as the first great Vietnamese nationalist uprising.

The Chinese then responded to the rebellion by deposing many of the local nobles who had either supported the Trung sisters or whose loyalty was in doubt. They also increased the level of sinicization, with Vietnamese being written in the Chinese script. For nearly 900 years, Vietnam remained firmly under Chinese rule. There were some revolts and rebellions, but most did not seriously threaten Chinese rule as much as that by the Trung sisters. In 412, a revolt in China had led some of the defeated Chinese rebels to flee to Vietnam where they tried to stir up trouble. A much more important event took place when a nobleman, Ly Bi, an ethnic Chinese whose ancestors had fled to Vietnam, launched an attack on the local Chinese administrators in 542, defeating a Chinese army sent against him the next year. He then tried to establish an independent kingdom but was unable to stand up to a large Chinese army in 545–546. At his death in 548, one of his aides, Trieu Quang Phuc, took command of the rebels and managed to use the disturbances in China to carve out his own kingdom, which survived until 603.

While the Chinese dominated northern Vietnam, in central Vietnam, the Kingdom of Champa was established in 192 C.E., becoming heavily influenced by Indian culture by the fifth century C.E. It maintained extensive trade connections with Muslim Indian traders, and with them, the Arab world, leading the kings of Champa and eventually the population to embrace Islam. Champa also established some trade ties with China and gradually became a problematic southern neighbor to the Chinese and later to independent Vietnam.

With the coming to power of the Tang dynasty in China in 618, there was a concerted effort to colonize Vietnam, which became the Protectorate of Annam ("Pacified South"). During this period Confucianism, Taoism, and Buddhism began to permeate through the peasant villages and was embraced by most of the people of Vietnam. When the Tang dynasty in China fell in 907 c.e., Vietnamese rulers decided to try to break away, and in 931, Duong Dinh Nghe made himself a regional governor. After his murder, the battle for independence was continued by Ngo Quyen. The Chinese attempted to deal with this uprising by sending a large fleet. According to popular folklore, Ngo Quyen sank iron-tipped stakes in the riverbed through which the Chinese were to attack. The Chinese launched their attack at high tide, with the Vietnamese fending them off until low tide. In the battle of Bach Dang, the Vietnamese then threw their full weight against the Chinese who tried to flee but ran aground either on sandbanks or on the stakes.

## EARLY MEDIEVAL VIETNAM

The Ngo dynasty ruled in Vietnam from 939 to 965. Led by Ngo Quyen, the dynasty marked the first time after a thousand years of Chinese rule that the Vietnamese had been independent. The kingdom was unstable, however, with local nobles forming factions. When Ngo Quyen died in 944, he was succeeded by his brother-in-law Duong Tam Kha, who was also a son of Duong Dinh Nghe who had started the rebellion against the Chinese. Officially Duong Tam Kha was a regent for one of the sons of Ngo Quyen, but being the son of the originator of the revolt, he thought he should rule the new kingdom. The son of Ngo Quyen took control, however, deposing Duong Tam Kha, and in 950 declared himself Nam Tan Vuong (king of Southern China). He sent an unsuccessful mission to the emperor of China with tribute to try to enlist Chinese support, but instead was killed in battle in 963, and the country was split among 12 local chieftains. The next three years became known as the "Period of the 12 Warlords."

In 966, Dinh Bo Linh, a chieftain from the Red River Delta, seized power and declared himself the emperor of the new kingdom, Dai Co Viet. He moved the capital from Co Loa, where it had been throughout Chinese rule, to Hoa Lu and tried to build up an administrative elite to rule the new entity. His main problem was succession, and when he designated his youngest infant son Hang Lang, as his heir, his eldest son Lien had his youngest brother murdered. A few weeks later, assassins killed both Dinh Bo Linh and Lien, leaving only a middle brother, 5-year-old Toan. With the court in chaos, the Chinese Sung Empire raised an army to retake Vietnam. To forestall takeover, Le Hoan, a general in the army of Dinh Bo Linh—also rumored to be a lover of the queen—took power and established the Le Dynasty. Because there was a later Le Dynasty, the one established by Le Hoan became known as the Early Le Dynasty.

Le Hoan ruled for 25 years, much of which was dominated by wars. In 981, he managed to defeat the Sung Chinese when they invaded China. Le Hoan then turned his attention to the Kingdom of Champa (in modern-day central Vietnam), seizing some of the land and forcing the inhabitants to move their capital from Indrapura to Vijaya. Le Hoan died in 1005 and was succeeded by his son Le Long Binh. He killed many members of his family and died two years later, leaving an infant boy to inherit the throne. With so many members of Le Hoan's family having been killed, a palace mandarin, Ly Cong Uan, took power and founded the Ly Dynasty, which is often known as the Later Ly Dynasty to differentiate it from the brief rule of Ly Bi in 544–545.

## THE LY DYNASTY

The Later Ly Dynasty became the first major dynasty to establish itself after the end of Chinese rule. Much of the success occurred because the Ly rulers were able to avoid the bloody succession disputes of the previous short-lived dynasties. This in turn allowed them to establish a series of political and social institutions. The founder, Ly Cong Uan, took the dynastic name of Ly Thai To. He had grown up as an orphan, being raised in a Buddhist temple in modern-day Bac Ninh Province near modern-day Hanoi. He then became a palace guard at Hoa Lu, which Le Hoan had turned into his capital. Ly Cong Uan managed to become a mandarin and, when Le Long Binh died in 1009, he used intrigue to take control.

The major administrative change during the reign of Ly Thai To was to move the capital to Dai La, which later became Hanoi. He named it Thang Long (Soaring Dragon) after he claimed that when he approached the site, he saw a dragon rise in the clouds above the place. The move of the capital from the mountains, where its location had primarily been chosen for defensive reasons, to the banks of the Red River, where it could be a major center of trade, signified increased confidence in the new nation. This decision might also have been heavily influenced by the terrible succession crises that had wrecked the previous dynasties, thereby creating a new power base away from the problems at Co Loa and Hoa Lu.

Ly Phat Ma succeeded his father Ly Thai To in 1028 and ruled under the name Ly Thai Thong until 1054. During that time, he strengthened the power of the state and also established a strong army. He created the Thien Tu Binh ("Army of the Son of Heaven") to serve as an Imperial Guard and also introduced conscription on an organized scale. To erode the power of the nobility, he created a professional class. The nobles continued to be granted large tracts of land, but their holdings were no longer hereditary, although in practice many did hold land for many generations. Philosophically, Emperor Ly Thai Thong was a follower of a form of Buddhism not unlike the Japanese Zen. He was also a strong believer in Confucian values. During his reign, the country was regularly at war with Champa to the south, and the lands captured from them were given to the nobles. In the north, his armies fought the Nung tribal people.

The third emperor of the Ly dynasty was Ly Thanh Tong, the first of the rulers to have been born during the life of the dynasty. He changed the name of the empire to Dai Viet and continued centralizing the power of the state. In 1068, he launched an attack on Champa, capturing their king and sacking their capital. He released the king of Champa in exchange for three provinces, which cover the modern-day provinces of Quang Binh and Quang Tri. His great achievement was the construction of the Temple of Literature in Thang Long (Hanoi) to serve as a center of learning for the country, the training of officials, and the contemplation of Confucian values.

Ly Nhan Tong was only seven when his father Ly Thanh Tong died, and during the regency of the mandarin Ly Dao Thanh, in 1076, the first competitive civil service exams were introduced based on the Chinese model. Taking place in the Temple of Literature, it provided opportunities for both talented wealthy and poor students to have access to careers in government service. These reforms were quickly overshadowed by the Chinese Sung Dynasty decision to attack Vietnam. Taking advantage of the Regency to launch a land and sea attack on the new state, the Chinese soldiers were repulsed by General Ly Thuong Kiet, who threw up a defensive line north of Thang Long (Hanoi). The Chinese, unable to maintain their long supply lines, had to sue for a peace agreement. There was then a period of stability and Ly Nhan Tong died in 1127, after a reign of 56 years.

As Ly Nhan Tong died childless, his adopted son Sung Hieu Hau succeeded him as Emperor Ly Than Tong. He was 13 years old and his reign saw continued fighting with Champa, as well as some trouble with the Angkor Empire in modern-day Cambodia. Ly Than Tong died in 1137 at the age of 23, and his infant son, Ly Anh Tong, became the next emperor. During his reign, Vietnam prospered and started trading extensively with its former enemies Angkor and Champa. Beset by illnesses, however, Ly Anh Tong handed over power to To Hien Thanh, a well-respected general, and died the next year, in 1175, at age 37. His son and successor, Ly Cao Tong, was only three when he became emperor and the regency lasted only three years. There was instability at court and when Ly Cao Tong did gain his majority, he became corrupt. As a result, in 1208, Pham Du staged a rebellion, forcing the emperor to flee the capital. The emperor managed to gain the support of the Tran family and staged a comeback, retaking Thang Long (Hanoi).

In 1210, Ly Cao Tong died, with the dynasty very weak and the Tran family helping to control the court. Ly Hue Tong succeeded his father, and when he became the emperor, he married Tran Thi whom he made his queen. Frequently ill and battling depression, in 1224, he was eventually persuaded to commit suicide by his wife's cousin, Tran Thu Do. The emperor's daughter Phat Kim then became the Empress Ly Chieu Hoang with another of the Tran family, Tran Tu Khanh, as her regent. She was then married to the eight-year-old nephew of Tran Thu Do, who was then declared the Emperor Tran Thai Tong, starting the Tran Dynasty in 1225.

## THE TRAN DYNASTY

Being a child when he became the Emperor Tran Thai Tong, the boy was dominated by his uncle Tran Thu Do. The scheming uncle managed to get the boy to divorce his wife and tried to force him to marry her elder sister who was already married to another member of the Tran family. In desperation, the adolescent fled to a Buddhist monastery, but was later persuaded to return to the palace where he reigned for 20 years. Although most of the country remained peaceful, there were some problems in the south with Champa, which was quickly defeated, and also in the north. In 1257, the new Chinese Emperor Kublai Khan demanded that the Mongol troops be allowed to enter Vietnam to strike at the Southern Sung—remnants of the previous dynasty. Tran Thai Tong refused and when the Mongols attacked, he was forced to flee Thang Long (Hanoi). The Mongols did not have enough men to hold the city, however, and, facing attacks on their supply lines, they retreated. Tran Thai Tong immediately abdicated the throne in favor of his son who was proclaimed the Emperor Tran Thanh Tong. He reigned for 20 years, with his father acting as his adviser for 19 of those years.

During the reign of Tran Thanh Tong, another threat came from the Mongols. Initially, the Vietnamese emperor decided to send tribute to the Mongol emperor, in the hope of avoiding war. He also massively strengthened the military. His reign, however, passed without the much anticipated attack from the north, and, in 1278, he abdicated in favor of his son, Emperor Tran Nhan Tong, acting as his royal adviser until he died in 1291.

The Mongols, who had established the Yüan Dynasty in China, finally decided to attack in 1279. They sent 300,000 soldiers into the Red River Delta region to try to restore full Chinese rule over the whole area. Tran Nhan Tong lost control of the capital, but waged a massive guerilla war against the invaders. The Mongols incurred so many casualties that they were forced to withdraw. In 1287, they attacked for a second time and were again driven back and were defeated at the second battle of Bach Dong. The Mongol weak point, for the third time, proved to be their supply lines, especially through the mountains that marked the Chinese-Vietnamese border. The Vietnamese commander-in-chief who defeated the Mongols was Tran Hung Dao; he is still revered for his brilliant defense strategies and his ability to wage a guerilla war against a foreign invader.

Tran Nhan Tong abdicated in 1293, in favor of his son, Tran Anh Tong, who managed to usher in a period of peace, not only with the Mongols, but also with the Chams. His daughter married the king of Champa, and peace was achieved in return for Champa ceding another two provinces. When the king of Champa died, Tran Nhan Tong refused permission for his daughter to be buried with her husband. The Chams saw this as a slight, which led to a major diplomatic incident and war. Although the Vietnamese were victorious, these wars had seriously weakened the country, which had lost many of its young men, as well as civilians in the fighting. Tran Minh Tong acceded to the throne when his father, as was by now the custom, abdicated. He tried to avoid war, but did launch an attack on Champa, seizing their capital in 1318. He was famous for issuing a decree to stop Vietnamese soldiers from being tattooed— many having the phrase "Death to the Mongols" marked on them. He was succeeded by his two sons, first Tran Hien Tong, and, when he died after a short reign, Tran Du Tong.

Tran Du Tong was an extravagant ruler, perhaps a trait made more obvious by his expenditure coinciding with a period of drought and disease. With the Yüan Dynasty in China collapsing, the Chams attacked the Vietnamese. In 1369, Tran Du Tong died without issue, and was succeeded by a younger brother Tran Nghe Tong who was, in turn, succeeded by Tran Due Tong, who was killed in battle in 1377. Tran Nghe Tong's son then became Emperor Tran Thuan Tong. He was deposed in 1398 and appealed to the Chinese for help.

## THE HO DYNASTY

Ho Quy Ly had emerged as a powerful court figure at the end of the Tran dynasty. Descended from a family that had migrated from China many generations earlier, he had married a cousin of the Emperor Tran Nghe Tong who then appointed him to the palace. During the 1380s, he had distinguished himself in commanding the Vietnamese armies in their fighting against the Chams. He was also a schemer and managed to influence the succession in the late 1380s. When he forced Tran Thuan Tong to abdicate in 1398, it was not long before he founded his own dynasty, assassinating Tran Thuan Tong soon afterwards.

Anxious about the succession, Ho Quy Ly abdicated after a year of being emperor in favor of his son, Ho Han Thuong, but he remained in actual power as his son's chief adviser. Although Ho was a usurper and keen on taking over power in the country, he was also anxious to reform the administration, and, within months of taking power, he had introduced reforms to the civil service, the administration, and the educational services, and reformed the system of raising taxes. He limited the amount of land that could be held by one person and redistributed the excess to poor peasants. It is possible that the support he built up in Vietnam might have led to a long and popular dynasty were it not for renewed Chinese intervention.

The new Ming dynasty in China decided to comply with the request of the last emperor of the Tran dynasty and, in 1407, invaded Vietnam. Although the Chinese stated that they planned to restore the Tran dynasty, they were actually interested in reestablishing Chinese rule over Vietnam. Ho Quy Ly was captured along with his son and senior officials, who were all taken to China. Ho, who was over 70 years old, was then conscripted into the Chinese army as a common soldier, where he died. Vietnam was once again ruled by the Chinese emperor from Beijing.

## THE LE DYNASTY

Chinese rule over Vietnam was unpopular and it was not long before rebel groups started to form. In 1418, a former Vietnamese imperial bureaucrat, Le Loi, staged a revolt. He took the title Binh Dinh Vuong ("Pacification King") and rallied his supporters for a battle with the Chinese. With other smaller guerilla and bandit bands roaming through Vietnam, it was not long before the Chinese decided to negotiate with some of them, and in 1423 reached a truce with Le Loi. When the Chinese Emperor Yung Lo died in 1424, Le Loi decided to attack and quickly won control of much of the land in the Red River Delta. In 1426, he defeated the Chinese forces near Hanoi, and two years later the Chinese left, leaving Le Loi in control of the country. Initially Le Loi had campaigned with the plan of restoring the Tran dynasty, and some of the family had accompanied him on his travels. With the final victory, however, he established himself as emperor and founded the Le Dynasty, which lasted from 1428 until, nominally at any rate, 1778.

Le Thai To, the second emperor of the Le dynasty, codified the legal system and promoted art, education, and literature. He also promoted better agricultural practices and prevented some powerful landowners from encroaching on communal land. As the population increased, the Le dynasty decided that territorial expansion would be the main way of accommodating landless people. The Chams had taken advantage of the fighting between the Vietnamese and the Chinese, and in 1446 they were able to retake Vijaya; however their successes were relatively short-lived. Under Le Thanh Ton (reigned 1460–1497), the greatest of the Le rulers, Champa was invaded for a final time and their capital Vijaya was sacked in 1471. Champa was then turned into a client state, with later rulers absorbing it into the Vietnamese Empire. Many of the soldiers started settling in the areas around Danang and Nha Trang, with subsequent incursions into Cambodian-held land in the Mekong Delta.

Le Thanh Ton then turned his attention to administrative reform and divided his empire into 13 parts. He instituted a national census, conducted an extensive geographical survey of the entire country, and introduced a new penal code known as the Hong Duc Code. This code, which had 721 articles, introduced heavy Confucian ethics into the civil and criminal laws. Containing six books, the Hong Duc Code remained in force until the nineteenth century. The Code granted women many rights including the right to own property and share equally with males in inheritance. Women were also recognized in common law marriages and even had some rights to gain a divorce from their husbands.

Between 1497 and 1527, ten kings came to the throne, four of them being usurpers. This great instability at court led a number of powerful landowners and mandarins to exert enormous power and amass vast wealth, the most prominent being the Nguyen family of Hue. The mandarin Nguyen Kim (d. 1545) helped the Le dynasty during the sixteenth century, and, when the military commander Mac Dang Dung established his Mac dynasty in 1527, the Trinh and the Nguyen families remained loyal to the Le. The Mac dynasty ruled in the northern part of Vietnam until 1591, when supporters of the Le seized the Mac capital at Thang Long (present-day Hanoi) and captured Mac Mao Hop, the last of the Mac dynasty, although some of his family managed to hold out at Cao Bang, along the Chinese border, until 1667 when they were finally defeated.

While the Mac dynasty had been able to establish itself in the northern part of Vietnam, the Nguyens consolidated the control of the south, a power vacuum having been created with the final destruction of Champa, and also the decline of the Khmer Empire at Angkor. In 1698, the city of Saigon was officially founded, and, by the mid-eighteenth century, most of modern-day southern Vietnam was ruled by the Le dynasty, but it was administered by the Nguyens, while the Le emperors became figureheads.

By 1757, Vietnam had reached its present size, with the exception of the province of Soc Trang, which was not annexed from Cambodia until 1840. The country was by no means unified, however, with the virtual partition of the country between the north, which supported the Mac, and the rest, which remained loyal to the Le. This division was perpetuated by the Trinh lords who had helped crush the Mac and then ruled northern Vietnam, although they continued to pay lip service to the Le emperors. The vast majority of the population was now ethnically Vietnamese, but there were also many Chinese, Khmer Krom (Cambodians in southern Vietnam), Muong tribesmen in the mountains, and the remnants of the Cham.

## THE TAY SON REBELLION

In the 1760s, there were some isolated peasant attacks on administrators of the Nguyen lords who controlled southern Vietnam. Initially the rebellions were leaderless and were fueled by resentment rather than by any major political goals. In 1771, however, three brothers raised the standard of revolt in the village of Tay Son, in modern-day Nghia Binh Province. The uprising became known as the Tay Son Rebellion and was specifically directed against the Nguyen lords and the way in which they were ruling their lands. Although the fighting started in the south, it quickly spread to central Vietnam and was soon imitated by other uprisings in the north. In 1785, the Tay Son rebels destroyed the Nguyen army sent against them, capturing Saigon; and in the next year, Nguyen Hye, the second of the three brothers, led an army into Thang Long (Hanoi). Nguyen Hue proclaimed that he wanted to restore the legitimacy of the emperor, Le Hien Tong, and the emperor gave his daughter in marriage to Nguyen Hue.

Le Hien Tong died in late 1786 and his grandson, Le Chien Tong, called on Chinese soldiers for help so that he would no longer have to rely on the support of the Tay Son brothers. In 1788, Chinese soldiers took Hanoi and Nguyen Hue replied by proclaiming himself the Emperor Quang Trung, launching a surprise attack on the Chinese soldiers who were forced to retreat into China. He established his capital at Phu Xuan (modern-day Hue) and sent tribute to China to try to placate the emperors of China. He also tried to improve the wealth of the country by promoting trade with European countries. A good administrator, Quang Trung died in 1792, at age 39, and was succeeded by his 10-year-old son Canh Thinh. This immediately weakened the new regime, and in 1802 the Nguyen lords were able to establish the Nguyen dynasty under Nguyen Anh, who in 1802 founded the Nguyen dynasty as Emperor Gia Long.

# 2

# The Nguyen Dynasty (1780–1887)

## EUROPEAN INFLUENCE IN VIETNAM

The reign of Gia Long, the first ruler of the Nguyen dynasty, saw increased foreign involvement in Vietnam. The first Europeans to arrive in the country had been Portuguese sailors who landed in 1516. Eleven years later some Dominican missionaries from Portugal came to Vietnam to seek converts to Christianity, and, in 1535, the Portuguese established a trading post at the city of Faifo (modern-day Hoi An) in central Vietnam. At that time Faifo had a significant Japanese population, which remained until 1637, when the Japanese government forbade any of its citizens to have contact with the outside world. At that time, most Japanese from Faifo returned to Japan.

By the time of the Tay Son rebellion, the French had become interested in trade with Vietnam. Alexander of Rhodes (1591–1660), a French missionary who had promoted Roman Catholicism in southern Vietnam, was responsible for writing the first Portuguese-Latin-Vietnamese dictionary and also developed a transliteration system for the Vietnamese language. This system would enable many French to study about Vietnam. In 1765, the French adventurer and missionary Pigneau de Béhaine arrived at Phu Quoc Island to reestablish a seminary that had been destroyed and some of the pupils murdered. Nevertheless, the intrepid priest kept going, and in 1770, to encourage his efforts,

Pope Clement XIV appointed him bishop of Adran, an ancient city in Asia Minor. The title was purely symbolic, but it helped give Pigneau increased prestige. Technically, the Portuguese still had a claim to the exclusive right to trade with Vietnam—at least as far as the papacy was concerned—and to have established a diocese there would invite diplomatic problems.

In 1775, Pigneau de Béhaine managed to make contact with Nguyen Anh who was believed to have fled to Phu Quoc. The bishop befriended the last member of the House of Nguyen and offered French greatly appreciated assistance against the Tay Son rebels. Although Pigneau did lobby the French authorities at Pondicherry in India, he soon decided that it would be best if Nguyen Anh accompanied him to France. Prince Canh, the son of Nguyen Anh, accompanied his father to the court of King Louis XVI in costume that was more Indian than Vietnamese, causing a sensation at Versailles. On November 28, 1787, the French foreign minister, Comte de Montmorin, signed a treaty giving Nguyen Anh 1,650 French officers and men, fully armed, in return for ceding the island of Poulo Condore and the port of Tourane (modern-day Da Nang).

The treaty was signed, but the French government had second thoughts and Louis XVI sent a message to Thomas de Conway, governor of Pondicherry, telling him that he need not provide the soldiers. While Conway was prevaricating, the outbreak of the French Revolution prevented France from involving itself too heavily in Asia. Pigneau de Béhaine, on his own account and with the support of French merchants, managed to organize some assistance, and Nguyen Anh was able to defeat the Tay Son.

Nguyen Anh had himself crowned the Emperor Gia Long in Hue on June 1, 1802, moving the capital of Vietnam to Hue and starting work on a vast palace complex, modeled on the Forbidden City in China, but more modest. The building focused on three structures. Work on the Kinh Thanh (Citadel) started in 1804, the site having been found auspicious by geomancers. Located on the northern bank of the Perfume River, the walls enclosed a large area, part of which was designated as the Imperial Enclosure, which contained within it the Forbidden Purple Palace. Tens of thousands of workers labored on the site and also on a lavish mausoleum that Gia Long built further up the Perfume River. By 1807, the Cot Co (flag tower), dominating the southern battlements, had been completed and the flagpole was erected. Outside the Ngo Mon Gate to the Imperial Enclosure, nine sacred cannons were placed symbolizing the five ritual elements (earth, fire, metal, wood, and water) and the four seasons. As with most Vietnamese and Chinese houses of the period, the buildings and walls from the southern Ngan Gate into the Thai Hoa Palace (the Palace of Supreme Harmony) in the Forbidden Purple Palace were staggered to confuse evil spirits.

Gia Long had renamed the empire Viet Nam, replacing the previous name Dai Viet. He was a Confucian in terms of his upbringing and had long been influenced by Chinese philosophy. With Chinese as the official language of Vietnam, Gia Long provided stability for a country that had been wracked by war for the previous 31 years. In 1815, he introduced the Gia Long Code, a penal code that replaced the Hong Duc Code and followed the Chinese legal approach, with less emphasis on local customs. Its central pillars were the maintenance of the power of the emperor and the Imperial Court and the provision of law and order for all the subject people. Gia Long died in 1820 and was succeeded by his second son, Emperor Minh Mang.

## EMPERORS MINH MANG AND THIEU TRI

In the year before Nguyen Anh had himself crowned as Gia Long in 1802, Prince Canh, his eldest surviving son, died. Undecided as to who should be his anointed successor, Nguyen Anh passed over the son of Prince Canh, settling instead on Minh Mang, the oldest son of his empress, Nhan Tuyen Tu Khanh-Thai. This decision was partly based on Minh Mang's own suspicion of the French, and Gia Long being worried about a boy emperor succeeding himself with the growing influence of the French.

Minh Mang was eager to reorganize the administration of the country so as to strengthen the power of the Nguyen dynasty. To do this he divided the country into 31 *tinh* (provinces), each of which was placed under the control of either a *tong duc* (governor) or a *tuan phu* (governor-general) who was appointed by, and loyal to, the central government in Hue. To improve the economy of the country, Ming Mang expanded the road network, and his local officials were encouraged to further irrigate the farmland to increase food production for a growing population. He also used some of the country's resources to enlarge the imperial palace complex at Hue, with the Ngo Mon gate into the Imperial Enclosure being rebuilt allowing for five entrances. The emperor alone was able to use the central entrance paved with stone; the mandarins and soldiers used the side entrances that were paved with brick.

The rise in population led to a foreign policy whereby Vietnam enlarged its borders at the expense of the Cambodians. Many of the Khmer Krom—ethnic Cambodians living in southern Vietnam—were forced off their land. From 1811 to 1812, the Vietnamese were involved in a war with the Siamese who contested Vietnamese influence in Cambodia. The death of King Ang Chan of Cambodia in 1834 led to another war after Queen Ang Mei came to the throne and ruled the country with Vietnamese advisers. In 1835, Cambodia was annexed by Vietnam and remained under Vietnamese control for the next five years.

Minh Mang disliked the way in which the French spread their influence through the use of missionaries. As a result he restricted the numbers of missionaries and their activities, prohibiting the practice of Christianity in Vietnam. His father had been lucky that France was more concerned about events in Europe during the Napoleonic Wars than in conquests in the East, but Minh Mang realized that the situation had changed when Louis XVIII of France requested that the French be allowed to increase trade in the country. The emperor said that this was possible as long as the merchants conformed to Vietnamese law. Although Minh Mang did not ban foreign traders, as some of his court advised, he was keen on restricting their number and keeping a careful watch on them and the money that trade generated. In 1820, Captain John White of Salem, New Jersey, sailed his clipper ship to Saigon in the hope of trading, but he was spurned.

Some Vietnamese officials disagreed with Minh Mang's policies and wanted further trade with the West. Le Van Duyet was a court official who had risen to power as one of the military commanders of the Nguyen forces who vanquished the Tay Son rebels. Gia Long had appointed him as regent of southern Vietnam, and he had been invested with the authority of conducting foreign relations with other Southeast Asian nations and the West. He protested when moves were made against Christian missionaries, and when he died in 1832, he was posthumously convicted of treason and his grave was desecrated. This enraged his adopted son Le Van Khoi, who staged a revolt against Minh Mang, seeking help from Westerners, including missionaries and the Siamese. The rebellion caused great consternation, and throughout Vietnam. Christian missionaries were rounded up with one of them, the unfortunate cartographer François Isidore Gagelin, being taken to Hue where he was slowly strangled by soldiers on October 17, 1833. Le Van Khoi held out in Saigon until the next year and died while his stronghold was being attacked by the imperial army.

Minh Mang died on January 11, 1841, and he was buried in his mausoleum near Hue. His son, Thieu Tri, became the third emperor of the Nguyen dynasty and was formally crowned at Hue on November 11, 1841. The change in emperor in Vietnam seemed to have encouraged Ang Mei, Queen of Cambodia, to try to amend her previous policy of subservience to Vietnam. The new Vietnamese administration quickly arrested her, which precipitated fighting throughout Cambodia. This conflict effectively ended Vietnamese rule, as the Siamese sent in large numbers of soldiers to occupy the country and support the new Cambodian King Ang Duang.

Thieu Tri was intellectually curious and eager to learn from the West but he had developed his father's wariness of French involvement in the country. He wanted to modernize Vietnam, but court officials frustrated many of his attempts. His arrest of a missionary Dominique Lefèbvre was to cause him much grief. Lefèbvre had been plotting to find another member of the imperial family who was more sympathetic to Christianity, if not himself a Christian, to replace the emperor. This was, of course, an act of treason, and Lefèbvre was arrested and held in prison at Hue. In the spring of 1845, he managed to smuggle a message to a U.S. naval captain, John Percival, whose ship, the U.S.S. *Constitution*, was at the nearby port of Tourane (modern-day Da Nang). The message arrived as Percival was hosting a party for a number of local mandarins on board his ship. Percival held the officials as hostages demanding that Lefèbvre be released. When the Vietnamese refused, Percival meekly released them and left, with the U.S. government subsequently disavowing Percival's actions and apologizing. In February 1847, Lefèbvre was handed over to a French ship and left for Singapore. A month later two French warships arrived at Tourane, unaware of the developments, and demanded the release of the missionary. After 18 days, when the Vietnamese prevaricated, the French bombarded Tourane, killing hundreds of the local people. They claimed that the Vietnamese had opened fire on their ships, but who attacked first remains a matter of academic dispute. The French ships then sailed away. Thieu Tri died on November 4, 1847, at the age of 40, leaving many sons, and being succeeded by his second son Tu Duc.

## TU DUC AND THE DECLINE OF THE NGUYEN COURT

Tu Duc, born as Huong Nam, was proclaimed emperor on November 10, 1847, and reigned for 36 years, the longest reign of any emperor of the Nguyen dynasty. For much of his reign Tu Duc suffered from ill health and faced dynastic and foreign threats. Court intrigue had sidelined the claim of his older brother, Hong Bao, to the throne, and Tu Duc's long reign was to be one of balancing the court against the French. Eventually he became resigned to Vietnam becoming a French protectorate.

The first problem facing Tu Duc was not the French but rather how he should deal with the supporters of Hong Bao. They had plotted a coup to put Tu Duc's elder brother on the throne, but the emperor's spies found out and Hong Bao was arrested and sentenced to death. Tu Duc's mother, Empress Mother Tu Du, intervened, however, and the sentence was commuted to life imprisonment. In jail, Hong Bao hanged himself, but conspiracies against Tu Duc continued. The main plot was the Giac Chia Voi Rebellion of 1866, which involved a group of noblemen and palace officials who planned to put Hong Bao's son on the throne. They also failed, but they did much to upset the politics at court.

The real threat to Vietnam was from the French. In July 1857, Napoleon III decided to invade Vietnam. He was eager to establish new markets for French goods and build a large empire in Asia that could compete with the British Empire. To this end, Napoleon III ordered his naval commander in East Asia,

Rigault de Genouilly, to attack and capture Tourane and to use it as a French naval base. Napoleon cited the agreement with Nguyen Anh (Gia Long) in 1787, and received support from the Vatican for defending the rights of missionaries and Christians in Vietnam. The French foreign minister, Comte Alexander Walewski, the illegitimate son of Emperor Napoleon I and his Polish mistress, and a powerful figure at court, opposed the move, claiming that as the French had not carried out their promises in the 1787 treaty, an attack on Tourane would be a declaration of war; however with Napoleon III so keen on taking the port, Count Walewski demurred.

Admiral Rigault de Genouilly's fleet of 14 ships, with 2,500 French sailors and marines, arrived off Tourane on August 31, 1858. They were also supported by the Spanish in the Philippines, who were also anxious to expand Christianity in the region. On September 1, the French marines landed and by the end of September 2, they had taken the entire city. The French soon recognized, however, that they could not use Tourane as a base to attack other parts of Vietnam, as their military strength was largely reliant on their naval guns, and the soldiers were already suffering badly from tropical diseases. After five months in Tourane, in February 1859, Rigault de Genouilly sailed for Saigon, which he captured two weeks later. These two campaigns left the French in control of two ports, but they were unable to advance beyond them without risking long lines of communication and making them vulnerable to guerrilla attacks. As a result of outbreaks of cholera and typhus among the marines, the French decided to leave a small detachment at Saigon and move the bulk of their forces back to Tourane in the hope of making contact with Tu Duc.

The situation changed on November 24, 1860, when Justin de Chasseloup-Laubat was appointed as French minister of the navy and colonies, and he decided to send Admiral Léonard Victor Joseph Charner to head an expeditionary force to Saigon in spite of the new-found French military commitments in Mexico. In July 1861, the French took Saigon and proclaimed it a French city. The Vietnamese court went into turmoil. Emperor Tu Duc was resigned to the French taking over Vietnam, and he eventually signed a peace agreement with them. In June 1862, he formally ceded to France Saigon and the three provinces around it, as well as the island of Poulo Condore. He also opened three ports to the French for trade and agreed that Roman Catholic missionaries would have the right to preach anywhere in the country. He also agreed not to cede any other part of the country to any power without French permission.

The next year the French, at the request of the Cambodians, established the Protectorate of Cambodia. The Cambodian king was concerned about a possible invasion from Vietnam and sought a Western ally to guarantee the borders of his country. The French move into Vietnam was unpopular, and small rebel forces continued to assault the French. Worried that the fighting might provoke the French into attacking Hue and possibly overthrowing the imperial dynasty, Tu Duc sent an envoy directly to Napoleon III in France offering to cede another three provinces in exchange for peace. Napoleon was tempted to accept, but Admiral Pierre Paul Marie Benoît de La Grandière moved first and in 1867 annexed three more provinces of southern Vietnam, which he formed into the colony of Cochinchina, which was to remain an entity until 1947.

Having lost a large section of his country, in 1867 Tu Duc retired from his palace in Hue and moved to his nearby mausoleum, where he spent the last 16 years of his life. He lived in palatial splendor surrounded by the empress, 103 other official wives, and many concubines. There he devoted his time to scholarship, poetry, and promoting literary endeavor. Tu Duc himself wrote several books, including 4,000 poems, a philosophical treatise, and some historical works. He also personally oversaw the construction of the mausoleum where he was buried after his death on July 19, 1883.

With the French defeat by the Prussians in the Franco-Prussian War of 1870–1871, the French were briefly rendered militarily impotent. Unable to afford another costly war, the French decided to embark on several geographical expeditions. Their hope was to trade with southern China, and several French geographers believed that the Mekong River might allow river traffic to reach into southwestern China. The Mekong River Expedition had actually started in 1866, four years before France's defeat by the Prussians, and was led by Francis Garnier. The concept caught the imagination of French businessmen, but it showed that the Mekong did not reach into China, and attention then focused on the Red River Delta, and Hanoi. In 1873, a French merchant, Jean Dupuis, who had been selling guns, managed to persuade Garnier to launch an attack on Hanoi, beginning with the storming of the city's citadel. Soon afterwards, on December 21, 1873, Garnier was killed while fighting Chinese mercenaries who were supporting the Vietnamese. The French held back for the next nine years. In April 1882, the French in Saigon, with the support of the French government, sent Captain Henri Rivière to Hanoi with 250 men with the aim of seizing part of the Red River Delta. Rivière was killed in May 1883, but the French did not give up their goal of taking Hanoi, as the French Prime Minister Jules Ferry was eager to restore French glory.

Despite having 104 wives, Tu Duc had no children, and when he died, the succession passed to his adopted son, his nephew Duc Duc. In some ways it was a relatively easy succession, but soon after becoming emperor, Duc Duc started inviting wayward friends and acquaintances to court. Vietnamese accounts of the time refer to the arrival of notorious gamblers, womanizers, and practitioners of black magic, along with their mistresses and hangers-on. Soon after the death of Tu Duc, and with the changes at court, the French had exploited the power vacuum to take control of northern Vietnam, which was named Tonkin, and central Vietnam, which took the name Annam, based on an early Chinese name for the area. Officially Annam was under a protectorate under the control of the emperor, with Tonkin a protectorate with an imperial regent, appointed by the emperor. In reality the concept of a protectorate was merely an administrative device. The French controlled both Annam and Tonkin, and when French warships arrived at Hue, the new emperor, Duc Duc, signed the Harmand Treaty in August 1883 and acknowledged French rights to the whole of Vietnam.

But that was not the end of the trouble for Duc Duc. When he was being formally enthroned as emperor on October 6, some conservative court officials read a suppressed portion of Tu Duc's testament in which he debarred Duc Duc from the throne because of, what was then only suspected, moral depravity. The ceremony was halted and the gathered officials decided to convene a court. They immediately sentenced Duc Duc to death for failure to observe the official period of mourning for Tu Duc and for forcing himself on his adopted father's concubines. Condemned to commit suicide by taking poison, Duc Duc was not even provided with a formal burial; his naked body was buried without any ceremony, although in 1899 a small mausoleum was built for the emperor who reigned for less than three months.

## TON THAT THUYET AND RESISTANCE AGAINST FRENCH RULE

After the death of Duc Duc, his uncle Hiep Hoa, a younger brother of Tu Duc, became emperor in October 1883. He took over at a delicate time in Vietnamese history with the disgrace of Duc Duc and the increased French demands on the country. The imperial court was split between those who were prepared to accede to increasing French demands and those who wanted to resist. The latter were led by Ton That Thuyet, one of the most powerful men at court, and the man who had led the move that deposed Duc Duc. It was not clear whether Duc Duc's mental state had only been the excuse to get rid of him. Ton That Thuyet and his supporters were keen on fighting the French, but they were unsure of when and how to act.

Soon after becoming emperor, Hiep Hoa was faced with an ultimatum from the French Admiral Courbet that the French had no intention of annexing the country, but that the emperor had to accept French protection as the only way the Nguyen dynasty could survive. Hiep Hoa reluctantly agreed to ratify the Harmand Treaty by which France controlled all of Vietnam's foreign relations, and the French territory of Cochinchina was further enlarged. When Ton That Thuyet found out about the treaty, he condemned Hiep Hoa for signing it and forced him to abdicate. The emperor was then sentenced to death and was given the choice of being beheaded by sword, strangled with a scarf, or poisoned with a mixture of opium and vinegar. He chose the last and died in the evening of November 29, 1883, after a reign of one month.

With Hiep Hoa dead, Kien Phuc, the previous emperor's nephew (and also another adopted son of Tu Duc), was proclaimed emperor. He was only 15 when he acceded to the throne, and his coronation took place all in one morning in the hope that the French would accept the succession as a *fait accompli.* The coronation was also a sign to the French that they did not have the right to advise on matters of dynastic succession.

Emperor Kien Phuc was never in good health and he rapidly became a puppet for Ton That Thuyet, who controlled the court and was a vigorous opponent of the French. On June 6, 1884, however, the French managed to get the Vietnamese emperor to agree to the Patenotre Treaty, which confirmed the French protectorates of Annam and Tonkin. Soon afterward, palace rumors revealed that one night Kien Phuc found his adoptive mother, Hoc Phi, with her lover Regent Nguyen Van Tuong. Although he vowed to get revenge for their infidelity, he was unsuccessful. Instead it was the emperor who was poisoned soon afterwards and died on August 1, 1884, after ruling for only eight months. The poisoners may have been settling a private score on behalf of the regent, or, alternatively, the deed may have been the work of officials who were against further French encroachments in the country.

The death of Kien Phuc brought his younger brother, Ham Nghi, to the throne. He was crowned on August 17, 1884, two weeks after his 13th birthday. Ton That Thuyet had appointed himself as regent, and the teenager became reliant on the anti-French official. In July 1885, the French demanded that Ton That Thuyet either resign or be fired, and when the emperor refused to agree, the French, in a show of force, surrounded the imperial palace in Hue, with more than 1,000 soldiers, and the French commander, General Roussel de Courcy, then demanded an audience with the emperor.

Ton That Thuyet overestimated his own strength and sent out imperial soldiers to attack the French. These were easily repulsed and the French then invaded the imperial palace, which they sacked. The French also destroyed the imperial library, and scrolls and documents dating back to medieval times were burned. Other parts of the palace were looted in a destruction that was reminiscent of the sacking of the summer palace in Beijing by the British in October 1860. Ham Nghi then decided to issue an appeal called *Can Vuong* (Save the Emperor) in which he urged the wealthy to donate money, for the strong to give their might, and the poor their bodies to defend Vietnam from the French. It was an attempt to rally the Vietnamese nationalists, but it was a disaster. Facing the French armed forces, three days after issuing his brave appeal, the emperor and Ton That Thuyet fled from Hue. They established a jungle stronghold in what is now Laos, and the people who came to support them formed the Can Vuong movement. The French responded in September 1885 by officially deposing the emperor and replacing him with his brother Dong Khanh. Ham Nghi was eventually captured in November 1888 after being betrayed by Hmong mountaineers, but Ton That Thuyet escaped to China. The French executed all members of the Can Vuong movement whom they captured except Ham Nghi who was sent into exile in French Algeria where he remained until his death in Algiers on January 4, 1943; he was buried in France. Another resistance group against the French arose in Annam in 1885 and was led by Phan Dinh Phung. It was active until his death in 1895.

# 3

# The French Protectorate (1887–1945)

## THE ESTABLISHMENT OF FRENCH RULE

In 1887, the French, having also annexed Laos, formed the Indochinese Union—French Indochina—which consisted of the colony of Cochinchina and the four protectorates: Annam, Tonkin, Cambodia, and Laos. The French administration was headed by the governor-general of Indochina, who had his headquarters in Saigon, with a *Résident-Superieur* in each of the capitals of the four protectorates: Hue (Annam), Hanoi (Tonkin), Phnom Penh (Cambodia), and Vientiane (Laos). The bureaucracy included a civil service that was controlled by the French who also held all the senior positions. The lower levels had many Vietnamese bureaucrats and minor officials including educated Vietnamese, some of whom moved to Phnom Penh and Vientiane to work in the colonial administration.

The office of the governor-general of French Indochina was a position of immense power. One governor-general, Paul Doumer, later became president of France and another, Albert Sarraut, served two terms as prime minister. The governor-general operated through three advisory councils involving government, economic interests, and defense. The civil service for Indochina provided the French and local employees for both federal and state functions, with 4,654 French civil servants working in Indochina in 1937, administering

Vietnam in the late 19th century. Oxford University Press.

a population of about 23 million. To illustrate the high numbers, a statistic often quoted was that the British employed a similar number of Britons to run India, which, in 1931, had a population of 352 million.

Unlike in Annam, Tonkin, Cambodia, and Laos, the administration of Cochinchina—southern Vietnam—was in the hands of a lieutenant governor (and after 1911 a governor) who was responsible for the day-to-day running of the colony. He was advised by a private council and a colonial council. The former had 10 members who were nominated by the governor-general and included the commander-in-chief of the army, the solicitor-general, the chief engineer of public works, and two Vietnamese officials. By contrast the colonial council was an elected body with 10 members chosen by the resident French citizens, and 10 "native" members elected by the Vietnamese on a restricted franchise, two delegates from the chamber of agriculture and two from the chamber of commerce. It met only once a year but set up a permanent committee that usually consisted of five members, two of whom were locals. In Annam and Tonkin, the French used the Vietnamese bureaucracy to run the two states, with municipal commissions running some of the cities in Annam, and municipal councils in Hanoi and Haiphong.

Officially the emperor of Vietnam, as well as the king of Cambodia and the king of Laos, held power in their respective protectorates, but in reality their power was purely symbolic. In Hue, Ham Nghi's older brother, Dong Khanh, was proclaimed emperor. The French had thought that Ham Nghi, being younger, would be easier to manipulate, but they were wrong. Dong Khanh was 21 when, on September 19, 1885, he became emperor. His accession coincided with the French desire for Vietnamese soldiers to put down the Can Vuong revolt being led by Ham Nghi. Dong Khanh contributed soldiers to this end, making him unpopular with Vietnamese nationalists. To boost support for himself and the French presence, Dong Khanh toured the countryside urging people to support the French. King Sisowath in neighboring Cambodia had a similar task. Soon afterward, Dong Khanh died suddenly on January 28, 1889.

Despite Dong Khanh's support for the French, the French overlooked his descendants and chose Thanh Thai, a son of the disgraced Emperor Duc Duc, to succeed to the throne. They were partly motivated by Thanh Thai's age (he was 11), but also because the French wanted to show that they could decide on the imperial succession. Some French even claimed that the family of Dong Khanh had an inherited trait of mental disease. The year after the death of Dong Khanh, work began on a modest mausoleum for him.

The first governors-general did not take great interest in the running of French Indochina, but they were interested in the rising importance of the rubber industry and the wealth that it generated. So the whole system of ruling French Indochina was overhauled by Paul Doumer who was the governor-general from 1897 until 1902. Albert Sarraut was to make significant changes and administrative improvements.

## CHARLES MAYRÉNA AND THE KINGDOM OF SEDANG

It was not long before Vietnam began to catch the imagination of Europeans. One of the more remarkable stories of Southeast Asia at this time centered on James Brooke, a British sea captain, who befriended the sultan of Brunei in Borneo and who had gained the title of sultan of Sarawak in 1846, establishing a dynasty that was to last for a century. Many other Europeans probably harbored the romantic idea of being ruler of some remote "country." One of these was Charles Mayréna, born as Charles David, in Toulon, France, in 1842. When he was 21 he had served in the French colonial forces who had captured Cochinchina, but then returned to France. After taking part in the Franco-Prussian War of 1870, he started working for a bank in Paris. In 1883, he was charged with embezzlement and, leaving his wife and two children, fled to the Netherlands East Indies, from where he was deported as an undesirable. Back in Paris he heard about the sultan of Aceh in northern Sumatra who was fighting a war to stop his country from becoming a Dutch colony.

Probably intending to head to Aceh, Mayréna arrived in Saigon in 1885 and ended up establishing a plantation in central Vietnam. Accused of gun-running, he disappeared for a short period, but returned in 1888 to offer his services to the French to stop English adventurers from making themselves a presence in the Vietnamese highlands. On June 3, however, Mayréna telegraphed a message to the French governor stating that he had proclaimed himself King Marie I of Sedang, and was quite happy to turn over his kingdom to the French in return for retaining economic control. He added that if he did not hear back from the French, he would contact their deadly enemy, the Germans.

The whole affair was greeted with some hilarity by the French population of Indochina, with the new king promulgating his own constitution, issuing several royal edicts, and creating orders of chivalry. He was briefly seen in Haiphong obtaining printers to produce elaborate certificates for the Order of Saint Marguerite and having uniforms made for his army. When the French governor decided to ignore him, the new king sailed for Hong Kong where the English governor greeted him, although the business community decided not to invest in Sedang. The next year Marie I went to Paris where he was a press sensation as he awarded people titles, issued some more decrees, printed his own postage stamps, and then, also with no support from business, moved to Ostend in Belgium.

With Marie I in Europe, the French officials went into Sedang and took down all his flags, dismantling his "kingdom." By January 1890, he had decided to return to Vietnam and left Belgium for Singapore where he tried to buy arms, but these were impounded, and the French refused him permission to return to Vietnam. Unable to get Siamese permission to return to Sedang through Siam and Laos, he retired to the island of Tioman, off the west coast of Malaya, where he died under circumstances that were never made clear. According to one account, he was bitten by a poisonous snake; another said that he was shot dead in a duel. The story of his life romanticized the Western view of Vietnam, which was reflected in the many postcards of French Indochina printed from the 1900s, showing temples, palace courtiers, the "noble savages" of the jungles, the peasants toiling in the fields, and some macabre scenes such as executions or severed heads. For many of the French posted to Vietnam, life was much more grim than they had imagined.

## THE INSTABILITY OF THE IMPERIAL COURT

The appointment of Thanh Thai as emperor signaled the exercise of French power to choose the emperor, and indeed Thanh Thai's father, Duc Duc, had signed the Harmand Treaty, which had acknowledged French control over Vietnam. The choice of Thanh Thai as emperor took everybody by surprise. He and his mother were in prison when guards brought him the news. His mother thought the guards had come to murder them, so both were pleasantly surprised!

Thanh Thai and his mother moved to Hue, but it was not long before the new emperor became eccentric and was even suspected of being mentally unstable, although some have subsequently argued that the incidents were staged to confuse the French. The emperor quickly accumulated a large number of concubines, and, in 1902, was involved in a scandal with two European women in Danang. The French administration was unhappy when Thanh Thai occasionally had servants and maids publicly flogged and was also concerned when he started inviting foreign visitors to have dinner with him during which time he recounted scandal and gossip much to the amusement of these guests, and probably to the detriment of the French authorities.

On a political front, in 1905 Thanh Thai tried to escape to China to join an anti-French resistance group; however, he was captured and sent back to Hue where he feigned madness for a period. In 1907, worried about his growing anti-French tendencies, the French decided to depose him and they exiled him to Vung Tau in the south, where he lived with his 4 wives, 10 children, and 20 female maids. During World War I he ran up large debts, some incurred from buying German products, and several mandarins paid the debts to prevent the shame that would have occurred had the ex-emperor been sued.

After Thanh Thai was deposed, the French chose his fifth son, Duy Tan, to become the next emperor. It was an odd choice because it was not long before Duy Tan revealed himself as even more anti-French than his father. When World War I broke out, many French officials and businessmen in Vietnam returned to France to serve in the French forces, defending their homeland from the Germans. Many Vietnamese also enlisted in the French colonial forces and served on the western front, where they also suffered significant casualties. In Vietnam, however, some nationalists decided the situation provided an ideal opportunity to move against the French, with Emperor Duy Tan announcing his support for an anti-French rebellion. On May 3, 1916, Duy Tan left the imperial palace in Hue and after urging people to rebel against the French, he took refuge in the nearby Thien Mu Pagoda. He was captured by the French and taken to the Mang Ca Citadel where he was held prisoner before he and his father were taken to Réunion Island in the Indian Ocean. In exile there, they were barred from returning home. Duy Tan's mother was eventually allowed to return to Vietnam in 1920, but the two ex-emperors were never allowed to return to their homeland.

## THE CONSOLIDATION OF FRENCH POWER

On May 17, 1916, Khai Dinh, the son of Dong Khanh, was proclaimed emperor. He was 30 years old when he acceded to the throne and avoided controversy during his nine-year reign, presiding over a period of considerable prosperity for Vietnam during which great wealth was generated for French companies and the small Vietnamese elite. Historians tend to view him as a French puppet, but he, no doubt, was constantly worried about being deposed, as had happened to his two predecessors. Even though he ruled for only 9 years, it took 11 years to complete the emperor's mausoleum, which was so expensive that extra taxes had to be levied to pay for its construction.

The commercial benefits of French rule in Indochina were paradoxical. On the one hand, the French taxpayer constantly had to subsidize the French administration; on the other hand, French companies made fortunes from their ventures in Indochina, especially rubber companies in Vietnam. The French taxpayer, as well as the Indochinese taxpayer, paid for the costs incurred in the roads, bridges, canals, railroads, and public works projects in Indochina. These allowed for rapid exploitation of the natural resources of Vietnam, with coal mines being established in the north of the country, the growing of rice in the rich river deltas, and the valuable rubber industry along the Cochinchina-Cambodian border region. In return the French were able to sell their own goods to a market that was unable to import from other countries owing to high tariffs for non-French goods. The French also constructed textile factories such as those at Nam Dinh in the north, which were built in 1913 and came to operate 54,000 spindles and employ more than 5,000 workers. There were also paper mills, cement and glass factories, and sugar refineries. By 1930, approximately 100,000 people were working in industries and mining in Vietnam, which began to generate considerable wealth for France. For most of the Vietnamese, apart from native crafts like pots and basket weaving, many of their own industries were unable to compete with cheap mass-produced French goods, leading to resentment from many artisans.

The life of the Vietnamese indentured laborer or factory worker was monotonous, and the people were often poorly paid. Novels such as Anthony Grey's *Saigon* (1982) and films such as *Indochine* (1992) have sought to portray the hard life of Vietnamese laborers in rubber plantations, but there are few contemporary accounts of the hardships that faced the peasants in the villages where extended families would work from dawn to dusk, often going hungry. In many places peasant farmers would have to pay up to 60 percent of their crop in rent. Starvation was not uncommon, with some descriptions of emaciated people lying on the side of roads in the hope of help from passers-by. As with other developing countries, many peasants left villages to find work on plantations or in the cities. Rice production per acre declined, and even through the amount of land devoted to rice quadrupled between 1880 and 1930, the land was either sold at auction to the highest bidder or taken over by French speculators or their Vietnamese friends. The result was that 45 percent of the land in Cochinchina was owned by 3 percent of the landowners, with 70 percent of landowners being peasant farmers who owned only about 15 percent of all land. Some of those in the cities worked as coolies. They labored at the docks or pulling rickshaws, and those who could afford it found solace in opium dens. Others chewed betel nut for its properties as a stimulant, although, as a cause of mouth cancer, it was to lead to the premature deaths of many of them.

Although the French boasted that they had made improvements in education and medical care, by 1939 only 15 percent of school-age children attended school, and four-fifths of the population was illiterate. One school, the lycée in Dalat, only took European children, and in 1937 there were only 4,611 secondary school students in the whole of Indochina out of a total population of 23 million. Although a medical school was established in Hanoi, in 1939 there were only 2 doctors for every 100,000 Vietnamese, compared to 25 per 100,000 in the Philippines, and 76 per 100,000 in Japan. High levels of infantile mortality persisted, and there was also a high prevalence of malaria, cholera, and other diseases.

The life of the Vietnamese elite changed considerably under the French. The political machinations at the imperial court in Hue during the first part of the Nguyen dynasty had rested entirely on the whim of the emperor. Now colonial officials made all the important decisions, and, with few of them staying long in their positions, astute mandarins were able to delay the implementing of policies they did not like, in the hopes that the succeeding official would change direction. One of these courtiers was Ngo Dinh Kha who had been the master of rites and the grand chamberlain to the Emperor Thanh Thai. He lived in Hue and became the headmaster of the Quoc Hoc, the National Academy, on the south bank of the Perfume River, facing the Imperial Citadel. Founded by Thanh Thi in 1896, it had replaced the earlier Quoc Tu Giam (Imperial Academy) and by the early twentieth century had emerged as one of the most important centers for education in the country. Ngo Dinh Kha's family had been devout Roman Catholics since the 1690s. Up to a hundred of the clan were murdered in an anti-Catholic attack on them in 1870, and like most Vietnamese intellectuals, he represented the paradox of being fascinated by French culture, but secretly disliking French control of the country. At least five of his six sons were all to share his beliefs; his third son become prime minister in 1954 and later became the first president of South Vietnam in 1955.

Born near Hue in 1867, Phan Boi Chau moved to the imperial capital and became an ardent nationalist leader by 1900, often meeting with pupils from the Quoc Hoc and talking with them about his views on Vietnamese independence. In 1905, the Japanese defeat of Russia in the Russo-Japanese War signified for Phan Boi Chau a great change in the nationalist climate in Asia, with an Asian country capable of defeating a European "Great Power." Believing that Japan might support a Vietnamese resistance movement, Phan Boi Chau went to Tokyo along with Marquess Cuong De, a great-great grandson of Prince Canh, the son of Emperor Gia Long. Styling himself Prince Cuong De, his plan of overthrowing the French won support from some Japanese politicians, and it was not long before numbers of young Vietnamese nationalists went to Japan where they studied at colleges and were also trained in the use of political propaganda, firearms, and explosives. The newly established Free School of Tonkin, opened in 1907, rapidly became a focus for anti-French dissent, and in the following year, there were mass demonstrations against the French, with hundreds of nationalists and others arrested, some being executed and the others being sent to the penal colony the French established on the island of Poulo Condore, off the coast of Cochinchina.

Phan Boi Chau's agitation for Vietnamese independence brought him into contact with other Asian nationalist leaders such as Dr. Sun Yat-sen who was planning for a revolution in China. When that was achieved in 1911, Phan Boi Chau had great hopes for the Chinese to support the Vietnamese, but problems in China prevented them from helping. While Phan Boi Chau went to Hong Kong, Japan, and Siam to raise support for his cause, Phan Chu Trinh, also from central Vietnam and the son of a member of the Can Vuong movement of Emperor Ham Nghi, which had opposed the French, became convinced that it was not the French that posed the main threat to Vietnam but the Vietnamese feudal system. He also saw Japan as a potential enemy rather than friend, influenced by the anti-Japanese Korean nationalism being espoused by Syngman Rhee. In 1926, Phan Chu Trinh died and his funeral in Saigon became the occasion for one of early massive nationalist protests in the city. In the same year, Phan Boi Chau was arrested in Shanghai by French agents and taken to Hanoi where he was tried for sedition and jailed, and later placed under house arrest in Hue where he died 15 years later.

## THE EARLY YEARS OF HO CHI MINH

In 1907, a local government official Nguyen Sinh Sac enrolled two of his sons at the Quoc Hoc in Hue. Both had both passed the entrance examination and been awarded scholarships. Nguyen Sinh Sac was a friend and colleague of Phan Chu Trinh, and his oldest son, Nguyen Tat Thanh, was 17, and a passionate believer in Vietnamese nationalism, remaining at school until he was 20. In 1910, Sac, the father, was dismissed from his government position for sentencing an influential local man to receive 100 strokes of the cane; the man later died from the punishment. Sac and his sons believed that he had been singled out because the dead man was well connected rather than because the punishment was unfair. Sac and his older son moved to Saigon, and, in 1911, the son managed to get a position as a cook's apprentice on a French ocean liner. He spent the next few years at sea, traveling around the world and visiting many of the major ports. In 1913, he was in the United States; and, by 1915, he had settled in England, living in London where he claimed to have worked as a snow sweeper and then as a pastry chef at the Carlton Hotel for the famous chef Auguste Escoffier, although some historians have doubted this last assertion. He also probably visited the United States again in 1917 or 1918, where he heard Marcus Garvey speak out against the treatment of African Americans.

Moving to Paris toward the end of World War I, he changed his name to Nguyen Ai Quoc (Nguyen the Patriot)—he later changed his name to Ho Chi Minh—and submitted a petition to the allied leaders at Versailles demanding that Vietnam should achieve the same rights of self-determination as being accorded to the people of Europe. The next year, 1920, he became a founding member of the French Communist Party, moving to the Soviet Union in 1923 and living in Moscow where he tried to get the Soviet government to support the idea of Vietnamese independence. In December 1924, Nguyen Ai Quoc moved to Canton (Guangzhou) in southern China, where he established the Revolutionary Youth League of Vietnam and in 1930 transformed it into the Indochina Communist Party.

On the run from the French, Nguyen Ai Quoc moved to Hong Kong where he was arrested by the British and held in prison until his release in 1933. He then returned to the Soviet Union, where he lived for several years. A recently published photograph of him soon after he arrived in the Soviet Union shows a rather haggard and gaunt man who obviously suffered, either from illness or ill treatment, in the prison in Hong Kong. During his time in the Soviet Union, he made his plans for the Vietnamese Revolution, although this did not come about until the end of World War II.

## EUROPEAN SOCIETY IN FRENCH INDOCHINA

Much is made of the luxurious life enjoyed by Westerners in colonial Vietnam, and there are many accounts of people dressing for exquisite dinners and being fussed over and waited on by servants who did all the menial chores in their palatial houses. Certainly this was the life of the colonial administrators, but many of the minor colonial officials lived in cramped quarters in a difficult climate and were susceptible to tropical diseases; many died g prematurely. The New York-born traveler and raconteur Harry L. Foster (1894–1932) visited Saigon in about 1922, and published his account in *A Beachcomber in the Orient* (1923). Foster wrote that the first time one travels in a rickshaw, one feels like a fool, on the second ride one has the feeling of being an inhuman slave-driver using one's coolie as a draught-horse, and on the third and subsequent ride one feels like a potentate being drawn around by a vassal. Although many colonial officials and Europeans in Vietnam were by no means rich, the miserable life of the coolies and rickshaw pullers certainly made them feel better.

The Hotel Métropole, founded in 1901, was regarded as *the* place to stay in Hanoi, and when wealthy visitors arrived in the city, their names appeared in the local papers. When the British writer W. Somerset Maugham went to Hanoi in 1922–1923, he was tracked down by a former acquaintance, a man who had dropped out of medical school in London, and worked for the Chinese Customs Service for 25 years. He finally managed to save enough money to return to England where he found the climate dreadful and eventually moved to Haiphong. Maugham's meeting with him was later recounted in *The Gentleman in the Parlour* (1930), by which time the presence of European drifters was common. In 1928, the British traveler Malcolm Macdonald also stayed at the Hotel Métropole, where his valet reported the shocking news that the French once turned up for dinner without bothering with evening dress.

Certainly petty jealousies were rampant in the European community, with not infrequent accounts of men taking mistresses, or having affairs with wives of other Europeans. The availability of cheap prostitutes, male as well as female, led to numerous scandals that were to rock French society in Indochina. In 1917, while France was preoccupied with World War I, an ambitious geologist, Jacques Deprat, was being arraigned in Hanoi on charges of placing some European fossils among samples he had collected from northern Vietnam and southern China. Deprat was dismissed from the French Indochina civil service and expelled from the Geological Society of France, ending the career of an aspiring French scientist. In another scandal several years later, charges of theft of ancient artifacts were made against André Malraux, a French Socialist. Surviving two trials in 1924–1925, Malraux believed the charges were brought against him as a way of trying to get him to stop protesting on behalf of the Vietnamese.

## THE 1930 UPRISING AND BAO DAI'S ATTEMPT AT REFORM

In 1926, the Emperor Khai Dinh died, and his 12-year-old son became the Emperor Bao Dai. The boy went to France to complete his education and did not return until 1932. In the meantime there had been a major uprising against the French. During World War I, the Thai Nguyen Rebellion had broken out in northern Vietnam in August 1917 and was quickly crushed. Although Ho Chi Minh had been establishing a communist movement in Vietnam, and among Vietnamese exiles, the major revolutionary nationalist movement at the time was the Viet Nam Quoc Dan Dang (VNQDD), the Vietnamese Nationalist Party, which had been founded in 1927 by Nguyen Thai Hoc, and was modeled on the Chinese Kuomintang from whom they gained some support.

Many Vietnamese peasant farmers worked in rubber plantations and mines in the 1920s, with French companies making large profits. With the slump in the world market from 1929, however, the decline in the price of rubber and other commodities led to many indentured laborers either having their pay cut or losing their jobs. Discontent allowed the VNQDD to recruit numbers of sympathizers, and on the night of February 9–10, 1930, the VNQDD managed to persuade a garrison at Yen Bay, Tonkin, to rebel and kill their French officers. The French reacted swiftly, however, by taking back Yen Bay and executing many of the mutineers, with the result that the rebellion quickly petered out, and the VNQDD leaders who managed to escape fled to southern China where they remained until 1945.

Although the other garrisons did not mutiny, from the late 1930s bands of peasants had been gathering and started attacking local landlords and Vietnamese officials. It was not long before communist ideas started spreading, and the peasants established communes in remote parts of Annam. The French ruthlessly suppressed these moves, in one instance using their air power to attack columns of demonstrators. Although some of the Vietnamese elite were happy that the French had restored law and order, many others were disgusted by the French actions. Although the French did crush the VNQDD and the Indochina Communist Party, with many nationalists either being executed, thrown in prison at Poulo Condore, or fleeing into exile, the nationalist cause was to gain many new recruits.

In September 1932, Emperor Bao Dai returned from France where he had completed his education. He was 19 years old, and on his return, his first actions, after paying his respects at his father's tomb and to the regent, were to visit a trade school and a girls' school. He promised judicial reform, the creation of a ministry of national education, recognition of a house of representatives, and inclusion of the president of the elected assembly in the council of ministers. Bao Dai was crowned as emperor, which ended the regency presided over by his domineering mother, known at Court as the "Tigress." A cosmopolitan figure, Bao Dai disliked the strictures of the court at Hue, and he appointed a little-known mandarin, Ngo Dinh Diem, as minister of the interior. It was a frustrating period for the emperor, and soon both he and Diem realized that the French made all major policy decisions, so Diem resigned after two months. Instead of trying to push ahead with his administrative and taxation reforms, Bao Dai resigned himself to an easy life as a playboy, inheriting from his mother an appetite for gambling. Suffering from neurasthenia, the young Emperor found relief in hunting wildlife in the jungles of central Vietnam.

As the Great Depression hit Vietnam, the plantations laid off large numbers of their workers and the French brutally crushed any attempts at agitation or rebellion. This continued until 1936 when the French people elected a Popular Front government, and Léon Blum became prime minister, taking over from former Indochina governor Albert Sarraut. Blum immediately introduced reforms into the running of Indochina, and, as a show of goodwill, he ordered the release of all political prisoners. These included Ton Duc Thang, who had been arrested in 1929, Le Duan, and Truong Chinh, all of whom would play a major role in the Vietnamese Communist movement for more than 40 years.

## WORLD WAR II

With the outbreak of World War II, there was a rise in the demand for rubber, and initially French Indochina—or, to be more precise, particular French companies—prospered. The French governor-general, Georges Catroux, was a supporter of the allied cause, and devoted his efforts in Indochina to boosting the production of rubber and other supplies. The French reinforced some of their positions in case of possible attack from saboteurs rather than any enemy forces.

In May 1940, when Germany invaded France, the French in Indochina were shocked. The fall of France in June 1940, after a campaign of only 5½ weeks, horrified them and breathed new life into the nationalist movement. On June 25, 1940, the new pro-German Vichy government in France appointed Jean Decoux as the new governor-general. Soon afterward French Indochina was attacked by Siam, and its defeat by an Asian power further encouraged the nationalists. On September 22, 1940, Decoux concluded a treaty with Japan, allowing for up to 30,000 Japanese troops to be stationed in French Indochina and able to use all Indochinese airports. The Japanese also established several more businesses in the region, including the Yokohama Specie Bank. The bank manager, Eisuke Ono, brought his wife and daughter, Yoko Ono (later the artist-musician and wife of John Lennon) to the Vietnamese northern capital.

The outbreak of World War II in 1939 had given ex-Emperor Duy Tan an opportunity to enlist in the French army, and in 1942 he rallied to the Free French navy serving as a telecommunications officer. In December 1945, he met with French leader, Charles de Gaulle, and soon afterwards was on his way back to Réunion when he was killed in a plane crash. There has been speculation that De Gaulle was planning to restore Duy Tan to the throne. His body was taken back to Hue where he was buried near Duc Duc's mausoleum. It was not until 1950 that Thanh Thai's son-in-law, Vuong Quang Nhuong, then the minister of education, managed to persuade the French to allow Thanh Thi to return to live privately in Saigon where he died four years later, and was buried in a grave near that of his father and his son.

In May 1941, Ho Chi Minh managed to get the Vietnamese Communists to agree to form a broad alliance with other nationalist groups. This was known as the League for the Independence of Vietnam, and subsequently as the Viet Minh. After December 1941, when Japan attacked British Malaya, Pearl Harbor, and the Philippines, the former from bases in Indochina, Ho Chi Minh decided to cooperate with the Allied war effort and started providing the United States and other allied nations with important military and political intelligence. In return Ho Chi Minh sought to get the Allies to recognize the Viet Minh as the legitimate representative of the Vietnamese people.

With the Chinese Communists supporting their compatriots in China, the Chinese Nationalists (Kuomintang) continued to do the same for the VNQDD. The nationalists hoped that they might be able to eject the French from Vietnam. Ho Chi Minh saw the importance of forging an alliance with the United States and managed to rescue a number of U.S. pilots before going on to meet General Claire Chennault of the Flying Tigers, whereupon the general gave Ho Chi Minh an autographed photograph of himself.

It was not until March 9, 1945, that the Japanese decided to strike. On the afternoon of that day they moved into place expecting the French to resist, especially in Tonkin. The Japanese worries were well founded. In Cochinchina and Cambodia, the Japanese rounded up all the French without much trouble. There was some fighting in Hue, where some of the French were captured by the Japanese at a cinema where they were watching a Tarzan movie. Those in one of the barracks were involved in a minor firefight with the Japanese and were forced to surrender the next day when they ran out of ammunition. In Hanoi, at 7:55 P.M., the French General Mordant heard about the trouble and organized a hurried resistance. The next morning Mordant finally surrendered along with many of his men. The French garrison in Haiphong also capitulated, but the French at Lang Son held out until March 13, when they, too, surrendered. The Japanese had suffered significant losses there and executed the most senior French officer in revenge. During all of this fighting, some 5,700 French colonial soldiers, nearly half being Europeans, managed to escape into southern China. Within a few days, the Japanese had interned 15,000 members of the Indochina armed forces, 80 percent of them European. About 2,100 European officers and men were killed in the takeover or disappeared soon afterwards, and hundreds of Japanese were also killed. Many lower level French civil servants and functionaries, however, were not interned; engineers, harbor pilots, doctors, and teachers were not easy to replace.

In Hue the private secretary to Emperor Bao Dai was informed that the Japanese had removed the French colonialists but would not be interfering with the court. Bao Dai himself was out hunting, and one cannot help but be reminded that Louis XVI was also hunting when the mob stormed the Bastille in 1789. When he was told of the Japanese move, Bao Dai was nervous. He knew the power of the Allies and that the Japanese seemed to be losing the war. He also knew, however, that the Japanese would deal harshly with him and his court if he refused to do what they wanted. He would also have known that Prince Cuong De, a pretender to the throne, had been living in Tokyo for some time, and that he might be deposed. On March 11, Bao Dai's decree abrogating the 1884 protectorate treaty with France was read to a hastily convened meeting of his ministers, along with a proclamation of independence. It was determined that March 14 was the most auspicious day to make this announcement. Tran Trong Kim, an historian and Confucian scholar, became prime minister of the newly independent Kingdom of Vietnam.

This turn of events had surprised Ho Chi Minh. He was in China at the time and he hastened back to Vietnam. Before leaving Kunming, Ho had written his American friends a note that "the French imperialist wolf was finally devoured by the Japanese fascist hyena." The note, which is now held in the U.S. National Archives, included a request for the Americans to consider landing in Vietnam. In Ho's absence, in April, the Central Committee of the

Communist Party of Vietnam ordered the creation of the Vietnam Liberation Army in preparation for a general insurgency at some later date. In May, Ho was back in Vietnam and mobilizing his forces. He was eager not to strike out too quickly. His men were no match for the Japanese in the same way that the resistance in France had been no match for the Germans. All knew, however, that an American landing on the beaches would change the military situation dramatically. Charles de Gaulle then issued his plan for the Indochinese Federation whereby the states of Indochina would come together in a federal union in which foreign policy and defense would still be controlled by France.

The Vietnamese Communists were holding a party conference when, on August 14, Japan surrendered. This had come after the bombing of Hiroshima and Nagasaki, and although the surrender had been expected and planned for over many months, the suddenness of it still came as a surprise. On August 19, there was a general uprising in Hanoi, and four days later the Communists seized control of Hue. An attempt to take over Saigon on August 25 was a little patchy, as other Vietnamese nationalists challenged the Communists there. These events are what became known as the August Revolution.

To act constitutionally, it was necessary for Bao Dai to abdicate, which he did on August 30. During the previous five months his government had floundered badly. They tried to move independently of the Japanese but could never shake off the public image of being a "puppet" government. A massive famine that struck in the poorest regions of Annam had only made matters worse, exacerbated by the Japanese constantly requisitioning supplies for their army. When members of the Viet Minh had approached him on August 25, the emperor had willingly handed over power to them and offered to live as a simple citizen. Traveling to Hanoi, he accepted a position as the supreme political adviser to the new provisional republic.

In July 1945, the Allied powers had met in Potsdam with the defeat of Japan imminent. The French, British, and Americans realized that the Communists might be able to seize power in Vietnam, so to preempt this move, they planned to send in two occupation forces. The Nationalist Chinese would take control of northern Vietnam and Laos, and the British would maintain order in the south and Cambodia. On September 6, a British advance party arrived in Saigon. Three days later, Chinese soldiers started arriving in Hanoi. Four days later British soldiers disembarked in Saigon.

Preempting the British move, on September 2, 1945, a massive crowd had gathered in Hanoi to hear Ho Chi Minh proclaim Vietnam's independence. It was the Feast of Vietnamese Martyrs, a day observed by more than a million Roman Catholics in North Vietnam, and more in the rest of the country. Read in front of tens of thousands of cheering people, from the balcony of the French Opera House, Ho Chi Minh's proclamation was modeled on the

U.S. Declaration of Independence: "All men are created equal. The Creator has given us certain inviolable Rights; the right to Life, the right to be Free, and the right to achieve Happiness." The few Americans who were there, such as Archimedes Patti, were placed prominently in the crowd—Patti had turned down a request to appear with Ho—and when a U.S. reconnaissance flight went over the crowd, the people of Hanoi saw it as a "fly-past" by their American supporters.

The new government quickly produced a small aluminum coin, which was joined in 1946 by additional coins showing crude portraits of Ho Chi Minh. The first banknotes were also produced in 1946 showing a youthful Ho Chi Minh. They also overprinted vast stocks of stamps of French Indochina, which were quickly sold in large numbers to U.S. collectors and others to raise funds for the new government.

Although the British, French, and Chinese had all been on the same side during the war, as had the Vietnamese nationalists, attitudes over what to do in Vietnam varied considerably. The British, as a major imperial power, were keen to help the French restore their colonial regime. Many of the Chinese Nationalists, however, were anticolonial after the experiences of the European powers in China, and they were also disinterested in Vietnam. The Chinese soldiers knew that a civil war was brewing in their own country, and that they were needed for the war there. Anxious to avoid fighting, the Chinese had tolerated Ho Chi Minh even though he was a communist, but they did allow the French to move back to Hanoi and a few other cities in the north. In the south, however, the British were determined to help the French restore their colonial rule.

Charles de Gaulle had tried to forestall the quagmire that was being created in Vietnam. As early as August 22, 1945, a French agent, Pierre Messmer (later to become prime minister of France), had parachuted into northern Vietnam but had been unable to make contact with other French agents there. Jean Cédile, in southern Vietnam, was more successful, although he was initially captured by the pro-Japanese militia. The French were adamant that their government of Indochina would be restored. They were helped by the British who were under the command of Major-General Douglas Gracey. In Saigon non-Communist nationalists and Trotskyites, as well as members of the Cao Dai and Hoa Hao sects, also started organizing.

On September 17, the Communists called for a general strike in Saigon and the British declared martial law four days later. On the next day after a meeting between Gracey and Cédile, the British armed 1,400 French soldiers and civilians to help with law enforcement. Released from the internment centers where they had been held by the Japanese, they went around Saigon exacting revenge on their Vietnamese jailers, people who had taken over their houses and businesses while they had been interned, and anybody else who was in the wrong place at the wrong time.

The general strike began on September 24, 1945, with the European population of Saigon cowering. They had good reason to be afraid. That morning the Viet Minh and the Binh Xuyen gangsters—an uneasy coalition at the best of times—managed to get into Cité Hérault, a European residential suburb. There they massacred 150 French and Eurasian men, women, and children. The British were horrified and immediately agreed with French plans to send a large force of French soldiers to try to restore order. The British had decided that if they withdrew quickly, this would be bad for relations with France; but if they stayed they might have to endure substantial casualties, as was to happen at Surabaya in Java where the British lost many men in their efforts to support the Dutch return to their former colony. Gracey's plan was to get the French troops to Saigon as quickly as possible and then withdraw. Some writers, such as the influential journalist Stanley Karnow, date the Vietnam War from the fighting on September 24, 1945. Certainly the first American casualty was not long in coming. With a large French force on the way, an American officer, Lieutenant Colonel Peter Dewey, son of a Republican Congressman, decided to leave Saigon. On September 26, he drove with a colleague to the Saigon airport. Finding that their plane had been delayed, the two drove back to Saigon and on their return they ran into a Communist roadblock. The Vietnamese opened fire with a machine gun and Dewey was killed instantly, as his friend escaped. Dewey's body was never found despite a search organized later the same day. He was the first American serviceman killed in Vietnam.

Large numbers of French soldiers arrived in Saigon during October 1945, and on October 16, the Viet Minh were forced to retreat from the city. At this juncture, with the possibility of losing control of the country they had taken over in August, the Communists decided to "reinvent" themselves. On November 11, the Indochina Communist Party was dissolved and its members became participants in an Association for Marxist Studies. In Hanoi Ho Chi Minh joined together with some remnants of the VNQDD and other nationalist groups to form a broader coalition against the French. This latter group came together on January 1, 1946, as the provisional coalition government of the Democratic Republic of Vietnam (DRV). Five days later some areas in the north elected a National Assembly in line with the new DRV Constitution. The Chinese Nationalist commander, Lu Han, was happy at the inclusion of the VNQDD, whom his government had long supported. His army, however, was far from popular in northern Vietnam where the soldiers, mainly drawn from poor peasants, pillaged many villages. By November there was a largely Communist government in *de facto* control of the north, albeit with a large Chinese Nationalist presence, and a restored French colonial regime was operating in the south.

On February 28, the Chinese finally agreed to leave Vietnam. In fact even without French pressure, they would have left anyway, as they were needed for the Chinese Civil War. On March 6, 1946, Ho Chi Minh signed an agreement with a French representative Jean Sainteny by which the DRV might become a "free state" within the French Union, with free elections in Cochinchina to see whether it wanted to join the DRV. There were further disagreements, however, and the Dalat Conference was held from April 18 to May 11 to try to resolve the impasse between the DRV and the French colonial authorities. Although the Communist commander Giap was present, as was the DRV's non-Communist foreign minister Nguyen Tuong Tam, no agreement was reached.

The French had been trying to work out a constitutional approach that would outmaneuver the Communists. Their idea was to rework de Gaulle's concept of an Indochinese Federation. By dividing Indochina into its five constituent parts—Annam, Tonkin, Cochinchina, Cambodia, and Laos—decisions would be made by a consensus or a majority. This constitutional setup made no attempt to resolve the unequal population in the five areas. With the Cambodian and Laotian governments, who controlled the smallest populations, openly pro-French, and Tonkin and Annam being largely in Communist hands, Cochinchina would cast the deciding vote. Thus on June 1, 1946, the Autonomous Republic of Cochinchina was formed by pro-French politicians in Saigon with the backing of the French army. It was the brainchild—if that word could be used—of Georges-Thierry d'Argenlieu, the former French high commissioner to Indochina, and an implacable anticommunist and believer in France's greatness. The aim was to undercut the Nationalist appeal of the DRV by making the Republic of Cochinchina its equal, constitutionally at any rate, and also preventing the French government in Paris from negotiating away the rights of the people of Cochinchina without their consent.

The French government was furious and refused to recognize the new entity. Instead Ho Chi Minh traveled to Paris to negotiate with the French government directly, but the government collapsed and its successor was even more right wing. Led by Georges Bidault, it refused to give any ground. Furthermore Ho Chi Minh, after having been left waiting in Biarritz, on the southwest Atlantic coast, then saw the conference moved to the old palace at Fontainebleau outside Paris, where it would receive less attention from possible demonstrators. Ho Chi Minh finally signed the Fontainebleau agreement with the minister of overseas France, which allowed for eventual French recognition of the DRV. In return, the French would be allowed to keep their soldiers in Vietnam but would progressively withdraw them over the next five years. For Cochinchina, the matter was left unresolved. It was at that meeting that

Ho Chi Minh told the French minister that if war broke out, "You can kill ten of my men for every one of yours I kill, but even at these odds, you will lose, and I will win." Ho Chi Minh returned to Hanoi where, confident that he had emerged triumphant, he purged his government of any non-Communists. In France he had also discovered that he could not rely on getting the support of French Communists, many of whom were passionately nationalist and supportive of the French colonial empire.

D'Argenlieu had not been idle during Ho's absence. He had managed to get some of the DRV representatives to meet him at Dalat where he hoped to drive a wedge between Ho Chi Minh and the moderates in his government. Dr. Nguyen Van Thinh, who had been chosen as president of the provisional government of Cochinchina, however, was so traumatized by the political machinations that he committed suicide in November.

The French generals in Indochina suspected that the Paris politicians would try to leave Vietnam, and on November 20–23, in what became known as the Haiphong incident, the French bombarded parts of Haiphong causing massive Vietnamese casualties. There had been tension in Haiphong for some weeks before the incident, with Ho Chi Minh announcing that he would be opening a customs house in the city, in line with the Ho-Sainteny Agreement of March 1946. The matter of who collected customs dues had not been resolved by the Fontainebleau agreement. On the morning of November 20, a French patrol boat had tried to stop a Chinese junk smuggling contraband, and the Viet Minh moved in on the French, opening fire briefly and then arresting the three French customs officials. The dispute quickly escalated, with the Viet Minh and their supporters throwing up barricades in the city. In response the French sent their tanks into the streets. D'Argenlieu decided to make an example of the Communists and ordered the Viet Minh forces to withdraw. He also obtained permission to use artillery if the Viet Minh did not budge. On the morning of November 23, d'Argenlieu ordered a massive bombardment of the Haiphong port area from artillery, planes, and a French cruiser in the harbor. The Viet Minh returned fire but were helpless against the French barrage. At the time, the Viet Minh claimed that 20,000 people had been killed, while the French estimated the number at 6,000. In 1981, one of the Communist leaders told an American reporter, Stanley Karnow, that the number of deaths was more like 500 to 1,000. Whatever the exact number of casualties, however, the destruction of the port area was horrendous. Anti-French riots started soon afterward, but the French quickly put these down. On December 19, 1946, the Viet Minh attacked French bases in North Vietnam, marking the beginning of the First Indochina War.

Although there was a ceasefire on Christmas Day 1946, the fighting was bitter. Indeed when it began Ho Chi Minh barely escaped from the house in which he was staying in Hanoi. A small group of Viet Minh held up the French while the rest withdrew from the city. The war began with the French in control of all the cities of Vietnam, including Hanoi and Haiphong in the north, Hue in central Vietnam, and Saigon in the south. They also controlled much of the countryside of the south, and many of the rubber plantations along the Vietnamese-Cambodian border. By contrast the Communists were in control of the large rural areas in north and central Vietnam, the border region with China and the southernmost part of Vietnam—the swamp land around the Mekong Delta. This last area was going to become a major problem not just for the French, but for the Americans later on.

Throughout 1947, the French, armed with British and American war surplus from World War II, and with a massively enlarged French Foreign Legion fought and captured much territory from the Viet Minh. The French, however, were in favor of the "Bao Dai" solution by which they hoped to create an independent South Vietnam to combat the view that the Indochina War was colonial in nature. In the first Ha Long Bay "agreement" in December 1946, and the second "agreement" in July 1947, Bao Dai believed that what the French were offering was inadequate. Both times he was tricked into accepting the agreements on a French cruiser in Ha Long Bay, off the coast of Vietnam. He was living in Hong Kong at the time, but both sides realized that for an agreement to be made, it had to be done in Vietnam, or at any rate in Vietnamese waters. Finally, in March 1949, the French president, Vincent Auriol, signed the Elysée Accords with a newly created Associated State of Vietnam (often known as the State of Vietnam) and also the Kingdom of Cambodia and the Kingdom of Laos. All achieved "demi-independence," with France retaining control over foreign relations and defense. In Cambodia, this immediately undercut the Communist forces, but in Vietnam the reception was more mixed.

On June 13, 1949, Bao Dai became head of state of the Associated State of Vietnam, which was officially proclaimed on July 1 and was immediately recognized by France. The Americans and the British, however, held back recognition until February 1950. Whatever constitutional headway this created, the Associated State of Vietnam and the French army started to suffer major reverses on the battlefield. On September 21, 1949, the Chinese Communists won the Chinese Civil War, and on January 18, 1950, they formally recognized the DRV, offering it large supplies of weapons and logistical help. The Soviet Union formally recognized the DRV exactly a week later. It was probably these moves that forced British and American recognition of the Associated State of Vietnam.

The French now faced a military situation whereby the Vietnamese Communists could bring (and indeed did bring) large quantities of arms across the Vietnamese-Chinese border. As a result the French had to try to bolster their forces in this region. In February 1950, France officially requested U.S. aid to continue the war. This request was approved by U.S. President Harry S

Truman on May 1, and $15 million was given to France. With the outbreak of the Korean War in June, it was not long before the U.S. government increased its aid to the French. The United States saw itself in a war against communism, and Ho Chi Minh, undoubtedly a communist, was portrayed by the French in as bad a light as they could.

In late 1950, the Viet Minh succeeded in destroying many of the French positions along the Vietnamese-Chinese border, but their attempt to incite an uprising in the Red River Delta in the following year failed. It seemed as though the French were unable to defeat the Viet Minh, but the Viet Minh did not have the power to launch an attack on many of the French positions. The French, trying to rally their flagging morale, appointed Jean de Lattre de Tassigny as their new commander-in-chief. He did inspire confidence for a while; he certainly was given more U.S. military aid. Bao Dai's government, however, lacked much credibility with many Vietnamese. Bao Dai's first prime minister, Nguyen Van Xuan, was a graduate of the French Ecole Polytechnique, and had spent most of his life in France. A French citizen, he is said to have spoken Vietnamese only falteringly. Few Saigon politicians trusted him. His son, Nguyen Van Hinh, was later made commander of Bao Dai's army, but he, too, was a French citizen who carried no Nationalist credentials. Xuan's successor was Nguyen Phan Long, a moderate reformist, but he lasted only two months before being replaced by Tran Van Huu, a wealthy landowner who held the post for two before he was also sacked. Both Long and Huu had tried to negotiate directly with the Americans and eliminate the French altogether. Both might have managed to increase the popularity of the Bao Dai government had they been allowed to continue their reforms. Huu's successor, Nguyen Van Tam, had a reputation as a French "puppet," but, to his credit, did try to promote land reform. He was voted out of office in January 1953. During this political infighting, General de Lattre managed to defeat two Viet Minh attacks, one in the Red River Delta and the other in Haiphong. De Lattre, however, lost his only son Bernard in an engagement that followed, and the general himself retired to France, succumbing to cancer a few months later.

By now many French people had become disenchanted by the war. De Lattre de Tassigny was replaced by Raoul Salan who adopted a cautious military policy, unlike his later actions in Algeria, after which he helped found the anti-Gaullist Secret Army Organisation (OAS) made famous in Frederick Forsyth's novel *The Day of the Jackal* (1971). In May 1953, under pressure from the Americans to launch a major blow against the Viet Minh, Salan was replaced by General Henri Navarre.

Navarre drew up his plan to win the war. Known as the Navarre Plan, it involved launching attacks on all the Viet Minh in central and southern Vietnam, and then, without any worry about being attacked there, have the French to concentrate their forces in the north. In a major military offensive in the spring or summer of 1954, he wanted to engage the Viet Minh in battle and destroy them. It was an ambitious plan but had support from the new Eisenhower administration in Washington, D.C. The U.S. government stepped up its aid and waited for the plan to bear fruit.

With the French finally going on the offensive, the Americans, and to a lesser extent the French, were having increasing doubts about the suitability of Bao Dai as a leader they should be backing. He was no longer the handsome playboy of the 1930s, but cut a rather plump figure, and the press was highlighting aspects of his corrupt lifestyle. He was not really interested in politics and preferred hunting and the nightlife. For the former, he wrote an introduction to *Just Elephants,* a book by a former hunting colleague, William Bazé, which was published in London in 1955. In it he invited hunters to pursue the "noble sport" in Indochina. He certainly was a well-known figure in nightclubs in Hong Kong and Paris, as well as casinos in Cannes. He was paid a massive allowance by the French and used this to live relatively modestly within the country—his main luxuy was maintaining four aircraft—and stash most of the rest in Swiss and French banks. He knew that he was living on borrowed time and was preparing himself for many years in exile. In Saigon the Binh Xuyen, formerly a gang of river pirates, were in charge of the city's police whom they used to curtail the activities of their rivals rather than stopping street crime. Drug taking and smuggling, prostitution, and gambling were rife; and it seemed as though the authorities were either unable to do anything about it, or, as most alleged, were actively involved in the illegal activities.

Compared with this corruption, Ho Chi Minh portrayed himself as incorruptible and living the life of an aesthete. He was certainly the latter and was popular with the peasants for his simple and uncondescending manner. Many politically conscious Vietnamese in Hanoi, Hue, and Saigon, however, questioned his political operations. When Ho Chi Minh was in a bad diplomatic or military position, he was all too ready to seem to compromise and introduce noncommunists into his government. This had happened several times already. As soon as he was in the diplomatic or military ascendancy, however, he was only too quick to purge them. Some, such as a former provincial governor, Ngo Dinh Khoi, along with his family, had been murdered in 1945. Many others had been assassinated by Viet Minh agents who roamed the lawless streets of Saigon picking off many of their opponents. A number of prominent Trotskyites had also been killed by the Viet Minh in Saigon in 1945.

The strength of Ho's government lay in the loyalty of several men who would stay with him throughout the wars in Vietnam. Pham Van Dong was from a mandarin family from central Vietnam and attended the National Academy in Hue, moving to China where he became active with the Communists there and joined the Revolutionary Youth League in Canton. He then trained at the elite Whampoa Military Academy before returning to Vietnam where he became involved in anti-French activities, leading to his arrest and imprisonment from 1931 to 1936. He then worked with Ho Chi Minh, based in southern China, and was regarded as a loyal and moderate supporter of Ho, accompanying him to Paris in 1946. In 1941, he had been a founding member of the Viet Minh. The other two men who formed the Communist Party leadership with Ho Chi Minh were Le Duan and Truong Chinh. In addition, while Saigon politicians had to put up with dissenters and demonstrators, often with not very good grace, Ho Chi Minh's position in charge of the Vietnamese Communist movement was unassailable.

The French soldiers were also criticized by the world's press. The top echelon included highly trained and disciplined regular soldiers, officers who graduated from St. Cyrienne, and quite a number who could speak Vietnamese fluently. Bob Denard, later famous as a mercenary leader in Africa, served in the French Navy in the Mekong Delta. The French Foreign Legion, the toughest and roughest soldiers in the French army, were some of its most effective in battle. Evidence gradually began to emerge, however, that many had been recruited after World War II from the ranks of the disbanded German army, with the possibility that some could have been S.S. war criminals. Books such as George Elford's *Devil's Guard* (1971) portrayed this idea to the public. By contrast, contemporary books such as Ensio Tiira's *Raft of Despair* (1954) paint a different picture of fairly simple men who were drawn into the hardship of the Foreign Legion and who, in the case of Tiira, almost died in their bid to escape. There was also a handful of British soldiers who served in the Foreign Legion. Henry Ainley; Colin John; and Adrian Liddell Hart, a former political journalist and son of the British writer Sir Basil Liddell Hart, all served in the Foreign Legion in Vietnam, and all three subsequently wrote their memoirs.

There were also many African soldiers from France's colonial empire who served in Vietnam including Jean-Bedel Bokassa, later emperor of the Central African Empire; Christophe Soglo, later president of Dahomey; Saye Zerbo, later president of Upper Volta; and Mohammed Oufkir, later Moroccan defense minister, executed in 1972 after a failed assassination attempt on King Hassan II of Morocco. While he was in Vietnam, Bokassa, later to rise to infamy for his lavish lifestyle in his impoverished country, fathered a Vietnamese child. In 1970, when Bokassa was at the height of his power, the girl, Martine, and her mother contacted him and he acknowledged his paternity, bringing both of them to Bangui.

The French, their Foreign Legion, and the Africans, however, constituted a minority of the soldiers the French were able to field. Most of their army was made up of Vietnamese—the Army of the State of Vietnam. These were Vietnamese who were trained by the French as an anticommunist corps to fight against the Viet Minh. Most of their officers were drawn from elite families.

Many of the rank and file were from peasant backgrounds. Although they formed a large, well-disciplined, and reliable force, the French command did not trust them and was worried that they might have split loyalties in battle, leaving most of them in garrison duties. Gradually as French losses mounted, they increased the number of Vietnamese soldiers. They called this process *jaunissement* (yellowing) in the same way that Richard Nixon in 1969 would refer to it as "Vietnamization." Against these soldiers, the Viet Minh was drawn from peasant farmers many of whom had family traditions of fighting the French and other foreign powers. They knew the terrain, many operating in and around their native villages, worked for little or no pay, and survived with little materiel.

As Navarre's plan started to bear fruit, the Viet Minh tried different tactics. While the French were anxious to pin them down, the Viet Minh decided to spread the area of conflict. The easiest way this could be done was to send soldiers into Laos and draw the French away. Because the Laotian government was a staunch ally of the French, the French authorities would feel that they had to protect them. In 1953, Viet Minh soldiers passed through a village called Muong Thanh, in the valley of Dien Bien Phu, and entered Laos. On November 20, the French, determined to prevent this from happening again, sent in soldiers to hold Dien Bien Phu. Worried about an attack, they expanded the fortifications they built, and gradually the French came up with a new plan.

This new strategy, "Operation Castor," involved constructing a massive base at Dien Bien Phu, which would then act as a magnet, forcing the Viet Minh to attack it. They would make Dien Bien Phu an irresistible target for the Communists and this would allow the French to use their firepower and aircraft. As the place was so remote, the French gambled that the Viet Minh would never be able to bring enough soldiers to the battle. Even if they did outnumber the French, the French and their Vietnamese allied soldiers would be in concrete bunkers defended with the best artillery in the world, and the Viet Minh would, so the French thought, be unable to bring large guns themselves. It was an offer that the Viet Minh commander, General Giap, was not going to refuse. He also decided to gamble on being able to defeat the French at Dien Bien Phu.

In early 1954, the Great Powers met in Berlin, Germany, and decided to hold a conference in Geneva to try to resolve the Korean War and the Indochina War. The French, the British, the Americans, the Soviet Union, and the Communist Chinese would all be represented. Both the French and the Viet Minh realized that the outcome of this peace conference might be decided at Dien Bien Phu and prepared accordingly.

General Vo Nguyen Giap was born into a peasant family but had managed to get a scholarship to attend the National Academy at Hue. At school during the 1920s, he had become interested in nationalist politics and was expelled from the school for taking part in demonstrations after the death of Phan Chu Trinh in 1926. He joined the Indochina Communist Party in 1930 and was imprisoned for two years, after which he studied law at the University of Hanoi. During World War II he emerged as the military commander of the Vietnamese Communists and became defense minister of the DRV. His wife had died in a French prison, after being arrested for pro-Communist activities. Hailed as one of the greatest generals in the twentieth century, in an interview in the 1980s he said "there is only one rule in war, and that is, you must win." At Dien Bien Phu he was to risk his entire army for an opportunity to defeat the French and end the Indochina War.

France was in a dangerous state of political flux. The French had suffered about 100,000 casualties, dead, wounded, missing, and captured. Opposition to the war was mounting. There were even a small number of Frenchmen who served with the Viet Minh, known as *Les Blancs Viet Minh*, nine being killed in combat. And the Viet Minh also had some supporters in France, although these were still a heavily marginalized minority. On the extreme left was a lawyer who was just about to become a member of the Paris Bar. Secretary of the International Union of Students Jacques Vèrges had managed to recruit several leftwing Cambodians to the communist cause, and would himself become famous many years later as the defense lawyer for Carlos "the Jackal" and numerous other infamous clients. His father was French from Réunion, and his mother was Vietnamese. When he was defending the Nazi war criminal Klaus Barbie many years later, he shouted at a witness "my mother didn't have to wear a yellow star—she was yellow from her head to her toes." It was a bitter exchange emanating from a man who suffered racist taunts during the Indochina War that were to haunt him for years to come.

Many French people had begun to have misgivings about the war in 1952. Problems were brewing in Madagascar, Morocco, and Algeria. Some, including a number of French army officers, thought it impossible to wage effective wars in Indochina and in Algeria. With northern Algeria being a part of France, not a colony, and 900,000 Europeans living there, they were more anxious to hold onto North Africa than to Vietnam. Socialist Pierre Mendès-France, a maverick, criticized the escalating cost of the war, which he saw as eating into the money France could otherwise have spent at home and in defense in Europe. Even some Americans saw France's commitment to Indochina as seriously challenging her ability to be a dependable member of the North Atlantic Treaty Organization.

French nationalists saw these factors as ploys to divert the attention of the French people from events in Indochina. They argued that France had a commitment to protect the non-Communist Indochinese from the Viet Minh. Laos and Cambodia had gained their independence on October 23, 1953, and November 9, 1953, respectively, and the governments of both countries supported the French and did not want the French to withdraw. The Vietnamese elite and many of the middle class in Saigon were terrified of a Communist victory, although large numbers were disparaging about Bao Dai. And then there were the French commercial interests.

Jean-Robert-Maurice Bonnin de la Bonninière, Comte de Beaumont, from a family ennobled during the reign of King Charles X, France's most reactionary king, ran the Sennah Rubber Company Ltd and the Compagnie du Cambodge, which controlled many of the rubber estates in southern Vietnam and Cambodia. A multimillionaire, he had worked as a journalist in Saigon and had been elected to the Assembly of the French Union for Cochinchina, a provision of the Elysée Accords. A member of the board of directors of many banks, and a keen hunter of big game, strictly speaking he was one of the elected representatives of southern Vietnam. When Cambodia had gained her independence, the new government there had undertaken to respect all French private and government property in the country. He wanted the same outcome, with suitable guarantees, for Vietnam; but he knew that Ho Chi Minh would not be interested in such undertakings, much less carry any of them out. Beaumont was prominent in the lobbying against a French withdrawal and had powerful business and social friends on whom he could call. After the French withdrew, he concentrated his interests in Cambodia and was a member and then honorary member of the International Olympic Committee from 1951 until his death in 2002 at the age of 98.

Thus there was much at stake when the Viet Minh met the French at Dien Bien Phu. General Navarre chose as his commander Colonel Christian Marie Ferdinand de la Croix de Castries, age 52, a lifetime soldier whose ancestors had fought since the Crusades and some of whom had served with Lafayette in the American Revolution. He was in the French international riding championship team from 1927 until 1939, holding two world championships (the high jump in 1933 and the broad jump two years later), and a daredevil pilot, with a string of girlfriends—and many brushes with outraged husbands—and a longer list of gambling debts. He was a tough commander, however, who had fought in Indochina since 1945, and Navarre knew he would do his best. His deputy was Colonel Charles Piroth, a one-armed artillery commander, who realized that the battle would probably be won or lost by the artillery.

The strategy adopted by the French was to entice the Viet Minh into attacking them at Dien Bien Phu. This would give the French the advantage of their concrete defenses in the center of the valley around the now-deserted village of Muong Thanh. They regarded their fortifications as impregnable. To help, they had also constructed three artillery bases on nearby hills. Gabrielle was located far to the north, with Huguette and Anne-Marie just north of the main base. Béatrice stood astride the main road to the northeast, with Françoise, Claudine, Marcelle, and Elaine to the south. Dominique and Elaine guarded the east. Isabelle was far to the south protecting an auxiliary airstrip. These were allegedly named after girlfriends of de Castries and would, according to French plans, draw away the Viet Minh.

General Giap spent months studying the dispositions at Dien Bien Phu and decided that if he was to take the fort, he would have to attack Gabrielle and Béatrice first. These were to the north of Dien Bien Phu. Isabelle was too far south to have to worry about, and also, he thought, too far away to give artillery support to the other French bases. The Viet Minh moved into position over a three-month period. The French had 13,000 men; Giap soon had 50,000 at his disposal, and another 20,000 securing his supply lines. During the three months of preparation, large numbers of Viet Minh and local villagers, some willing, others forced, built roads for the Communists to bring their weapons to the battle zone. Large artillery pieces were literally hauled up the side of mountains, and when all was in position, Giap gave the order to attack.

The Viet Minh attack started on the afternoon of March 13, 1954. He brought his guns to bear on Béatrice, which fell quickly. This allowed Giap to bring his own artillery within range of the main base, and he then turned to Isabelle. There the Foreign Legionnaires were bombarded and at 8 P.M. it was clear that ammunition was running low. The men were then instructed to use as little ammunition as possible until 9:30 P.M. At that time those still capable of the final effort fixed bayonets and shouted "Vive la Légion," charged at the Viet Minh machine gun positions, and were wiped out to a man. On March 14, Piroth, the deputy commander of the French garrison, shot himself. Much of his artillery had been destroyed and he said before he died that he was dishonored.

Although the Viet Minh were able to make rapid advances, they were not as fast as Giap had hoped. A direct Viet Minh "human wave" attack on the central French positions was repulsed. Giap then changed his entire plan, drawing back his artillery and getting his soldiers to dig trenches, and then surround Dien Bien Phu, laying siege to it and gradually building more trenches to narrow the "noose."

The Viet Minh artillery then started bombarding the French bases again, and French planes bringing supplies had to fly so high to avoid antiaircraft fire that some of the materiel they were dropping by parachute started landing in Viet Minh hands. On March 20, news of the possible fall of Dien Bien Phu reached the U.S. capitol. There U.S. Secretary of State John Foster Dulles was shocked and heard plans drawn up by Chairman of the Joint Chiefs of Staff Admiral Arthur Radford that he could use planes to bomb the Viet Minh bases. The raid would involve using between 60 and 98 B-29 heavy bombers, with an escort of 450 fighter aircraft in case the Chinese decided to intercept. There was even mention of using battlefield nuclear bombs to totally destroy the Communist bases, as well as sending in paratroopers elsewhere in Vietnam and mining Haiphong harbor for good measure. On March 25, the National Security Council approved the Radford Plan, and on April 7, at a news conference when discussing Dien Bien Phu, President Eisenhower used the analogy "You have a row of dominoes set up, and you knock over the first one, and what will happen to the last one is the certainty that it will go over very quickly." This later became developed into the "Domino Theory" that came to dominate U.S. policy thinking during the Cold War.

Although the U.S. government supported the Radford Plan, Eisenhower was not keen on escalating the conflict or using nuclear weapons without consulting the British. On April 24, Radford and Dulles met Anthony Eden, the British foreign minister, in Paris. They said that Eisenhower would be asking Congress for a joint resolution to approve U.S. air strikes, with no mention of nuclear escalation. Eden told them that he was against escalating the war, but promised to relay their request to British Prime Minister Winston Churchill. Churchill had worked with Eisenhower in the last years of World War II, and the two respected each other's judgment. Churchill was unimpressed by the Radford Plan and claimed that the U.S. idea would involve misleading Congress. He refused British support for a U.S. nuclear strike, which might have been the only way of saving the day for the French.

On April 26, 1954, the Far Eastern Conference began in Geneva, with discussion of Korea. It was scheduled to start discussions on Vietnam on May 8, and on the days leading up to this, the Viet Minh redoubled their efforts to try to take the French base. Finally on May 7, the Viet Minh managed to capture General de Castries's headquarters at Dien Bien Phu, and the French surrendered. It was a humiliating defeat for the French, with 15,000 French and colonial soldiers killed or taken prisoner, even though the Viet Minh lost 25,000 men and women.

When the Far Eastern Conference in Geneva turned to discuss Indochina on May 8, John Foster Dulles paid tribute to the French at Dien Bien Phu stating that they had lost "after a heroic defense." For the U.S. delegation the conference had not gone well. It was the first time that the People's Republic of China had representation at any conference involving the Great Powers; their enemies, the Republic of China (Taiwan), held the United Nations seat until October 1971. Dulles refused to shake hands with the Chinese foreign minister Zhou Enlai and left Geneva after a week.

With neither side able to agree about what to do in Vietnam, the Chinese took over the negotiations. They and the Soviet delegation were worried that if the conference was not able to resolve anything, the war might intensify, and the United States might want to become involved; and this might lead to a Communist defeat. Also, they feared that the French might pull out of the talks and try to take the military offensive. Pressure mounted when, on June 17, Pierre Mendès-France, the new prime minister of France, declared that he would resign if he could not obtain a ceasefire in Indochina by July 20. It was clear that the only way to get a ceasefire would be a partition of Vietnam. As the deadline approached, two major issues were outstanding: the exact boundary between the DRV and the State of Vietnam, and the length of time before a referendum would be held to decide Vietnam's future. In Korea, the 1945 partition along the 38th parallel had proven unworkable, and in Vietnam it was finally decided to partition the country along the Ben Hai River, although most commentators wrote that the partition was along the 17th parallel.

As to the referendum on the possible unification of Vietnam, the Communists had wanted it to be held within six months. This would give them an advantage, as Ho Chi Minh was far more popular than Bao Dai, and six months would not allow enough time for a new non-Communist leader to emerge to establish himself. Even Eisenhower admitted in his memoirs that an open election in Vietnam would lead to a Communist victory. As a result, the anti-Communists—the delegations of the State of Vietnam and the United States—wanted an election in five years. The eventual compromise, on the night of July 20–21—Mendès-France's deadline—was for a referendum to be held in two years. The delegations of the State of Vietnam and the United States both accepted the delineation of the border but refused to agree to the deadline for the referendum, with neither signing the agreement.

Thus the First Indochina War ended with the Communists having won on the battlefield, but managing to get control of less than half the country. The French had to evacuate Hanoi, along with their other bases and settlements in the north, but the anti-Communists kept control of Hue, with the Communists having to pull out their supporters in the pro-Communist areas of central Vietnam. It was agreed that people who wished to move from one area had six months to do so. An International Control Commission consisting of Canadians, Indians, and Poles would monitor the Geneva Agreement.

# 5

# From Geneva Agreements to the Start of War (1954–1960)

## NGO DINH DIEM

At the Far Eastern Conference in Geneva, a new Vietnamese politician emerged on the international scene. Ngo Dinh Diem was a politician from central Vietnam who had been appointed prime minister of South Vietnam, a new entity created at Geneva that included the city of Hue where he had grown up. He faced many problems—many of the South Vietnamese politicians had fought alongside the French and viewed the new country as a betrayal of the sacrifice of the French soldiers and their Vietnamese allies. They saw that the promise of a referendum in two years on reunification as a proverbial "sword of Damocles" hanging over them, and many left the country, or made plans to do so. For the Vietnamese Communists who lived south of the new boundary, some decided to leave for the north, but others decided to stay and organize for the referendum they felt sure they would win.

The United States undertook, privately and publicly, to help South Vietnam and immediately organized a flotilla of boats to assist 900,000 North Vietnamese, mainly Catholics, to resettle in the south. These people, the United States thought, would be loyal to the new South Vietnamese government and allow it, backed by the United States, to become a bastion against communism.

This commitment coincided with the signing of the Southeast Asia Treaty Organization, which was organized by the United States to help with its new policy of containment of communism. Drawing together France, the United Kingdom, Australia, New Zealand, Thailand, the Philippines, and Pakistan, member states, unlike those in the North Atlantic Treaty Organization, were not automatically obliged to mount a mutual defense if any one of them was attacked. It did allow the United States, however, to send advisors to South Vietnam.

Born in 1901 in Hue, Ngo Dinh Diem was a devout Roman Catholic, but was influenced by Confucianism. He attended the Quoc Hoc school where his father was headmaster and declined a scholarship to study in France, briefly considering becoming a monk, or at any rate joining the priesthood as had his brother Ngo Dinh Thuc. He had then entered the civil service as had his oldest brother Ngo Dinh Khoi, which led to his appointment as minister of the interior in 1932. However he had resigned after two months in a protest against French interference in what he felt was his area of responsibility. Diem then spent the decade from 1933 until 1945 living with his mother in Hue, and in 1945 was traveling from Saigon to Hue to urge Bao Dai not to form an alliance with Ho Chi Minh when he was captured by the Viet Minh and taken to a highland village near the Chinese border. There he learned that Ngo Dinh Khoi and his son had been murdered by the Viet Minh. Six months later Diem met Ho Chi Minh who denied having any part in the killing of Khoi. Diem then returned to Hue and, in 1950, left Vietnam. He had stated that he planned to attend the Holy Year celebration at the Vatican, but instead he went to the United States and spent two years in New Jersey at the Maryknoll Seminary at Lakewood where he started training for the monkhood. While in the United States he made important connections with U.S. Roman Catholic political figures such as Cardinal Spellman of New York and John F. Kennedy.

In May 1953, Diem moved to a Benedictine monastery in Belgium, which served as his base for frequent visits to the French capital. In Paris his youngest brother, Ngo Dinh Luyen, was urging the Vietnamese community there to endorse Diem as their leader, and on June 18, 1954, Bao Dai had placed a crucifix before Diem and made him pledge to defend Vietnam against the Communists. After leaving Bao Dai's chateau, Diem returned to Paris and from there flew to Saigon, arriving on June 26, 1954. He was greeted by about 500 mainly Roman Catholics who had gathered to support him.

In the true Confucian mold, Diem was to rely on his family who were his most loyal supporters. His older brother Ngo Dinh Thuc, a priest, became archbishop of Hue and the dean of the Catholic Episcopacy of Vietnam. Ngo Dinh Nhu became Diem's "Supreme Advisor" and was minister of the interior, controlling the police. Ngo Dinh Can was later appointed governor of central Vietnam, and Ngo Dinh Luyen was sent to London as ambassador to the Court of St. James. Nhu's father-in-law, Tran Van Chuong, became ambassador to Washington, D.C., and his brother, Tran Van Do, served as foreign minister between 1954 and 1955.

When Diem arrived in Saigon he faced a major political battle with General Nguyen Van Hinh, the chief of staff of the armed forces who insisted he should control the country—Bao Dai initially felt it was unsafe to return, and then Diem refused to let him come back. Diem persuaded Bao Dai to invite Hinh to France for consultations. Hinh, a French citizen, then went into exile. In this move, as in so many others in the next few years, Diem had the help of the U.S. government. The Americans were eager to see a strong anticommunist government established in a viable South Vietnam with a popular government.

## THE CONSOLIDATION OF THE DIEM GOVERNMENT

Although the United States had sent advisers to Vietnam to assist the French, a few weeks before Diem arrived in Saigon, Edward Lansdale, an agent with the Office of Strategic Services, moved to Saigon and established the Saigon Military Mission. Lansdale was the model for the character of Alden Pyle in Graham Greene's *The Quiet American* (1955) and for Colonel Edwin Hillendale in *The Ugly American* (1958) by William Lederer and Eugene Burdick. His aim was to assist the new South Vietnamese government and used in this endeavor Major Lucien E. Conein, an American who had been born in Paris, France. Conein had grown up in Kansas, returning to France to fight alongside the French resistance during World War II. Lansdale and Conein formed groups of Vietnamese "stay-behind" agents who remained in North Vietnam and sabotaged the Communist efforts. At the same time Lansdale organized the transportation of the 900,000 northerners who were settled in South Vietnam from whom the new Diem government could recruit soldiers.

After winning the confrontation with General Hinh, Diem then moved against the Binh Xuyen gangsters who controlled the Saigon police. Diem ordered them out of his capital on April 27, 1955; the Binh Xuyen responded by shelling the presidential palace. By the end of May, Diem was victorious and Bay Vien, the gangster leader, went into exile in France. In a curious twist, some of the Bin Xuyen supporters ended up allied to the Communists. He also moved against the Hoa Hao, a millenarian sect; and their leader, Ba Cut, was finally captured in 1956, tried, and publicly guillotined soon afterwards.

Deciding to test his popularity, Diem held a referendum on October 23, 1955 on whether he should run the country, or whether Bao Dai should remain in charge. The ballot papers for Diem showed him in a suit and were red, signifying good luck. Those for Bao Dai were green, the Vietnamese color for misfortune, and Bao Dai was in imperial regalia, which he had not worn for nearly 10 years. Official returns showed that Diem had won with 98.2 percent of the vote. There was certainly intimidation of Bao Dai supporters at the polling stations even though it was unnecessary. Diem would have clearly won a free vote, but his U.S. advisers had come to realize that he was becoming intolerant of dissent. On October 26, 1955, the Republic of Vietnam was proclaimed, with a new flag—yellow with three red stripes. These signified the three parts of Vietnam: Tonkin, Annam, and Cochinchina, as well as the three rivers of Vietnam, the Red River in the north, the Perfume River in central Vietnam, and the Mekong River in the south, with yellow representing the soil of the country.

Other symbolic changes were made in Saigon. Many streets were renamed: Rue De Gaulle was renamed *Duong* Ngo Dinh Khoi, after Diem's older brother who had been killed by the Viet Minh; and Boulevard de la Somme was renamed *Dai Lo* Ham Nghi after the emperor who fought the French. Armand Rousseau, a street named for the French governor-general of Indochina in 1895–1896, was renamed Jean-Jacques Rousseau, after the French philosopher, in an attempt to keep much of the name, while also illustrating the French influence on the Diem government. The Boulevard named after Lord Kitchener, the British World War I soldier and statesman, was renamed after Nguyen Thai Hoc, the man who had founded the Vietnamese Nationalist Party, the VNQDD. The street named for the French Commander de Lattre de Tassigny did not change.

Diem started a series of highly publicized tours of the countryside where he met with many villagers who, for the first time in their lives, were able to see the leader of their country. Rallies staged to show support for Diem were probably unnecessary, as the villagers appreciated his visits and his popularity grew. A massive land reform program was undertaken, which the U.S. government supported and financed. The aim was to break up the landholdings of the landlords and allow the peasant farmers to own their own land. It was a system that had worked well in Taiwan and Japan, and would have been successfully implemented in South Vietnam had Diem not insisted on raising the size of land that landlords could keep and exempting land that had been used for family burials. With many wealthy families having grave sites around their properties, the real redistribution of land to the peasants slowly ground to a halt with less and less land available for redistribution. Diem also insisted that the peasants pay for the land they had seized during the war against the French.

It was not long before Diem started moving against the Communist movement itself. The Communists had expected a referendum to be held in 1956, but with neither the South Vietnamese government nor the U.S. government having signed that part of the Geneva Agreement, it was clear by early 1956 that Diem had no intention of holding the referendum. He argued that not only had he not signed any undertaking to hold a referendum, but that any referendum that was held would be unfair. Communists had been able to organize in

South Vietnam, certainly up until the start of 1956, but the non-Communists were not allowed to campaign in North Vietnam, and a referendum where nearly half the population would be used as a bloc vote by the Communists would deliver an inevitable Communist victory.

Diem's security forces drew up lists of Communists and suspected Communists—or to be more precise they updated already existing French lists. They identified people who had relatives who had gone north or who had fought alongside the Communists and earmarked them for arrest and interrogation. By the end of 1956, it was clear that no referendum was going to be held in South Vietnam, and there were, curiously, only muted protests from North Vietnam.

It was also necessary to move against the Cao Dai (High Tower) sect. It had been founded in 1926 by Ngo Van Chieu, a civil servant in the colonial government whose ideas merged the philosophical concepts of Buddhism, Confucianism, Islam, Daoism, and Christianity, gaining much support in Cochinchina. The religion involved the teachings of Buddha, Confucius, Moses, Jesus, and Mohammed, with a focus also on Joan of Arc, Rene Descartes, William Shakespeare (who had not been mentioned in mainstream Cao Dai literature since 1935), Victor Hugo, Louis Pasteur, and V. I. Lenin. From its headquarters at Tay Ninh, the main church of the Cao Dai, the sect managed to avoid a direct confrontation with the Diem government, reluctantly supporting the South Vietnamese government against the Communists.

## THE CREATION OF NORTH VIETNAM

During the establishment of Communist rule over North Vietnam in 1954, Ho Chi Minh and the Viet Minh returned to Hanoi, which they had left nine years earlier. Some of the Communist leadership assumed that the referendum in 1956 would easily deliver them the south of the country, or that the South would collapse of its own accord, and they set about turning North Vietnam into a communist economy.

Unlike Diem, Ho Chi Minh never had any sects or army dissidents to challenge his rule, and the French left the north in an orderly fashion, although they did take with them many prefabricated buildings and the contents of post offices, schools, libraries, and hospitals. They even took their dead from the Hanoi Military Cemetery. The first problem faced by Ho Chi Minh was feeding the people of the north, and the Soviet Union paid for emergency rice shipments from Burma.

Many of the Communist Party leaders did not fit in well with their new role as leaders of the government of a country. They had been leading a resistance war against the French for nine years, and many had been fighting the French for a great deal longer than that. They now had to set up and operate a health service and schools, repair roads and bridges that were destroyed in the war or had simply worn out, and build up the infrastructure of the country. The first postage stamps were issued in October 1954, showing Ho Chi Minh with the Soviet Prime Minister Malenkov on his left and Mao Zedong on his right. It was not until 1958 that North Vietnam was able to print new banknotes to replace those printed in Czechoslovakia in 1951 that had been the official currency of the country from 1954. Also in 1958 the first North Vietnamese coins were issued.

The first process of turning North Vietnam into a communist country was to categorize all the people into five groups: the landlords; the bourgeoisie; members of religious groups; and workers and peasants. The "landlord" class represented 5 percent of the population, and the Communists sought to identify them and, in many cases, execute them out of hand. Tribunals had to achieve their quotas, with some peasants manufacturing evidence against rivals either to settle old scores, or to be able to seize their land when the family that they had denounced had been executed. According to several accounts, tribunals were unable to find enough landlords to meet their quotas and chose people at random. Anybody who had a family member who worked for the French was suspect, and suspicions often led to denunciations, which could, in turn, lead to execution.

By August 1956, the land reform program in North Vietnam had gone horribly wrong with, tens of thousands of people held in forced labor camps. Even Ho Chi Minh was forced to publicly admit to errors having been made. This situation led to more chaos, as prisoners were then quickly released, and perpetrators of the "errors" were denounced and arrested. On November 2, 1956, a peasant uprising took place in Nghe An province, Ho Chi Minh's home area, with peasants protesting to members of the International Control Commission. Ho Chi Minh urged for moderation, and with much of the world focusing on the crushing of the Hungarian uprising in Europe, the specter of international communism looked bad.

Reacting to the situation, the Communist government purged Truong Chinh, the general secretary of the Communist Party, and he was made the scapegoat for the excesses of the government. During 1956, North Vietnam was hardly able to hold its own referendum for the reunification of Vietnam even had it wanted so to do. By 1959, with their currency in tatters, the North Vietnamese were forced to introduce a currency revaluation.

## DISSENSION IN SOUTH VIETNAM

When Ngo Dinh Diem first arrived in Saigon in 1954, the people he most feared were the South Vietnamese elite. By 1958, however, he had shown them that he was capable of restoring and maintaining law and order in the country, and he had the support of the United States. Many had even accepted that Diem would use his family to run the country; after all Vietnam had been a feudal country for much of its history. Reports on the activities in North Vietnam horrified people in South Vietnam, many of whom had a liking for "Uncle Ho," as Ho Chi Minh was affectionately known, even if they were not Communists.

Gradually, however, resentment grew regarding the high-handed way in which Diem ran his government. Many of the intellectuals in Saigon and Hue were not that concerned about the lack of true democracy. Vietnam, after all, did not have a democratic tradition. Some did resent the promotion of Roman Catholics in the civil service and the army, but they were more troubled by the seeming inflexibility of the new regime. Initially the dissent showed itself in minor ways, with some people not opting to use postage stamps with Diem on them. For the U.S. government, it seems to be an awkward period, but it still did not flinch in its support for Diem.

In 1959, Vietnam celebrated the anniversary of the Trung sisters who had led the rebellion against the Chinese 1,920 years earlier. Diem's sister-in-law, the vivacious Mme. Nhu, organized the construction of a statue in Saigon to commemorate the sisters, modeling them on her own image and thereby implying she was a reincarnation of them. The statue was unveiled in 1962. When North Vietnam revalued its currency in March 1959, the first postage stamps they issued with the new currency symbolically commemorated the sisters, although the South Vietnamese postal service did not commemorate them until 1974.

Soon after the celebrations for the anniversary of the Trung Sisters, in August 1959, legislative assembly elections were held in South Vietnam. The aim was to introduce a democratic system, and opposition candidates were invited to stand against members of Diem's Can Lao (Personalist Labor) Party. Although peasants were encouraged to vote, many found themselves pressured into voting for Diem's candidates, with troops based in Saigon delivering bloc votes for the regime. The official returns showed a turnout of 86 percent, with 460 candidates standing for the 123 seats—333 standing as independents. The results were never in doubt, with all but two seats won by parties or independents who supported Diem.

Not long after the election some South Vietnamese politicians and military figures drew up plans for a coup d'état. The coup centered on Lieutenant Colonel Vuong Van Dong, originally from northern Vietnam, who had fought for the French. An anticommunist, he had trained at Fort Leavenworth, Kansas and had become angry at the way that Diem interfered with military operations. On the morning of November 11, 1960, the rebel soldiers surrounded the presidential palace. It was certainly a naïve coup attempt. No one had cut the telephone lines from the palace, allowing Diem to call loyal units. In the fighting that resulted, 400 were killed—rebels, loyalists, and civilians who wandered into the line of fire.

The real problems facing South Vietnam, however, were not rebel commanders, but the Communists. In October 1957, Communists in South Vietnam received instructions from Hanoi to start organizing armed groups. Ho Chi Minh still urged the southern Communists as late as 1959 not to engage in armed attacks on the Diem government. With the southern Communists anxious for action, however, the government of North Vietnam was split. Le Duan had come from Quang Tri province, part of South Vietnam, in fact on the southern side of the border, and he constantly urged North Vietnam to support the southern Communists, eventually managing to persuade Truong Chinh and then Ho Chi Minh.

On December 20, 1960, the National Front for the Liberation of South Vietnam was proclaimed at a secret location near the Vietnamese border with Cambodia. Its aim was to mobilize public sentiment against the Diem government by bringing together a range of political groups opposed to Diem. It proclaimed its support for land reform, personal freedoms, and democracy, with no reference to communism. The formation of the National Front for the Liberation of South Vietnam (NFL), as it became known, marked the start of a civil war between those who saw the NFL as a southern group that received support from the North, or a foreign invasion for those who saw it as a communist "front" organization founded and controlled by Hanoi.

# 6

# From the Formation of Vietcong to U.S. Soldiers (1960–1965)

The National Front for the Liberation of South Vietnam (NFL) claimed that its members were made up of nationalist and patriotic individuals who opposed the Diem government of South Vietnam. Certainly it acknowledged that some of them were communists, but its leader, from his release from prison in 1961, was Nguyen Huu Tho, a French-educated lawyer from Saigon who had been a member of the French Socialist Party. Captured by the Viet Minh in 1947, he was won over to their cause. From 1954 until 1961, he was imprisoned in South Vietnam and then became leader of the NFL, which supported land reform, democracy, and peace. Initially its program did not refer to the reunification of the two Vietnams, and it made no reference to communism. Ostensibly the NFL was an umbrella group of anti-Diem forces, which were starting a civil war against a government they opposed.

By contrast, the South Vietnamese government took the view that the NFL, which often became known internationally as the NLF, was established by the North Vietnamese Communists as a "front organization," with the clear aim of waging war in South Vietnam on a pretense of being opposed to Diem; in reality, it was actually spearheading a North Vietnamese "invasion" of South Vietnam, and was set on destroying South Vietnam as an entity. The Diem government denounced the members of the NFL as communists and urged the United States to support South Vietnam in the worldwide battle against communism.

The NFL gained international support from the Communist world, who viewed continued U.S. support for South Vietnam as meddling in a civil war. Its stance was championed by the United States who saw a pro-U.S. government in danger of falling to a Communist invasion. As a result, fighting started in parts of South Vietnam as the NFL's armed wing, the People's Liberation Armed Forces (PLAF), formally established in February 1961, tried to try to take control of parts of the country. In October 1963, the NFL issued its own postage stamps proclaiming "Independence—Democracy—Peace—Neutrality," and the stamps were posted in Hanoi.

The Diem government quickly renamed the PLAF with the pejorative term "Vietcong," and it was not long before the term was used in the press around the world. The PLAF was split into three groups. The command and the main armed forces operated with full regular units. Below them were guerillas organized at the provincial or district level. The lowest tier consisted of the village militia. Initially the aim was to attack Diem supporters in isolated villages and settlements throughout South Vietnam and to attack lines of communications in a method similar to that used by the Malayan Communist Party from 1948 in British Malaya. By striking at government supporters and destroying the economy of the country, the government might see the need to negotiate.

As the NFL was becoming established, a fundamental change occurred in the United States with the election of John F. Kennedy as President of the United States in November 1960. In his inauguration address on January 20, 1961, Kennedy stated that he "would pay any price, bear any burden, meet any hardship, support any friend, oppose any foe in order to assure the survival and the success of liberty." At the time he made the speech, few U.S. commentators saw Vietnam as a major issue. President Dwight D. Eisenhower, in his memoir *Waging Peace*, makes only a few incidental references to Vietnam. Robert McNamara, the incoming U.S. secretary of defense, in his account of the briefing that took place on January 19 between the outgoing administration and the incoming one, noted that most of the focus was on events in Laos.

President Diem of South Vietnam believed that the new U.S. government would be more supportive of his government, as Kennedy was a Roman Catholic and sympathetic to the plight of Catholicism in Asia. The appointment of Frederick Nolting as the new U.S. ambassador, replacing Elbridge Durbrow, also encouraged Diem in this belief. Nolting had served in Paris and then on the North Atlantic Council and quickly came to realize the difficulties that Diem faced in South Vietnam, as well as the high level of support that he had achieved in a relatively short time.

The problem that many in South Vietnam saw, and that the U.S. administration began to understand, was that Diem's strong support did not extend to the entire South Vietnamese government, and especially not to Diem's younger brother Nhu. Ngo Dinh Nhu had studied in France where he had become fascinated by the philosophy of "personalism" developed by Emmanuel Mounier, a French Roman Catholic thinker. This philosophy emphasized that human dignity was more important than materialism, and it had been adopted as the national ideology of South Vietnam, even though many of Mounier's supporters in France claimed that what had been introduced in South Vietnam bore only a superficial similarity to Mounier's actual beliefs. Nhu was a great organizer, however, and he transformed support for Diem into a political movement, the Personalist Labor Party, with the formation of cell-like structures capable of operating in the same manner as the Communist Party, which they were dedicated to destroying. These cells provided excellent intelligence by school teachers, doctors, nurses, and others who were sent to villages presumed to be hostile during the late 1950s. Almost the entire Communist infrastructure in South Vietnam had been identified and its ringleaders arrested. In fact the very declaration of the NFL occurred because the Communists in the South could see that Nhu was smashing their structure, and there is even some evidence that the amount of initial northern support for the NFL illustrates how effective Nhu's intelligence tactics had been.

As Diem never married, Nhu's wife, Madame Nhu (née Tran Le Xuan), was an influential figure and a major aide to the president. Officially she was the First Lady of the Nation, hosting important national receptions. Vivacious, intelligent, and also quite obstinate, she promoted hardline Roman Catholic policies by which abortion and contraceptives were banned, divorce prohibited, adultery made a criminal offense, and nightclubs and boxing matches made illegal. These changes altered the face of Saigon, Dalat, and other places in South Vietnam. It also opened up the police to corrupt practices, with police chiefs taking bribes to allow these operations to flourish in secret.

With the start of an insurgency war in South Vietnam, the situation became comparable to the Malayan Emergency, 1948–1960, when the British were able to defeat the Malayan Communist Party through military and political means. Nhu felt that he might be able to win the political battle, but he and his advisers looked to Malaya for possible military tactics. In Malaya the British had instituted what became known as the Briggs Plan. This plan established "New Villages" where Chinese squatters on jungle frontiers, and others, were herded into settlements that were surrounded by defenses that prevented them from giving food supplies and intelligence to the Communist guerillas in nearby jungle camps. Ngo Dinh Nhu inaugurated what became known as the Strategic Hamlets Program. In essence it was similar to the Briggs Plan, but there were crucial differences. Whereas in Malaya the villagers were moved from land they did not own to land that was given to them as freehold title, as an incentive to help with the relocation, those in Vietnam were being moved from land they owned to what was generally less fertile land that was also given to them. Unlike in Malaya, the peasants in South Vietnam were not turned into landowners, and they were also forced to move from land their family may have cultivated for centuries and where their family and ancestors had been buried. As a result the Strategic Hamlets Program led to simmering resentment against the Diem government.

The first major attack on Diem, however, did not come from the PLAF or disgruntled peasants. In the early morning of February 27, 1962, two fighter aircraft attacked the presidential palace in central Saigon in an assassination attempt on Ngo Dinh Diem. Diem, Nhu, and Madame Nhu took refuge in the cellar of the palace, with Madame Nhu later describing for television how a bomb, "the size of a small pig" landed near her and failed to explode. Diem was quickly able to make a radio broadcast and calm down Saigon, which, for an hour, was in a panic. Of the two pilots, one bailed out and was captured, but not executed. The other managed to escape to nearby Cambodia where he was subsequently interviewed by the press. He claimed that his actions had been forced on him because of blatant favoritism by the Diem administration to their Roman Catholic supporters, and that not enough was being done to fight the NFL who were making substantial military progress.

The attack showed the U.S. government the differences between the South Vietnamese elite and the Diem family. Eisenhower had referred to Diem and Nhu as the "king and his brother," and several members of the U.S. administration were becoming increasingly critical of Nhu and the first family. By now Diem's surviving brothers, Thuc, Nhu, Can, and Luyen, were respectively bishop of Hue, minister of the interior, governor of central Vietnam, and ambassador to London. In addition, Madame Nhu's father was ambassador to Washington, and many members of the extended family held important positions of influence, leaving Diem clearly open to charges of nepotism.

## THE BUDDHIST PROTESTS

The problems with Diem became public in mid-1963. On May 8, the South Vietnamese government violently broke up a demonstration in Hue where Buddhists, celebrating the 2527th anniversary of the birth of Lord Buddha, illegally flew the Buddhist striped flag. Only a week previously, also in Hue, Roman Catholics had flown papal banners to commemorate the 25th anniversary of Ngo Dinh Thuc's ordination. The reaction to the Buddhist demonstration was seen as discriminatory and heavy-handed; a woman and eight children died, either killed by the special forces or in the crush that followed their arrival.

The Buddhist leadership in South Vietnam started to condemn Diem and Nhu, using the deaths as a rallying cry. This protest quickly gained momentum with many others who had simmering resentment of the Diem government, or of Nhu, seeing it as an opportunity to put on record their disapproval of the South Vietnamese administration. Nhu believed that these protests were organized by the Communists, with well-planned Buddhist demonstrations in Saigon and Hue in which English-language placards were displayed and English-language leaflets were handed out for the benefit of the press who began to see the event as a major news story.

The U.S. government was horrified that their entire endeavor in South Vietnam might collapse and Ambassador Nolting urged conciliation. The U.S. administration was split as to what to do. Diem categorically refused to sack his brother Nhu, and some talk started in Washington, D.C. of a possible U.S.-supported coup to oust Diem. As these discussions started, the whole nature of the protests in Saigon changed on the morning of June 11. On that day at a Buddhist protest, a monk sat down in the road in central Saigon, and other monks doused him with gasoline. Soon afterward he erupted into flames. Photographs of the self-immolation of the monk, Thich Quang Duc, appeared on the front pages of newspapers all over the world.

The reaction of the Diem administration was stubborn and Madame Nhu, when interviewed, referred to the monk as having been intoxicated by colleagues who abused his confidence and barbecued him. She then added that the barbecuing "was done not even with self-sufficient means because they used imported gasoline." More Buddhist monks set themselves on fire, and the U.S. press coverage of Diem went from bad to worse. When Nolting, a supporter of Diem, was replaced by Henry Cabot Lodge, the new U.S. ambassador appointed by Kennedy, the laissez-faire attitude the U.S. administration had adopted to political developments in South Vietnam changed.

In Washington, a number of senior officials decided that the only way to force the government in South Vietnam to become more conciliatory was to get rid of Nhu, and if Diem refused, to oust Diem himself. In other words, members of the U.S. government became deliberately involved in supporting a coup d'état against a loyal ally. On August 20, some South Vietnamese generals, notably Tran Van Don, asked for extra powers for the army in their fight against the PLAF. This strategy was to help them stage their coup d'état, but Diem also felt it would allow him to use the army against the Buddhist protestors in Saigon. At midnight on August 21, Nhu struck at the Xa Loi Pagoda in central Saigon, where 400 monks and nuns were arrested. In Hue, hundreds of monks and nuns, aided by thousands of their supporters, fought off for eight hours an attack on their temple by Nhu's special forces. Both actions were seen as heavy-handed, but Nhu's supporters were quick to point out that South Vietnam's very survival was being threatened by the Communists and that their reaction to the Buddhist protests was mild. As Morris West noted in his novel *The Ambassador*, based on the relationship between Diem and the new ambassador Henry Cabot Lodge, demonstrations in parts of the United States were taking place at the same time, and with far more violence, in many U.S. cities, notably Little Rock, Arkansas and Birmingham, Alabama.

With Robert McNamara, the U.S. secretary of defense, on vacation, Roger Hilsman, the assistant secretary of state for Far Eastern affairs, drafted a telegram to Henry Cabot Lodge in Saigon, which was sent to President Kennedy for approval before being transmitted. McNamara wrote that Hilsman completed the telegram on August 24, and it was then sent to Kennedy. The telegram stated that clearances were being sought from Undersecretary of State George Ball and the Defense Department. Kennedy agreed to send the telegram if his advisers agreed. Dean Rusk, the secretary of state, was unenthusiastic but said he would go along with it if the president agreed. With the CIA director absent, his deputy director of planning said he would go along with it because Kennedy had already done so, and Deputy Secretary of Defense Ros Gilpatric, standing in for McNamara who was on leave, concurred, as the president and secretary of state both agreed with it.

The telegram instructed Henry Cabot Lodge to urge Diem to sack Nhu, and if he did not do so, then to "examine all possible alternative leadership and make detailed plans as to how we might bring about Diem's replacement if this should become necessary." With Diem adamantly refusing to get rid of Nhu, it was basically an instruction to the U.S. ambassador to organize a coup d'état against a president the U.S. government had publicly backed for nine years. Lodge met with Diem and tried to urge him to sack Nhu, but Diem refused to let Lodge bring up the question, much to the ire of Lodge. By this time serious planning had started for a coup and the U.S. administration through Lucien Conein had promised the Buddhist generals, the main group mobilizing against Diem, that they would have continued U.S. support should their coup be successful.

## THE OVERTHROW OF DIEM

At around the same time that the U.S. administration was contemplating the overthrow of Diem, Nhu made secret overtures to the Communists whom he publicly called "lost sheep." Much has subsequently been made of this move, and the exact nature of Nhu's plans has never been ascertained. Suffice to say that the possibility of Nhu, a passionate Nationalist, albeit anticommunist, and Ho Chi Minh, also a Nationalist, and a member of the Communist Party, establishing a coalition government, filled the U.S. administration with horror.

The main problem facing the coup plotters and their U.S. backers was that Diem had become extremely popular in South Vietnam, even if Nhu was hated. No other person had the personality to take over if Diem was overthrown or be able to unite the country against a growing communist threat. The concept of ousting a regime with the veneer of democracy—Diem had, after all, held elections—with an unelected military junta, had been openly discussed as a genuine possibility in Washington for several weeks.

With the coup planned for October 26, 1963, and then delayed until October 31, the date for it was finally set by astrologers for November 1. Even though the plotters, led by General Tran Van Don and General Duong Van Minh—nicknamed "Big Minh" because of his size—had received the consent of the U.S. embassy, they refused to tell the embassy the date of the coup. Nhu had been expecting the coup and had prepared two plans. According to the first plan, known as Bravo I, Nhu would deploy his most loyal soldiers, under the command of Colonel Le Quang Tung, in the countryside outside Saigon. Then a number of Nhu loyalists would pretend to stage a coup. This would "flush out" opponents of Diem while Diem and Nhu took refuge at Vung Tau, a small coastal resort near Saigon. During the crisis, some of Nhu's supporters would seize control of the Saigon radio station and broadcast support for the Communists. This would then associate, in the minds of most people, any anti-Diem generals who had joined the fake coup with the Communists. According to Operation Bravo II, Colonel Tung would force his way back into Saigon, restoring Diem and Nhu to power. The coup plotters, and anybody else who was troublesome, could then be arrested. The main problem with Nhu's plan was that it relied on General Ton That Dinh, age 37, who had betrayed Bravo I and II to the actual coup plotters. In another twist, the plotters did not trust General Dinh and feared that Bravo I and Bravo II were just the cover for another of Nhu's machinations.

From 10 A.M. until noon on the morning of November 1, the U.S. ambassador, Henry Cabot Lodge, talked with Diem in the Gia Long Palace—the presidential palace having been badly damaged in the February 1962 air attack. The meeting went cordially, and with Lodge heading off for lunch, at 1 P.M., the plotters were ready to strike. A "routine meeting" was held at the staff headquarters in Saigon where the plotters planned to arrest the loyalist generals. Lucien Conein brought with him 3 million piasters (about $40,000) in cash in case the plotters needed money. One of the loyalists, Captain Ho Tan Quyen, had decided not to attend. As the commander of the navy, he had noticed unexplained troop moves and drove off to consult with some confederates. Outside Saigon, the car was ambushed and he was killed in a nearby field while trying to escape. As the "routine meeting" began, the army officers present were told of the coup, and some congratulated the plotters. Colonel

Tung was taken to a nearby room and killed. The plotters felt that he was too dangerous to be allowed to live.

When the coup began, Diem and Nhu descended into the bunker under the Gia Long Palace. It was not long before they found themselves unable to contact General Dinh whom they still believed was loyal. Thinking that he might have been captured, Diem telephoned General Tran Van Don, the leader of the plotters, and offered to meet with the conspirators and negotiate a solution to prevent loss of life. Many of the conspirators feared that Diem would outwit them in negotiations and persuaded Don not to meet the president. An hour and a half later, Diem telephoned Ambassador Lodge and asked him what the U.S. attitude was to the coup. Lodge prevaricated and replied that it was early in the morning in Washington, D.C., but he offered to look after the physical safety of Diem and Nhu. Diem declined while rebel soldiers started firing on the barracks of the presidential guard.

At about 8 P.M., Diem and Nhu, along with two aides, left the palace and drove to the house of the Chinese merchant Ma Tuyen in Cholon, the Chinese suburb to the west of Saigon. There Diem was able to telephone the coup plotters who still believed him to be in the Gia Long Palace. At midnight Diem was able to contact General Dinh who, surrounded by the other plotters still unsure about which side he was on, shouted obscenities at Diem. Several hours later, one of Diem's aides who had escaped with him telephoned the plotters to say that Diem and Nhu had fled to Cholon. Soon afterward, rebel soldiers led by Colonel Nguyen Van Thieu, later president himself, attacked the Gia Long Palace, finally breaking in after hours of fighting. They were able to confirm that Diem and Nhu had escaped.

At that point Diem and Nhu clearly realized that they had nowhere else to turn. Diem rang General Don and offered to hand over power to the vice president or the parliamentary speaker in line with the country's constitution. Don rejected this plan. Diem then offered that he and Nhu would leave the country provided he was given the "honors due a departing president." Don again refused, although he had promised to guarantee the brothers' safety if they surrendered. Diem then telephoned Don and told him that he and Nhu were at the Cha Tam Church, in Cholon, well known as the burial place of François Xavier Tam Assoa, the vicar apostolic of Saigon who died in 1934, and would surrender unconditionally. Don contacted Conein to see how the two brothers could be escorted out of the country. Conein suggested a U.S. plane but that would take 24 hours to organize, and with the United States undoubtedly not wanting to give them asylum, it might take a few days to find a place for their exile.

General Don then sent General Mai Huu Xuan, a secret police chief, to get Diem and Nhu. The brothers had taken communion and left the church where an armored personnel carrier was waiting. Xuan told the brothers it was for their protection and ushered them in while he clambered into one of the accompanying jeeps. The convoy headed for the staff headquarters where the now successful conspirators were meeting. The cars stopped at a railway crossing where two officers in the armored car machine-gunned Diem and Nhu, and one of them then stabbed Nhu. The convoy then made its way back to the staff headquarters where General Xuan reported to General Minh, "Mission accomplished."

Madame Nhu was in Los Angeles when news had arrived of the coup. She had been visiting the United States in the hope of raising support for the South Vietnamese government in the same manner that Madame Chiang Kai-shek had done in the 1940s; however Madame Nhu lacked the political acumen of Madame Chiang. When the coup started, Madame Nhu said she knew her brother had suspected a coup, and when rumors spread of the murder of Diem and Nhu, she said that if the brothers had been "treacherously killed, in that effect it will be only the beginning... the beginning of the story."

General Minh had undoubtedly organized the killing of the two brothers, but he told Lucien Conein that they had both committed suicide. Conein told Minh that the story was ridiculous, and when President Kennedy heard of the deaths, he was badly shaken. At a meeting with senior officials, he rejected the idea of suicide, although Roger Hilsman who had initiated the U.S. support for the coup, suggested it was possible that the brothers could have killed themselves. To that suggestion, McGeorge Bundy, the national security adviser, replied that it was highly unlikely that the two shot and stabbed themselves with their hands tied behind their backs. Three weeks after the assassination of Diem, Kennedy himself was assassinated. Worried that the Soviet Union might get blamed for Kennedy's assassination, the Soviet leader, Nikita Khrushchev, had the KGB investigate the death of the U.S. President. They concluded that it was possible that the assassination could have been linked to the murders in South Vietnam, although this view has not been held by any of the other major investigations into the Kennedy assassination.

## INSTABILITY IN SOUTH VIETNAM

Soon after the assassination of Ngo Dinh Diem and Ngo Dinh Nhu, General Minh, as one of the coup leaders, became chairman of the Revolutionary Military Committee and titular head of state. Although he was a capable general, he was unable to operate politically, and he was badly tarnished by his close involvement in the killing of his predecessor. In December the Central Committee of the Vietnam Workers' Party decided to escalate the war in South Vietnam by providing more weapons and supplies to the PLAF. By mid-January 1964, the war was progressing badly and a group of middle-ranking officers decided that they wanted to oust Minh and the older coup plotters. On January 30, 1964, they staged a coup d'état and General Nguyen Khanh became president. On February 8, however, Minh launched his own coup, ousting Khanh.

The South Vietnamese government remained highly unstable when the U.S. presidential election campaign started in early 1964. The incumbent, Lyndon Johnson, was assured of a relatively easy victory over his Republican opponent, Barry Goldwater. In May 1961, when Johnson had been Kennedy's vice president, he had visited Saigon to bolster the Diem government. By now, Johnson's main focus was on civil rights in the United States. Although for most people, Vietnam was not a major election issue, Johnson wanted to assure the American public that he was a strident anticommunist. When Barry Goldwater stated that he would contemplate the possible use of nuclear weapons in war, Johnson was able to portray Goldwater as an extremist. Goldwater's slogan "In your heart you know he's right" was lampooned by the Democrats as "In your heart you know he might," suggesting that Goldwater might send the world into oblivion with a nuclear war.

On August 2, 1964, the U.S. navy became involved in what became known as the First Gulf of Tonkin Incident. North Vietnamese gunboats attacked the U.S.S. *Maddox* while it was sailing off the North Vietnamese coast monitoring radar capabilities while the South Vietnamese were launching a commando attack on North Vietnam. The United States immediately sent in the U.S.S. *C. Turner Joy,* another destroyer, to the area and claimed that the two destroyers were attacked on August 4. Johnson's administration was convinced that the two attacks were part of a major threat posed by the North Vietnamese to test U.S. resolve, Congress passed the Tonkin Gulf Resolution, which gave the U.S. President the power to take actions he deemed necessary to protect U.S. security interests in mainland Southeast Asia. As this meant that the president no longer needed to consult Congress, it allowed Johnson to match any Communist threat or escalate the war if he wanted to do so. It subsequently emerged that the second incident never took place, a fact acknowledged publicly by Ray Cline, Deputy Director of the Central Intelligence Agency, when interviewed by Stanley Karnow for a television series on Vietnam. On August 16, Minh was overthrown by Khanh who, after 11 days, was overthrown by a Provisional Leadership Committee, with Minh and Khanh acting together. This regime lasted only until September 8, after which Minh became chairman of the Provisional Leadership Committee, and hence titular head of state. On October 26, Minh stood down in favor of Phan Khac Suu, a moderate who established the first civilian government in South Vietnam since the killing of Diem. The stability that the generals had promised would follow the overthrow of Diem eluded everybody, as the United States headed to the polls.

On November 3, 1964, Johnson was resoundingly reelected, winning the largest share of the vote of any candidate in recent times. Not only was

Johnson elected in his own right, but the Democrats won control of many of the Congressional seats being contested; and with the Tonkin Gulf Resolution, Johnson was prepared to meet the Communists. Used to organizing political deals, Johnson, at a speech at Johns Hopkins University, on April 7, 1965, offered the North Vietnamese a massive financial package to develop the Mekong River if the North Vietnamese would either abandon their war in the South, or postpone it. The Communists rejected this offer and war escalated, with the PLAF attacking the U.S. base at Pleiku in the central highlands of South Vietnam. They had attacked the Brinks Hotel in Saigon just before Christmas in 1964, but the attack at Pleiku provided Johnson with a pretext to order a bombing campaign against the North, and hopefully bringing together the different factions in the South Vietnamese government.

## THE FIRST U.S. GROUND SOLDIERS

Since 1954, U.S. military advisers had played a major role in the support of the various South Vietnamese governments. By 1963, these numbered as many as 11,000, although with support staff and others, the total for the U.S. presence was probably much larger, perhaps closer to 17,000. The U.S. Embassy telephone directory for 1963 lists approximately 8,500 U.S. government personnel—military and civilian—compared with 890 six years earlier, proving that the U.S. presence in the country was considerable. Many pilots, both for fixed wing aircraft and helicopters, were involved in ferrying South Vietnamese soldiers around the countryside.

Lyndon Johnson was planning air strikes against North Vietnam from bases in South Vietnam. Because Johnson was certain that the South Vietnamese would be unable to protect the U.S. aircraft, on March 8, 1965, the first 3,500 marines in South Vietnam arrived at Danang. These were the first U.S. combat soldiers deployed on mainland Asia since the end of the fighting in Korea, and the event marked a crucial change in the war. Johnson acted cautiously, sending another 3,500 soldiers soon afterward, but restricting U.S. soldiers to a 50-mile radius of their air bases. In an interview with the press soon afterward, General Wallace Greene confirmed that the marines were also involved in operations "to find these Vietcong and kill them." By July 1965, there were 75,000 U.S. soldiers in the country, fighting alongside as many as 600,000 South Vietnamese soldiers.

The arrival of the U.S. marines led to the continuation of Operation Rolling Thunder by which the United States, from March 2, 1965 until November 1, 1968, embarked on a massive program of aerial bombing of North Vietnam. The plan was to bolster the morale of the South Vietnamese and badly damage so much of North Vietnam's infrastructure that it would be unable to continue its military program of supporting the PLAF, or it might feel the

# 7

## From U.S. Involvement to Tet Offensive and Death of Ho Chi Minh (1965–1969)

The new government in Saigon centered on three emerging political figures. The leader, Nguyen Van Thieu, was from a family of small landowners in a coastal village in central Vietnam. He had briefly served in the Viet Minh in 1945 before enlisting with the Vietnamese National Army established by the French. In 1956, Thieu was appointed head of the South Vietnamese National Academy and took part in the attack on the Gia Long Palace in November 1963, which resulted in the overthrow of Ngo Dinh Diem. Thieu had then emerged as a leader of the "Young Turk" faction that finally overthrew the civilian government of Phan Khac Suu in June 1965. In this coup, Thieu was assisted by Nguyen Cao Ky, a flamboyant air force officer who became prime minister in the new government. The civilian arm of the new regime was Tran Thien Khiem, who became prime minister when Ky assumed the vice presidency.

Initially this triumvirate, held together with massive restrictions placed on the press and numbers of political opponents, including militant Buddhists, were arrested or placed under house arrest. Although these decisions were criticized in the Western media and also, obviously, in North Vietnam, they provided stability for Saigon for the first time since the overthrow of Diem two years earlier.

Facing the South Vietnamese, the North Vietnamese government was still headed by Ho Chi Minh who was still revered by many Vietnamese—North and South—who cherished the role he had played in the struggle against the French. The governments of North Vietnam faced many problems; for example, few of the new leaders had any experience in civilian administration. In war they were able to give orders, but to run a country, there had to be some degree of negotiation and persuasion, and many of the Communist leaders had been uneasy with these concepts. They had gradually adapted, but their government had been badly tarnished by the disastrous land reform program in the mid-1950s. Although the divisions in the country were gradually healed, there were still some who favored rebuilding the North rather than fighting the war in the South. By contrast there were also numbers of Communists from southern Vietnam living in the north who were anxious to overthrow the southern government.

By 1965, the civilian institutions of both North and South Vietnam had now become established, with schools, hospitals, postal services, communications, and other arms of government starting to function well, albeit with occasional problems in isolated parts of the South where there were outbreaks of fighting.

By September 1965, the North Vietnamese decided to launch a major campaign to try to destroy South Vietnam. The plan was essentially to seize the central highlands in the South, and then use their troops there to take over the nearby coastal region around Nha Trang. This would cut South Vietnam in half, leaving the southern part around Saigon and the northern coastal region around Danang and Hue isolated and render the country unviable. With reports of massive North Vietnamese troop concentrations, the United States sent their Air Cavalry in search of the Communists. They located them in the Ia Drang Valley at the foot of the Chu Pong Mountains. Soon afterward the North Vietnamese braced for battle, and the United States deployed large numbers of troops into the Ia Drang Valley.

In the battle of the Ia Drang Valley (November 14–18, 1965) U.S. soldiers engaged for the first time in a full-scale battle against the North Vietnamese. With the U.S. marines unable to dislodge the North Vietnamese soldiers without suffering massive losses, B-52 bombers were deployed, bombing the North Vietnamese lines and destroying most of their soldiers. For the North Vietnamese it was a major defeat, and they realized that the massive U.S. firepower could give the United States and the South Vietnamese victory in any set-piece battle. As a result the North Vietnamese and the People's Liberation Armed Forces (PLAF) decided to embark on different tactics.

After the battle of the Ia Drang Valley, the North Vietnamese and the PLAF began a guerilla war in which they attacked isolated South Vietnamese villages, winning support in some of them and intimidating people in others. Gradually, they started to destroy the infrastructure of the South Vietnamese government. At the same time, the U.S. government, aware of the problems that had been caused by the instability that followed the overthrow of Diem, decided to support Ngyuyen Van Thieu. Elections for a Constituent Assembly in South Vietnam were held in September 1966, which led to the approval of a new constitution in April 1967. As a result, in September 1967, elections were held throughout much of South Vietnam. With five major slates of candidates, Nguyen Van Thieu was elected president with 38 percent of the vote; Ky became his vice president.

As a symbolic gesture, Thieu also introduced a new series of banknotes, showing three heroes from Vietnamese history: Le Van Duyet, Nguyen Hue, and Tran Hung Dao, a curious choice, as the first two had fought each other bitterly during the Tay Son Rebellion. On November 1, celebrations were held in Saigon to commemorate the third anniversary of the overthrow of the Diem government, although with the political instability that had resulted, few people outside the military command or the diehard opponents of the Diem family actually celebrated.

## ESCALATION OF THE VIETNAM WAR

To try to prevent the North Vietnamese from reinforcing the PLAF, the U.S. military established bases along the border between North and South Vietnam, one of which was Khe Sanh. Located in an isolated part of the countryside to make attack by the PLAF or the North Vietnamese difficult, it might also serve as a target for attack in the same way as the Viet Minh capture of Dien Bien Phu had managed to lead to the defeat of the French in Vietnam in 1954.

The Vietnamese Communists initially decided not to launch any major attacks on Khe Sanh and instead opened up what became known as the Ho Chi Minh Trail, a series of jungle paths through Laos and northeastern Cambodia. These paths had existed as routes for smuggling, and also were used during the Indochina War against the French for taking supplies. With the need to bring large numbers of men and also materiel to South Vietnam, the Vietnamese Communists widened the trail to allow for the passage of trucks.

The South Vietnamese and the U.S. forces soon became aware of the use of the Ho Chi Minh Trail and in Laos used hill tribes to try to attack the Communist military convoys. In Cambodia, which was neutral, the U.S. government tried to put pressure on the Cambodian leader Prince Norodom Sihanouk. By this time Sihanouk was playing a dangerous game of trying to keep Cambodia out of the war. He was sure that the Communists would eventually win the Vietnam War. For this reason, he had reached an agreement with the North

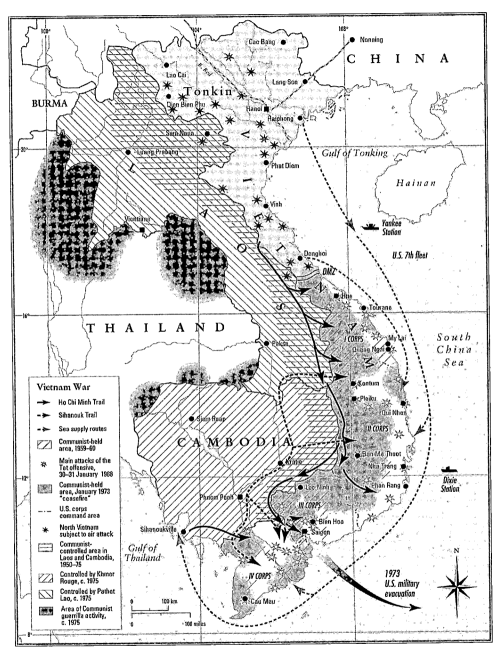

Map showing the Vietnam War. Cartography courtesy of BookComp, Inc.

Vietnamese that they would be able to use Cambodian territory, provided they did so discreetly. In return when they won the war, North Vietnam guaranteed that they would respect the Vietnamese-Cambodian border.

The PLAF also started building a massive network of tunnels, soon to become famous as the Cu Chi tunnels, in farmland northwest of Saigon. There they were able to hide large numbers of supplies, train people, and hide when the United States sent in ground forces. The area, along with the Mekong Delta region, had long been a hotbed of dissent against the French, and Diem had tried to pacify it by settling significant numbers of northern Catholics in the region.

With as many as 500,000 U.S. troops in the country, the United States rapidly found itself overcommitted to the war. With Lyndon Johnson rejecting calls from the Pentagon to mobilize the Reserves, the United States introduced the draft to raise enough soldiers to maintain their military presence in Vietnam. Young men continuing their education were exempt, as were members of pacifist religions and those with medical certificates. Moreover, those people serving in the National Guard and other units based in the United States were rarely being posted to Vietnam. As a result, the war gradually led to increasing numbers of poor men being conscripted, with an over-representation of African Americans. The conscription was to quickly lead to the increasing unpopularity of the war. Large numbers of young Americans fled to Canada and to other countries.

Before the Vietnam War, the Majestic Hotel was the most famous in Saigon, with its address as 1 Rue Catinat (subsequently renamed Tu Do). By the 1960s, however, the Rex Hotel and the Brinks Hotel were favored heavily by the Americans. The Caravelle Hotel, boasted 75 first-class rooms, and the Continental Palace Hotel, with 95 rooms on the far side of Lam Son Square, was made famous by British writer Graham Greene. Now with over half a million servicemen in the country, the cities of Saigon and Danang were transformed quickly. The nightclubs, which had been closed down during the last years of the Diem government, reopened and catered to the large number of soldiers on "rest and recreation" leave. Many of them also visited nearby countries, with a boom in the tourist trade in Thailand, Malaysia, and the Philippines.

The war also attracted large numbers of war correspondents to the country. Some of these, such as Neil Sheehan of United Press International, David Halberstam and Homer Bigart of the *New York Times*, and Peter Arnett of Associated Press, rapidly became household names. Four won Pulitzer Prizes for their work, with Seymour Hersh also winning for his story of the My Lai massacre. Of the hundreds of reporters who covered the war, 70 covering the U.S./South Vietnamese side were women. A total of 135 war photographers covering the war from both sides of the conflict, died in the war. As well as the press reports in newspapers and on the radio, the footage shot by the journalists ensured that the Vietnam War appeared regularly on the television news.

## INVOLVEMENT OF AUSTRALIA
## AND OTHER U.S. ALLIES

Although the United States provided the majority of the foreign forces to support the South Vietnamese, they were by no means alone. Some U.S. allies such as Britain made clear their opposition to the war, but others, such as Australia, New Zealand, South Korea, and Thailand, contributed soldiers. Altogether nearly 50,000 Australians, 3,890 New Zealanders, 1,450 Filipinos, 320,000 South Koreans, and 38,958 Thais served in the Vietnam War, along with a small contingent from Spain. Australia was unable to raise enough soldiers, so the government introduced conscription in 1964, leading to major political repercussions and widespread demonstrations against the war. South Africa offered to send soldiers to the conflict, but the United States was critical of the apartheid policy and felt that the presence of South African soldiers could cause dissension among African Americans in the U.S. forces.

As a member of the Southeast Asia Treaty Organization, Australia became committed to the defense of South Vietnam providing what became the "Australian Army Training Team Vietnam." In December 1964, Tran Van Huong, the South Vietnamese prime minister, asked for further Australian support, and soon afterward Australian Prime Minister R. G. Menzies managed to get his South Vietnamese counterpart, Phan Huy Quat, to request Australian soldiers, to which he gave, as promised, a positive response.

On a diplomatic front, following the severing of relations between South Vietnam and Cambodia after the Buddhist crisis in 1963, and the severing of relations between Cambodia and the United States two years later, the Australian Embassy in Saigon was looking after Cambodian interests in South Vietnam, and the Australian Embassy in Cambodia was helping to deal with U.S. interests in Cambodia. As a result, it was requested that Australian troops in South Vietnam not be deployed near the Cambodian border.

Initially the Australian soldiers were full-time professionals, but in November 1964, conscription was introduced. In June 1966, Australian soldiers based near Xa Long Tan, east of Saigon, were attacked by a large number of PLAF soldiers; 18 Australians and 245 PLAF were killed. The battle of Long Tan soon became symbolic of the Australian commitment to the war. In November 1966, the federal elections in Australia were fought largely over the issue of sending soldiers to Vietnam, with the Labor Party, who opposed the war, losing heavily. In the 1969 elections, the Labor Party was able to make up much of the ground, and although it lost, its policy of ending the Australian troop commitment to South Vietnam was becoming steadily more popular.

The troops were finally withdrawn in 1971, with the Labor Party coming to power in the 1972 federal elections, and offering an amnesty for those who had evaded the draft.

Overall, for the approximately 50,000 Australian service personnel in Vietnam, 512 died, of whom 415 were killed in action. These included Kevin Arthur Wheatley, Warrant Officer Class II, who was killed after trying to save a colleague during an action in the Tra Bong Valley in November 1965, and Major Peter John Badcoe, also of the Australian Army Training Team, who was killed in action near Hue. Both were posthumously awarded the Victoria Cross, the highest British and Commonwealth award for valor, as were Warrant Officers Class II Rayene Stewart Simpson and Keith Payne for actions in 1969.

## THE TET OFFENSIVE

Although the Communists were eager to destabilize the South Vietnamese government, their high command was still reeling from the disaster at the Ia Drang Valley. As a result, they planned their new action carefully. In late 1967, the Communists started infiltrating large numbers of their supporters into Saigon, Hue, and other South Vietnamese cities. Their plan was to launch a large number of urban attacks on the South Vietnamese. Part of this was in response to U.S. Commander General William Westmoreland who, on November 21 in a speech at the National Press Club in Washington, D.C., proclaimed that the U.S. forces were heading to victory, saying that "the end begins to come into view."

The other timetable that affected the plans of the Communists was, undoubtedly, the U.S. presidential election, which was beginning with the New Hampshire primary on March 12. Most of the U.S. public was sure that the South Vietnamese, supported by them, were wining the war, with news coverage showing fighting largely taking place only in the countryside. In the U.S. presidential elections, the Republicans, after doing so badly in the 1964 elections, started to re-form around Richard Nixon, the vice president who had lost the 1960 elections to John F. Kennedy. Against them, the Democrat Party started their primaries with Lyndon Johnson uncertain whether or not he was going to stand in the elections and antiwar candidate Eugene McCarthy urging an end to U.S. troop involvement. McCarthy suggested that the United States should push the South Vietnamese government to be more inclusive and agree to the formation of a coalition government with the Communists.

Into this climate, on the night of January 30–31, Communists in Saigon, Hue, and every other major city and town in South Vietnam, as well as at Khe Sanh, attacked U.S. and South Vietnamese government targets. Approximately 100 places were assaulted. Initially the U.S. government thought that the attacks were to try to draw their soldiers away from Khe Sanh, which would allow for a significant victory there similar to that in Dien Bien Phu. It was not long before they came to realize that the attack on Khe Sanh was actually the diversion, and the real focus was the fighting in Saigon and Hue.

In Saigon, a PLAF unit seized control of the Saigon radio station and blew it up. Another group attacked the U.S. Embassy, blasting their way in, and holding out there for six hours. Television footage of U.S. marines and CIA agents fighting them in the grounds of the embassy was broadcast all around the world. It was later discovered that the two PLAF commanders had been killed as the group broke into the embassy, and, leaderless, the group provided little resistance and all were killed. Elsewhere in Saigon, fighting in Tan Son Nhut Airport and other places, especially in downtown Saigon, continued sporadically over January 31, and in a few places for a few days after that.

In the old imperial capital of Hue, a concerted PLAF attack resulted in the Communists seizing control of part of the imperial citadel and the university. Much of the former was blown up as the South Vietnamese and U.S. soldiers fought their way into it. In the latter, the Communists vented their rage on some of the university staff and students, massacring hundreds of them. When the PLAF were finally driven from Hue, mass graves were uncovered, revealing the bodies of 2,800 people killed by the Communists. Initially when the Communists had taken the city, they turned on supporters of the South Vietnamese government, but most of the killings took place when they withdrew and killed anybody who might have been able to identify them. Elsewhere in other towns, the PLAF attacks were either repulsed or their soldiers were quickly driven back.

In much of the Western press, however, attention focused not on the fighting throughout the country, nor even the shooting in the U.S. Embassy, but rather on a single incident that took place on February 1. General Nguyen Ngoc Loan, the chief of the South Vietnamese police, shot dead a captured Communist, later identified as Nguyen Van Lem, in front of the U.S. photographer Eddie Adams and Vo Suu, a Vietnamese cameraman for NBC. Adams and Vo Suu had spotted a group of South Vietnamese soldiers leading a captive and went over to photograph them. As the soldiers brought the captive to General Loan, he briefly waved his gun to indicate that the solders should back off slightly, and then clearly aware of the journalists, he shot the captive in the head. The photograph appeared in newspapers all around the world, later winning Adams the Pulitzer Prize. The news footage appeared on the television news throughout much of the world.

The photograph and the film footage showed the brutality of the war. General Loan was soon demonized all over the world. He was a close political ally of Vice President Ky and was alleged to have been involved in narcotics, although nothing was ever proven. He was also an effective military commander, popular with his soldiers. During the fighting in the Tet Offensive, some of his family had been killed, as had a number of his men. He was determined on revenge and meted out summary justice to the first captive who came into his hands. The photograph became one of the most famous of the war.

The South Vietnamese and the U.S. forces were able to defeat the Communists during the Tet Offensive with relatively little difficulty. The "mopping up" took several days, and by the end of it the Communists had been decisively defeated. The public perception, however, was that the Communists had won, and in a sense they had. They were able to show that they were capable of attacking into the heart of Saigon and, through the photograph of Eddie Adams, were able to portray the South Vietnamese as the villains.

## THE MY LAI MASSACRE

It was not long after the end of the Tet Offensive that U.S. soldiers became involved in one of the most notorious atrocities of the war. C Company of the 1st Battalion of the 20th Infantry, 11th Infantry Brigade, was involved in an assault on the village of My Lai, south of Danang. They entered the village expecting to find Communist soldiers, but instead they found only women, children, and old men who were eating breakfast. The U.S. soldiers were out of control and started firing at the unarmed civilians. Lieutenant William L. Calley's first platoon not only shot people whom they encountered, but rounded up others who were taken to a nearby ditch where they were murdered. As the marines set fire to some of the houses and blew up others with hand grenades, more civilians were killed.

As the remaining villagers tried to escape, marines followed, firing at them, but they had to stop when Warrant Officer Hugh Thompson landed his helicopter between the soldiers and the fleeing civilians. Estimates of the number of people killed range from 200 to about 500, with the Vietnamese Communists maintaining that 504 were killed and publishing a list of names. The U.S. government estimate of the dead puts those murdered at 347.

It was not until a year later that the My Lai incident was discovered by army investigators. The resulting board of inquiry tried to blame the killings on the soldiers becoming frustrated after attacks on them by guerilla snipers, the inexperience of the leadership, and various other mitigating factors. Eventually 14 soldiers were charged with crimes; only one, Lieutenant Calley, was found guilty of personally killing 22 civilians, his platoon having been responsible for about 200 deaths. Sentenced to life imprisonment, his sentence was subsequently reduced to 20 years, then to 10 years. Calley was released after 4½ months in a military prison, pending his appeal. He then spent 3½ years under house arrest, with one judge ruling that pretrial publicity had prejudiced Calley's ability to get a fair hearing. He was subsequently paroled and moved to Columbus, Georgia, where he managed a jewelry store.

## THE 1968 U.S. PRESIDENTIAL ELECTIONS

At the New Hampshire Democratic Party primary, Eugene McCarthy, as an antiwar candidate, was able to make a strong showing, getting 42 percent of the vote against Lyndon Johnson who was a "write-in" candidate who managed only 49 percent. This strong showing by McCarthy encouraged Robert Kennedy, younger brother of John F. Kennedy, to decide to offer himself as a candidate, with Lyndon Johnson finally announcing that he would not stand in the election and endorsing Vice President Hubert Humphrey. Throughout most of the rest of the primaries, the competition was between Humphrey and Kennedy, with the war rapidly becoming the major issue in the election campaign.

While Humphrey tried to distance himself from Kennedy and McCarthy, the Republican candidate Richard Nixon denounced all the Democrats for the longest war that the United States had had to endure and promised that a vote for him would lead to "peace with honor." On the political fringe, George Wallace of the American Independence Party campaigned in the South against the Civil Rights movement, with his vice presidential candidate, General Curtis E. LeMay, declaring that he could win the Vietnam War by bombing the Communists "back into the Stone Age."

Many people had protested against the Vietnam War since its start. Initially these included large numbers of Quakers and peace campaigners who were against all war. Gradually with increasing numbers of young men being drafted into the U.S. military, many people, both draftees, would-be draftees, and their families, started taking part in protests. These were joined by other people who were against U.S. involvement in Vietnam. There were also former U.S. service personnel who, after returning from Vietnam, started taking part in demonstrations, and there were also a number of people who took part in marches and protest movements who were clearly campaigning for a Communist victory in Vietnam. Although these subtle differences were evident to most observers, gradually the image of the antiwar movement changed, as the press started concentrating on a violent minority, and also on known Communists who took part in demonstrations waving North Vietnamese or NFL flags.

As the electioneering intensified, Martin Luther King, the leader of the Civil Rights movement, was murdered in Memphis, Tennessee. He had been one of Lyndon Johnson's closest allies during the moves to introduce the Civil Rights Act of 1964; a believer in nonviolence, however, he heavily opposed the war.

As the fighting intensified in 1967 and the number of U.S. casualties rose, the number of casualties among African Americans was so large, especially since African Americans were over-represented in the U.S. military, that many of their leaders such as King wanted the United States to pull out its soldiers. Many other African Americans who had supported Johnson had also become critics of the war, with the actress Eartha Kitt, who was also of Cherokee ancestry, publicly criticizing Johnson at a White House luncheon and soon thereafter finding herself unable to find work in the United States.

Martin Luther King's opposition to the war had led to increased FBI surveillance of him, with some prowar politicians accusing him of siding with the North Vietnamese. The murder of King on April 4, 1968, was followed by Robert Kennedy winning the California primary, and then Kennedy's own murder on June 6, with the Democratic nomination within his grasp.

When the Democratic Party Convention took place on August 26–29, in Chicago, thousands of antiwar protestors went to make their voices heard. Hubert Humphrey was guaranteed the party's nomination, but supporters of Eugene McCarthy wanted to be recognized on the convention floor. On the night of August 28, as the Democratic Convention was ready to vote on its presidential candidate, thousands of demonstrators marched on Convention Hall, the International Amphitheatre, determined to make a presence, with hundreds of police blocking their way. Hundreds were injured in the fighting that resulted, and Humphrey was easily chosen as the candidate of the Democratic Party. As Walter Mears of Associated Press wrote, "Humphrey, a man of peace, received the Democratic nomination tonight under armed guard." Lyndon Johnson had been advised by the Secret Service not to attend.

A number of demonstrators were arrested in Chicago and subsequently charged. The most well-known group, including Abbie Hoffman, an anarchist and co-founder of the Youth International Party ("Yippies"); Jerry Rubin; and David Dellinger, became known as the Chicago Eight, and later the Chicago Seven. They were charged with incitement to riot and other offenses. The trial dragged on into 1970, and five were found guilty of having "crossed state lines with the intent to incite a riot." They were all fined and sentenced to five years in prison, but in November 1972 the convictions were reversed.

In the week after the Democratic National Convention in Chicago, Richard Nixon traveled to the city and vowed that in the United States, "no one is above the law, no one is below the law, and we're going to enforce the law. And Americans should remember that if we are going to have law and order." Antiwar protestors followed Humphrey around the country with the call "Dump the Hump." With Lyndon Johnson announcing a bombing halt in Vietnam beginning on November 1, support for Hubert Humphrey increased. Many voters feared, however, that if neither Nixon nor Humphrey managed to win the election outright, then George Wallace would hold the balance of power in the electoral college. Nixon narrowly won the election, and on January 20, 1969, he was sworn into office to carry out his promise of "peace with honor."

## THE GUAM DOCTRINE AND VIETNAMIZATION

Essentially Nixon's plan to deliver "peace with honor" relied on a policy of Vietnamization. This policy would increase the number of soldiers in the South Vietnamese armed forces, who would be trained and armed by the United States. These forces could gradually take on more of the fighting, reducing the number of U.S. soldiers, and as a result, U.S. casualties. With U.S. hardware, the South Vietnamese government might be able to survive without any U.S. soldiers. This plan relied on what was known as the "decent interval" concept.

The "decent interval" concept—the name was coined by CIA agent Frank Snepp in his book *Decent Interval*—involved the United States bolstering South Vietnam before its withdrawal. This would then delay any possible collapse of South Vietnam to a "decent" interval of time. If the South Vietnamese government collapsed several days after the U.S. withdrawal, the two could be clearly linked. If the South Vietnamese managed to retain its independence for 10 years after a U.S. withdrawal, however, the connection between the two events could be denied. Somewhere between several days and the 10 years lay this "decent interval."

The problem with this plan was that none of the new U.S. administration believed it was possible. As a result the concept of a "decent interval" was mooted, which was made famous by the book of the same name by Frank Snepp, a CIA agent in Saigon. The book, initially banned in the United States, was published in Britain.

To embark on this policy, the U.S. administration started secret talks with the North Vietnamese. In fact Lyndon Johnson's administration had already begun talks, and Henry Kissinger, Nixon's national security adviser, continued them with some urgency. The main U.S. demands in the negotiations were that the United States would be able to withdraw from the country, that all their prisoners of war—many held in Hanoi, the North Vietnamese capital—would be returned, and that there would be some security guarantees for the South Vietnamese. The North Vietnamese quickly realized that the U.S. administration was keen to withdraw and that what they essentially had to do was undermine the security guarantees, which would enable them to take over South Vietnam and proceed with the reunification of the country.

To try to reduce pressure on the U.S. and South Vietnamese troops, in March 1969, the U.S. Air Force started bombing the Ho Chi Minh Trail, attacking targets in neighboring Cambodia in complete violation of Cambodian neutrality. With Cambodia's leader, Prince Sihanouk, denying that the Vietnamese Communists were using the Ho Chi Minh Trail, the United States felt justified in their secret bombing known as Operation Menu. Although Sihanouk was critical of the U.S. actions, he stopped short of openly criticizing the bombing, eager not to offend the United States as the peace talks started.

During the secret bombing of Cambodia, the United States had also made considerable use of defoliants to try to destroy the tree cover. Agent Orange, the most well known of the "herbicides" had been used from 1961 until its use was phased out in 1971. Containing dioxins, these defoliants have been blamed for causing birth deformities in children of U.S. soldiers who used them or who served in affected areas, as well as even worse cases affecting the Vietnamese. These claims have been continuously denied, but many commentators have protested that if the chemicals sprayed from airplanes were able to destroy jungles by attacking broad leaves, it must have some effect on people living there, with large numbers of Vietnamese having subsequently suffered horribly.

The continual U.S. bombing of North Vietnam had led to significant numbers of U.S. planes being shot down, and U.S. airmen taken prisoner. Many were held in Hanoi in the Hoa Lo prison, which became known as the "Hanoi Hilton." One of the most well known of these prisoners of war was John McCain, whose plane was shot down by an antiaircraft missile near Hanoi. As he regained consciousness after bailing out of his plane, he was attacked by a large number of villagers who had gathered. The son of the U.S. commander-in-chief, Pacific Command, McCain was offered his freedom by the North Vietnamese, but he refused and was held a prisoner of war for 5½ years, along with hundreds of other U.S. prisoners of war.

By this time the main "unknown" factor for the U.S. administration was the South Vietnamese government. By 1969, Thieu had been head of state for four years and had been democratically elected in 1967. The South Vietnamese legislature was a forum for much debate, with opposition to Thieu centering on Tran Ngoc Chau, a nationalist who had been elected to the South Vietnamese legislature. Thieu's police, however, accused him of communist sympathies—Chau's brother had sided with the Communists—and Chau was dragged out of the South Vietnamese National Assembly building in 1970 and spent the next five years in jail.

Thieu was initially unaware of the extent of the secret U.S.-North Vietnamese talks, which started in January 1969, when he met Richard Nixon on the island of Midway on June 8, 1969. —Thieu had traveled to the island via Seoul and Taipei, using diplomatic support from both countries to bolster his position. Nixon and Thieu reaffirmed their alliance and discussed the peace negotiations. Nixon made security promises to Thieu in exchange for reducing the U.S. troop commitments to Vietnam. In return the South Vietnamese government took on more of the military tasks in their country. According to the schedule drawn up by Nixon, U.S. troops would be gradually drawn down, with the final withdrawal in June 1972, just ahead of the next U.S. presidential election. This soon became known as the Guam Doctrine, or the Nixon Doctrine.

With the prospect of a negotiated settlement to the Vietnam War, the Communists reformed the NFL into the Provisional Revolutionary Government of the Republic of Vietnam (PRG), which was proclaimed on June 8, 1972. Officially it was a merger of the NFL; the Alliance of National, Democratic, and Peace Forces; and the People's Revolutionary Party and was nominally noncommunist, although its communist sympathies and its control from North Vietnam were obvious. It was no longer a resistance group, however, but a rival government to that of the Republic of Vietnam (South Vietnam), which meant that the South Vietnamese Communists could be represented at any future peace talks. Nguyen Huu Tho of the NFL and Huynh Tan Phat, also a prominent member of the NFL, became the leaders, and it gained international recognition from North Vietnam, neighboring Cambodia, and most communist countries, with "missions" in all of these, as well as Algeria, Egypt, Indonesia, Syria, and Tanzania. Internationally, members of the PRG traveled on North Vietnamese passports. To try to publicize the PRG, Huynh Tan Phat embarked on a number of foreign visits including to Cambodia where he received a good reception from the neutralist leader, Prince Norodom Sihanouk, who was trying to win favor with the Vietnamese Communists.

## THE DEATH OF HO CHI MINH

On September 2, 1969, 79-year-old Ho Chi Minh died of heart failure. The announcement of his death was initially reported as being on September 3, so it would not clash with National Day, but it was subsequently corrected to September 2. As soon as news of the death was made public, the North Vietnamese government immediately proclaimed a period of mourning, with many North Vietnamese openly crying, their weeping being captured by the film *79 Primaveras* ("Seventy-Nine Spring Times of Ho Chi Minh"), made by the Cuban filmmaker Santiago Alvarez. The North Vietnamese government then invited world leaders to attend Ho Chi Minh's funeral. The only non-Vietnamese head of state who attended the ceremony was Prince Norodom Sihanouk, the neutralist leader of Cambodia who was anxious to show his support for the Vietnamese Communists whom he believed would win the Vietnam War. Huynh Tan Phat, the leader of the PRG, was also present, as was Ton Duc Thang, Ho Chi Minh's successor; thus three heads of state were in attendance. Rather than be cremated, which had been Ho Chi Minh's wish, his body was embalmed and put into the newly built Ho Chi Minh Memorial to the west of The Citadel in Hanoi where Vietnamese and foreigners go to pay their respects to the man who led the Vietnamese Communist movement for 40 years.

# 8

# From the Death of Ho Chi Minh to Reunification (1969–1976)

The death of Ho Chi Minh marked a period of great sadness for the North Vietnamese. They had hoped to reunify the country while he was still alive. By early 1970, however, it seemed as though the war was to be long and drawn out, with some Vietnamese Communists expecting that it might last another 10 or 15 years. That situation changed on March 18, 1970, when Prince Norodom Sihanouk was overthrown in Cambodia. He was in the Soviet Union at the time where he was trying to get the Soviet leadership to put pressure the Vietnamese Communists to decrease their use of Cambodian territory. During his absence, the rightwing Cambodian, Prime Minister Lon Nol, seized power with the support of the Cambodian National Assembly and ordered all Vietnamese Communist soldiers to leave the country within 72 hours.

The demand by Lon Nol was clearly impossible. Instead the Communists rallied the Cambodian peasants, who supported the deposed Prince Sihanouk, and, arming them, struck back at the Lon Nol government and destroyed much of the Cambodian army. Richard Nixon then decided that this was an opportunity to destroy the Ho Chi Minh Trail. On April 29, he sent South Vietnamese and U.S. soldiers into Cambodia, destroying the eastern border area of the country and causing the Communists there to flee westward where they were, incidentally, to pose a far greater threat to the pro-U.S.

Lon Nol government. The "invasion" of Cambodia—Lon Nol first heard about it on the radio and gave his consent after the U.S. soldiers had already entered Cambodia—led to what became known as the Second Indochina War, although for much of the period the war in Cambodia was separate, militarily, from what was happening in Vietnam.

With the U.S. invasion of Cambodia, protests increased throughout the United States. One such protest was held at Kent State University in Ohio where students had burned down a Reserve Officer Training Corps building. On May 4, with National Guard troops facing students, guardsmen opened fire, killing four students and injuring nine others. In Melbourne, Australia, on May 8, 1970, more than 100,000 people gathered in what was the largest protest in the history of the country, with the same number gathering elsewhere in the country.

## PREPARATIONS FOR THE PEACE TALKS

With the peace talks in Paris making progress, in early 1971, Nguyen Van Thieu offered himself for reelection as the president of South Vietnam. To prevent the large number of candidates that had contested the 1967 elections, the rules for the new election were that any candidate needed to get his nomination papers signed by at least 40 of the 197 deputies of the South Vietnamese legislature, or senators; or 100 of the 545 members of the provincial or city councils, countersigned by the relevant provincial chief or mayor. Thieu faced two major opponents. General "Big" Minh, who had overthrown Diem in 1963, and was anxious to contest the election, and ex-Vice President Air Marshal Nguyen Cao Ky. Both Minh and Ky chose Roman Catholic vice presidential running mates, respectively, Ho Van Minh, the deputy speaker of the House of Representatives, and Truong Vinh Le, a former chairman of the National Assembly.

Minh and Ky agreed privately that the former would seek the required number of legislators, and the latter would try to find 100 councilors. When the time came for the nomination papers to be filed, Minh had found 16 senators and 28 deputies to sign his papers, but Thieu's nomination papers were signed by 15 senators, 89 deputies, and 452 councilors, meaning that only 93 councilors were free to sign Ky's papers. Thus when Ky filed his nomination papers on August 4, it was supported by 101 signatures, but 39 of the signatories had already signed Thieu's papers and their signatures were not validated by their provincial chiefs.

Thieu had quite rightly feared that Ky might defeat him, given Ky's popularity with the war veterans and many other groups. Ky denounced the election procedure in a press conference later on August 4, and the next day the Supreme Court ruled his nomination as invalid. Eight days later Ky denounced the election process as a fraud, and decided that he would not stand.

With Thieu looking as though he might be the only candidate in the presidential election, the Supreme Court, with support from the president, decided to revalidate Ky's nomination papers even though he had not appealed to them. On August 21, the day after Minh's withdrawal, the Supreme Court declared that as Thieu had the required number of deputies and senators, all the signatories from the councilors were invalid. Accepting Ky's nomination papers, they then stated that the posting of the final list of candidates be done straight away, in a move to prevent Ky from withdrawing from the race. Ky, however, was able to extricate himself from the election, a move deemed legal by the Supreme Court on September 1.

Thus Thieu remained the only candidate in the presidential elections. So as to ensure that he was not reelected with 100 percent of the vote, Thieu then declared that anybody who wished to oppose his candidacy need only cross his name out on the ballot paper, and indeed any ballot paper that was damaged would be regarded as a vote against him. After the election was held on October 3, Thieu was declared the winner with 94.3 percent of the vote, the turnout being 87.9 percent. In Hue as many as 36 percent of the people cast invalid votes, as did 25 percent in Danang and 16 percent in Saigon.

By early 1972, the next U.S. presidential election was starting, with the incumbent president, Richard Nixon, facing a challenge from George McGovern of the Democratic Party. The shooting of George Wallace during the campaign effectively ruled out Wallace as a serious contender. With Vietnam still a major item in the news, on June 8, 1972, a British news cameraman Alan Downes filmed a number of Vietnamese civilians as they fled a napalm attack by the Americans near Trang Bang, which was a village being attacked by the North Vietnamese. The napalm, a flammable liquid used in bombs, had initially been used in Vietnam to clear vegetation for landing areas for helicopters. By this time it was being used against insurgents, inflicting terrible chemical wounds on anybody who survived. The sight of one of the civilian victims, a naked nine-year old girl, later identified as Phan Thi Kim Phuc, became famous around the world. Richard Nixon initially doubted the authenticity of the image, but there was no doubt in many people's minds that it showed the poor peasants getting horribly injured or killed in war.

At the time Nixon was anxious to win the election, which led to the Watergate incident in which five men were found inside the Democratic Party headquarters in the Watergate Hotel in Washington, D.C. on June 17, 1972. The men were arrested and charged, with some evidence starting to link them to people in the Nixon White House. It gradually emerged that Nixon had been using agents to damage his political opponents, and that the incident at the Watergate Hotel was only one of many similar events that had been organized by Nixon and his aides, although for the time being there was no evidence directly connecting Nixon to Watergate. By this time a number of foreign antiwar critics were visiting North Vietnam, including author and critic Mary McCarthy, and actress Jane Fonda, who went to Hanoi in July 1972. Nixon and the White House were critical of these actions, and they might have helped him gain support, as it allowed Nixon to portray antiwar critics as supporters of North Vietnam.

To try to show their strength, the North Vietnamese had launched an Easter Offensive in South Vietnam in March and April. The offensive failed to generate the media attention of the Tet Offensive four years earlier, but in Paris the North Vietnamese negotiator Le Duc Tho gradually stepped up his demands knowing how desperate the Americans were for a peace settlement ahead of the elections. Finally Nixon decided that what was offered was dishonorable and broke off negotiations. After a lackluster election campaign, Richard Nixon won a landslide victory carrying every state except for Massachusetts, which went to his rival, George McGovern, along with the District of Columbia. Nixon, with a renewed mandate, then turned to the issue of ending the Vietnam War.

## THE "CHRISTMAS DAY" BOMBINGS
## AND THE PARIS PEACE ACCORD

Fresh from his overwhelming election victory, Richard Nixon, and Henry Kissinger, now his national security advisor, but about to become the secretary of state, decided to launch what was officially known as Operation Linebacker II. The bombing raids, which lasted from December 18–20, became known as the "Christmas bombings" and were the heaviest bombing raids by the U.S. Air Force since the end of World War II. The Christmas bombings destroyed parts of Hanoi and other areas of North Vietnam; it also caused the death of several thousand people including those who died when the Bach Mai Hospital, one of the largest hospitals in Vietnam, was destroyed. The objective of the raids was to force the North Vietnamese to concede ground at the negotiations in Paris.

Immediately after the bombing, Henry Kissinger reported that his North Vietnamese counterpart, Le Duc Tho, became more cooperative, and finally, on January 27, 1973, the Paris Peace Accord was reached. The agreement included a ceasefire "in place," by which there would be a ceasefire, with all soldiers, South Vietnamese, North Vietnamese, and PLAF, remaining where they were. It stipulated that within 60 days, all U.S. forces in Vietnam would be withdrawn, and the North Vietnamese would hand over all prisoners of war held by them. In addition North Vietnam undertook to help with inquiries into the U.S. service personnel who were listed as missing in action.

The Paris Peace Accord also made references to a possible political settlement that would establish a National Council of Reconciliation and Concord to organize "free and democratic general elections" in which people could vote on a new government for South Vietnam. Before the elections were held, however, President Nguyen Van Thieu would remain in office. The United States saw the Peace Accord as the way to extricate itself from the war; the Vietnamese Communists saw it as a staging post on the way to the takeover of the entire country. The South Vietnamese government, however, violently opposed the Peace Accord and had initially refused to sign it. They objected to the ceasefire being "in place," which allowed as many as 200,000 North Vietnamese troops and their South Vietnamese allies to hold large tracts of the country. Thieu signed the agreement only when faced with massive pressure from the United States, and even then only after two concessions. First, South Vietnam received what became known as Operation Enhance, followed quickly by Operation Enhance Plus. These two operations at the end of 1972 transferred large amounts of U.S. military materiel to the South Vietnamese and handed over U.S. bases in South Vietnam to the South Vietnamese military. In addition, Richard Nixon made a written promise that if the Vietnamese Communists broke the ceasefire, his U.S. government would reintervene militarily, including bombing North Vietnam. It was only after Nixon sent Thieu two letters promising this action that Thieu reluctantly, and under heavy pressure, signed the Peace Accord.

Nobody expected the Paris Peace Accord to end fighting forever. Indeed, before the Peace Accord was enacted, the South Vietnamese tried to take back crucial territory from the PLAF, with a measure of success. As the Accord came into force, public buildings, shops, and private houses throughout South Vietnam flew the South Vietnamese flag as a sign of support for their government. It was, at best, an extremely uneasy peace. Later that year, Henry Kissinger and Le Duc Tho were both awarded the Nobel Peace Prize—Le Duc Tho refused to accept the prize, stating that there was still no peace in Vietnam. He became only the second person to decline the prize—the other being Jean-Paul Sartre who declined the Nobel Prize for Literature as he refused all official honors. The U.S. songwriter and satirist Tom Lehrer dryly commented that satire was now obsolete after Kissinger received a prize for peace.

The Paris Peace Accord held until September 1974, although in neighboring Cambodia war continued with increasing ferocity during this entire period. Many of the South Vietnamese elite, however, realized that it was only a matter of time before the Communists came to power and they started sending some of their assets abroad, with a number departing for a new life in the United States, France, Canada, and other countries. Fighting began in September 1974 and increased in October. As a result, the North Vietnamese military high command drew up a plan to attack South Vietnam the next year.

The North Vietnamese plan was also influenced by a change in administration in the United States. Throughout early 1974, the U.S. government had been unable to act because of the Watergate crisis, which linked Richard Nixon to the break-in at the Watergate Hotel in 1972. Finally as the evidence mounted, and several of Nixon's staff turned on him, on August 9, Nixon resigned the presidency, and Vice President Gerald Ford, appointed by Nixon eight months earlier, was sworn in as president.

Soon after being sworn in, Gerald Ford made a foreign policy speech in which he promised to carry out the policies of the Nixon administration. Henry Kissinger remained as secretary of state, reinforcing the confidence of the South Vietnamese who believed that the United States would honor its commitment to defend their country if attacked. By contrast, the North Vietnamese believed that it was highly unlikely that the United States would want to reintervene in Vietnam and it secretly began to redeploy their soldiers.

## THE BATTLE FOR SOUTH VIETNAM

With all-out war inevitable, on January 6, 1975, the North Vietnamese and their South Vietnamese allies launched a general offensive against the South Vietnamese government. The aim was to take control of the South in a two-year campaign. With North Vietnam going on the offensive, the dry season, from January until April, was the best time to attack, but few North Vietnamese leaders thought it would possible to capture the whole of South Vietnam in four months. Communist ideologue Le Duan argued that a general uprising in South Vietnam in 1976 would make a Communist victory certain.

The first North Vietnamese attack was at Phuoc Binh in the central highlands, and initially they acted cautiously, unsure what the United States would do. Soon it became obvious that the United States was not prepared to bomb North Vietnam and was certainly not going to send in soldiers. The North Vietnamese leadership then gave General Van Tien Dung, the commander-in-chief of the People's Army of Vietnam, instructions to try to capture as much of South Vietnam as he could by the end of April when the rainy season would prevent large-scale troop movements.

U.S. Ambassador Graham A. Martin, who had replaced Ellsworth Bunker in 1973, passionately asked the U.S. government to send weapons and financial aid to the South Vietnamese government. A career diplomat and former ambassador to Thailand whose wife's son had died during the war, Martin was dedicated to supporting the beleaguered Saigon government, but some visiting U.S. politicians felt he was not able to view the conflict dispassionately and rejected his requests. As Republican congresswoman Millicent Fenwick was to say, "we have sent, so to speak, battleship after battleship, and bomber after bomber, and 500,000 or more men, and billions and billions of dollars. If billions and billions did not do at the time when we had all our men there, how can $722 million save the day?"

The North Vietnamese decided to try to capture the central highlands first, as they had attempted in 1965, so they attacked the cities of Pleiku and Ban Me Thuot. The attack on the former was a diversion, with the full force of the North Vietnamese thrown against Ban Me Thuot. Thieu fell for the feint and moved his special forces to Pleiku, weakening the defenses of Ban Me Thuot, which fell on March 13, after a heroic resistance by a vastly outnumbered South Vietnamese garrison. The North Vietnamese, having captured their first major city in South Vietnam, then pushed on to Pleiku.

It did not take long before panic broke out among the South Vietnamese armed forces and civilians. Those in the north fled to Danang, although those in the south were able to hold their position. Ships were sent to Danang to evacuate troops, their dependents, and other civilians from Danang, while the South Vietnamese government officially stated it had no intention of retreating. Privately it became obvious that the South Vietnamese government was about to prepare for something it had never previously contemplated—a repartition of Vietnam, with the government holding onto only the southern part of the country. The morale of the South Vietnamese was sapped, and it was not long before their forces in the northern part of South Vietnam retreated to Danang and took part in the evacuation. Tens of thousands of soldiers and civilians streamed into the port of Danang where the United States had brought in supplies for its forces on so many occasions. Many of them were able to be evacuated by ship to Saigon, and many soldiers left behind abandoned their weapons and their uniforms and surrendered to the incoming North Vietnamese and PLAF soldiers. On March 29, Danang fell and the North Vietnamese film camerawoman, Thu Van, was able to film desolate groups of South Vietnamese soldiers surrendering to her film crew as she went into the city. She was finally reunited with her mother whom she had not seen since the original partition in 1954.

With the South Vietnamese forces retreating, General Dung then increased his attacks on them, driving them back toward Saigon. The South Vietnamese desperately pleaded to the United States for help, but the Ford administration was noncommittal about sending in military help, and Congress even cut off financial help to South Vietnam. This left the South Vietnamese unable to run many of their vehicles, because the escalating fuel price had made gasoline unaffordable.

In the first week of April, General Le Minh Dao regrouped the South Vietnamese soldiers of his 18th Infantry Division for what was effectively the last place the South Vietnamese could realistically hold back the North Vietnamese. At Xuan Loc, he proudly stated to visiting journalists that he would fight there even if the North Vietnamese outnumbered him—"I will knock them down, even if they bring here two divisions or three divisions." In well-prepared positions, the South Vietnamese soldiers realized it was their last chance to save their nation. What remained of the South Vietnamese Air Force flew mission after mission against the North Vietnamese, using cluster bombs and inflicting heavy casualties on the attackers. Fighting raged from April 9–16, when the Vietnamese Communists broke through the lines. The South Vietnamese forces had finally been defeated as General Dung threw nearly 50,000 soldiers against them. After a massive weeklong battle, the South Vietnamese army was in tatters, and those who survived the battle of Xuan Loc fled to Saigon.

## THE EVACUATION OF SAIGON

The U.S. Embassy in Saigon had realized that if the war went badly for them, they would have to evacuate not only their own staff, but all other Americans in Saigon, some of whom were married to Vietnamese, and also people from countries allied to the United States: Australians, British, New Zealanders, South Koreans, Thais, and French (in spite of the French scheming with General Tran Van Don, the South Vietnamese minister of defense, to install his co-conspirator from the 1963 coup, General Duong Van Minh as the new leader of a figurehead Saigon government that might be able to broker an agreement with the Communists). In addition, the U.S. embassy and administration felt duty-bound to evacuate all its South Vietnamese allies—government officials, army leaders, South Vietnamese who had worked for the Americans, and their families. This could amount to as many as 200,000 people.

To achieve an effective evacuation, the U.S. government sent the Seventh Fleet to a position just off the South Vietnamese coast, while aircraft started evacuating as many South Vietnamese as possible. Henry Kissinger later said that he deliberately tried to make it look as though the fleet was there to help the South Vietnamese government in the hopes of dissuading the Communists from attacking Saigon. He was also cautious about ordering the evacuation of all Americans and other foreigners straight way for two reasons. First, he thought that some South Vietnamese might turn on the Americans, and second, he thought that the presence of Americans in Saigon might delay a Communist attack, for the Communists wanted to be careful about endangering Americans, which might lead to a U.S. military response.

With the survivors of the battle of Xuan Loc streaming into Saigon at the news of the terrible defeat, and the Communist victory in neighboring Cambodia on April 17, President Nguyen Van Thieu, persuaded that there was some hope for a coalition government without him, resigned the presidency on April 21 and left Saigon five days later. He took with him a large amount of gold, and retired to a comfortable exile just outside London. Former Vice President Nguyen Cao Ky left for Taiwan four days later, calling the U.S. inaction in failing to defend South Vietnam "an inhumane act by an inhumane ally."

Thieu's resignation left Tran Van Huong, the 72-year old vice president as the new president of South Vietnam. He had served in several governments since the overthrow of Diem and was increasingly frail. Although he wanted to negotiate with the Communists, they saw little reason to make a treaty with a government that was about to collapse. On April 28, Tran Van Huong finally resigned—he had apparently told friends that he always wanted to be president for at least a week. On the seventh day, he handed over the office of the presidency to Duong Van Minh. The inauguration of Minh was disturbed by thunderclouds—the North Vietnamese forces were now at the Newport Bridge, ready to enter Saigon, and the rainy season was just about to begin.

On April 29, the Communists blasted Saigon's Tan Son Nhut Airport, and the United States started the largest helicopter evacuation in history, Operation Frequent Wind. Using 70 helicopters, they managed to evacuate 6,000 Vietnamese and 1,000 Americans and third-country nationals to aircraft carriers offshore. In one of the memorable incidents at the end of the war, helicopters were pushed off U.S. aircraft carriers to provide more room for refugees arriving on them. Although highlighted in popular culture as an act of wastefulness, it was actually a significant humanitarian decision that allowed many more people to be evacuated than would otherwise have been possible.

Remaining in the presidential palace to meet the attacking North Vietnamese and PLAF, Duong Van Minh, president for 44 hours, watched as a tank flying the PRG flag broke through the gates of the presidential palace and drove toward the palace itself, an event filmed by the Australian war reporter Neil Davis. This tank was followed by others, as well as Colonel Bui Tin, the leading North Vietnamese war correspondent. Waving the PRG flag—symbolically not the North Vietnamese flag—the Vietnamese Communists entered the building and President Minh announced to them that he was there to transfer power. Bui Tin replied that he did not have any power to transfer. But he added that "there are no victors and no vanquished...The war for our country is over."

## THE COMMUNIST VICTORY

As North Vietnamese and PRG soldiers made their way through the streets of Saigon, a large crowd symbolically gathered around the statue in central Saigon, erected to commemorate the sacrifice of the South Vietnamese soldiers in the war against the Communists. Tying rope around it, it was pulled down and crumbled into dust.

Legally, the Communists maintained the line that it was the PRG, and not the North Vietnamese, who were leading the fight—the North Vietnamese were merely helping their South Vietnamese allies. As a result, Huynh Tan Phat, the leader of the PRG became the titular president of South Vietnam.

How much power he actually possessed is debatable. Certainly within hours of the Communist victory, there was retribution against the people who had supported the South Vietnamese government. Some of those who were caught were shot, especially members of the secret police. Many of their files, including their personnel roll, were captured at the fall of Saigon. Many others were also beaten up and/or arrested; however, a number of senior South Vietnamese leaders remained in Saigon. The last two presidents of South Vietnam, Tran Van Huong and Duong Van Minh, were both placed under house arrest. In 1977, Huong was declared to have "reformed" and had his civil rights "restored," although he rejected this offer, as many South Vietnamese officials were still held in prison. Minh remained in his villa for the next eight years where he grew exotic orchids and raised birds; he finally went to France in 1983.

Many others were not so lucky. Officers in the South Vietnamese armed forces were arrested and sent for lengthy "reeducation," often lasting many years, with noncommissioned officers also undergoing "reeducation," albeit for shorter periods. Although privates were generally pardoned, many had no jobs, and were refused employment in the new regime, with many having to survive in menial jobs as wharf laborers, cyclo-drivers (operating cycle rickshaws), and the like. The North Vietnamese were worried that the entrepreneurial nature of the south and greater wealth would overwhelm the north. For that reason, as well as a keenness to punish the losers in the war, the South Vietnamese had their currency massively devalued by the victorious North, effectively wiping out the savings of millions of people. Soon afterwards a new currency was introduced, recognizable by small aluminum coins that contained a hole in the middle of them.

On April 25, 1976, elections were held throughout Vietnam for a new National Assembly. In all, 249 deputies were elected from the north and 243 from the south. Altogether 60 seats were reserved for members of minorities. The new National Assembly met for the first time on June 24, 1976, and on July 2, the body proclaimed the official reunification of Vietnam, with Hanoi becoming the capital of the country, and the Constitution of North Vietnam being the country's constitution. Furthermore, the North Vietnamese flag, its anthem, and emblems became those of the new country. The president of North Vietnam, Ton Duc Thang, was the new president of the Socialist Republic of Vietnam (SRV), and the prime minister of North Vietnam, Pham Van Dong, became the prime minister of the SRV. The only major office to go to a South Vietnamese politician was Huynh Tan Phat of the PRG, who became the vice president.

# 9

# From Reunification until the Withdrawal from Cambodia (1976–1989)

The period from the end of the Vietnam War until the reunification of the country on July 2, 1976, had allowed for a gradual merger of the organs of both states—the education and health systems, the public works boards, and the like. The first new coins of the Socialist Republic of Vietnam (SRV) bore the emblem of North Vietnam, but now referred to the whole of Vietnam. The symbol also appeared, along with various portraits of Ho Chi Minh, on the new banknotes. The first postage stamps, issued on July 27, were less controversial. One commemorated the 30th anniversary of the Vietnamese Red Cross; the other two were issued specifically for use by disabled war veterans. By December, stamps were being produced commemorating the capture of Ban Me Thuot, Danang, and Saigon's presidential palace in the previous year. With the formation of the SRV, one of the other issues concerned the reorganization of the Vietnamese Olympic Committee, which took place on December 20, 1976, although it did not receive official recognition until 1980 when a team competed in the Moscow Olympics.

As with the ending of all civil wars, there was a spate of name changes, the most obvious being Saigon, which was renamed Ho Chi Minh City, although it was a city that Ho Chi Minh had had little to do with during his life. The one building that did have a genuine association with him, the *Nha Rong* (Dragon

House), which had been the headquarters of a French shipping company, was turned into the Ho Chi Minh Museum, as it was from this building that Ho Chi Minh left Vietnam in 1911. The South Vietnamese Presidential Palace was renamed the Reunification Palace, and was used for state functions; it is now a major tourist attraction. Although guides maintain that it has remained unchanged since 1975, its bookshelves crammed with the works of Kim Il Sung tend to indicate that its library has been updated since Duong Van Minh surrendered there in April 1975.

The street names were also changed. Rue Catinat, one of the most fashionable streets in French Saigon, had been renamed Duong Tu Do ("Tu Do" Street) by Diem, and was now renamed Dong Khoi. The road at the southern end of it, which ran along the Saigon River, had been named Quai le Myre de Villiers by the French (after the governor of Cochinchina from 1879 to 1883) and was now renamed after Ton Duc Thang, the man who had succeeded Ho Chi Minh as president of North Vietnam. North of the presidential palace, the formerly French Rue Legrand de la Liraye was now renamed Dien Bien Phu. Many streets kept the same name, however, with the French Rue Taberd having been renamed by Diem after the early modern writer Nguyen Du (1765–1820), a name retained by the Communists who also respected the official who led a mission to China in the early nineteenth century.

## ECONOMIC PROBLEMS

Vietnam was desperately poor and survived largely on donations by the governments of the Soviet Union and other Communist countries. The United States maintained a boycott on political contact with, and economic ties to, Vietnam, and Vietnamese Americans and their supporters kept up the pressure on successive U.S. administrations. President Ford, President Carter, and especially President Reagan pressed the Vietnamese government to release the tens of thousands of former South Vietnamese officials and army officers and noncommissioned officers held in reeducation camps, some in the same prisons that international human rights groups had criticized the South Vietnamese government for maintaining in the early 1970s. There was also pressure by the U.S. government to account for the American service personnel still listed as "missing in action" and to deal with reported sightings of American prisoners still being held in Vietnam.

The French government had played an ambivalent role in much of the latter period of the Vietnam War. Trying to pursue an independent foreign policy, the French were certainly involved in negotiations with the Vietnamese Communists, as well as the Communists in Cambodia. Indeed, French rubber plantation owners worked tracts of territory along the Ho Chi Minh Trail during the 1960s and early 1970s and seemed never to notice the use of the trail to bring

Communist supplies into South Vietnam, much to the annoyance of the U.S. and South Vietnamese army commanders. Only in 1976 did the Vietnamese government finally take over the rubber plantations, and the French commercial presence in Vietnam ended. During the 1980s, the French government was to systematically exhume all French graves throughout Vietnam and transport the bodies to France, where they were reburied in a massive cemetery at Fréjus, near Toulon in the south of France. A massive memorial commemorates by name the 39,000 soldiers who died for the French—as well as the tens of thousands of French, Germans, Africans, and others who died in the French Foreign Legion or in the French colonial forces.

With nearly a million people made homeless by the war, and as many as one-eighth of the population injured in the war, the problems facing the SRV were extremely formidable. Furthermore, many children had been unable to attend school for years, and the healthcare system was fairly rudimentary in large parts of the country. Many foreign-trained doctors from South Vietnam had fled the country, and those who remained operated, for the most part, in heavily under-resourced hospitals and clinics. Although the fighting had ended, there were large numbers of unexploded mines and other ordnance littering the countryside, adding daily to the number of people injured by the war. The aftereffects of the defoliants on people living in affected areas still remains a major problem.

To try to overcome these problems, the government of the SRV drew up plans to try to revitalize the economy, which had been on a war footing since 1945. Essentially, the plan was to encourage the expansion of industry in the north of the country and to increase agricultural land in the south. The former ran into technical problems with a shortage of Western-trained personnel, and the latter was even more problematic because of the massive amount of un-expended ordnance, mines, and defoliant such as Agent Orange used during the war. The defoliants and the bombing had destroyed 5 percent of the total tree cover of the country and had damaged half of what remained. Most of the Communist bureaucracy had spent its energy during the last 30 years providing for the war effort. In the south, there was continual resentment, especially in Saigon, which had been renamed Ho Chi Minh City, although many of its residents continued to call it Saigon.

The commercial sector was dominated by ethnic Chinese who refused to cooperate with the new economic directives from Hanoi and who opposed the establishment of the "new economic zones" created in depressed parts of the country. The nation was also battered by major floods in parts of the country and a drought in some of central Vietnam, which reduced food production. As a result, the Hanoi-based bureaucracy decided to embark on the "socialization" of industry and agriculture in the south, seizing control of private property and starting to establish communes. Protests were brutally repressed and hundreds of thousands of people, most of whom were ethnic Chinese, left Vietnam, either to head over the mountains into China, or by boat for China, Hong Kong, or places farther away. Known as the "Boat People," tens of thousands of them were attacked by pirates in the South China Seas, with men being hacked to death and women and girls raped. Most countries were eager not to want to be seen to encourage refugees arriving by boat, and many of those who did arrive were put into internment centers, from where some managed to get resettlement as a part of refugee programs, but others languished for long periods, with some being forcibly returned to Vietnam.

Because of the ethnicity of many of the refugees, China willingly took in several hundred thousand who were resettled in the south of the country. The relationship between the Vietnamese and Chinese Communists, enjoyed so much during the Vietnam War, started to sour badly. On May 24, 1978, a spokesman of the Overseas Chinese Affairs Office of the State Council of the Chinese government publicly accused the Vietnamese government of mistreating Chinese residents. He stated that more than 50,000 people of Chinese ethnicity had been forced over the Vietnamese border into southern China and compared the actions of the SRV to those of Ngo Dinh Diem in 1957, when he introduced regulations to make Chinese in South Vietnamese into Chinese citizens. Three days after the Chinese statement, the SRV's foreign ministry issued its own statement denying the facts at issue.

On June 9, 1978, the Chinese attacks on the Vietnamese government's policies became even more pointed when the Chinese ministry of foreign affairs stated that it was well known that there were more than 1 million Chinese in Vietnam and urged for reconciliation, as "China and Vietnam are linked by common mountains and rivers, and the two people share weal and woe." Many of these refugees in China were settled at the port of Beihai, but there was little likelihood of any reconciliation, as incidents along the Vietnamese-Cambodian border soon led to war.

## THE WAR WITH CAMBODIA

The Communist Khmer Rouge had taken control of Cambodia two weeks before the Vietnamese Communists captured Saigon. The Cambodian Communist Party had long operated underground, and few knew that their leader was Pol Pot (formerly Saloth Sar), a longtime communist who harbored a passionate hatred of Vietnam. Pol Pot yearned for a rebirth in Cambodia's importance in Southeast Asia, and, having been able to win the civil war there ahead of the end of the war in Vietnam, he soon had an overblown idea of the strength of the Cambodian soldiers he commanded.

On December 3, 1975, the coalition government in Laos was abolished by the Communist Pathet Lao, who, in control of that country, ended the 600-year old Laotian monarchy, proclaiming the People's Democratic Republic of Laos. The new ruler of Laos was Prince Souphanouvong, a member of the Laotian royal family who had a long history of anti-French activism, having spent much of the time since 1945 heading a guerilla force in the countryside. Prince Souphanouvong was to remain a loyal supporter of Vietnam, with Kaysone Phomvihan as his prime minister.

While the Vietnamese Communists were able to start to dominate Laos, the new Cambodian Communist government became increasingly xeno-phobic and, in fact, claimed parts of southern Vietnam as Cambodian terri-tory, citing the Cambodian ownership of them for the period up to the 1800s. Border clashes began, with the Cambodians massacring villagers along the Vietnamese-Cambodian border. In 1977, there was a simmering border dis-pute, and by mid-1978, the Vietnamese government made clear that it in-tended to confront, militarily, the Khmer Rouge who was also arming for a confrontation along the border.

A wave of arbitrary arrests in eastern Cambodia in 1977 and early 1978 had led to a number of Khmer Rouge fleeing into Vietnam. These included Cam-bodian Communists Heng Samrin and Hun Sen and in August 1978, Chan Vèn. It was not long before the Vietnamese decided to help these exiles, pos-sibly providing them with weapons and even using the Vietnamese army. In early 1978, large numbers of copies of a Vietnamese-Cambodian dictionary were published in Vietnam, which Cambodian nationalists later cited as clear evidence for Vietnam's plans to colonize Cambodia.

As tensions heightened along the Cambodian-Vietnamese border, the Cam-bodian government suddenly decided to invite three Westerners to its country to show that it was about to become the victims of a Vietnamese invasion. The Scottish academic, Malcolm Caldwell, the American journalist Elizabeth Becker, then with the *Washington Post*, and Richard Dudman, of the *St. Louis Post Dispatch* arrived in Phnom Penh, the Cambodian capital, on December 3, 1978. The country by that time had been cut off from the world since 1975, apart from a brief visit by a Yugoslav camera crew who had portrayed a very bleak view of the country. Early in the morning of December 23, a group of armed people broke into the government guest house where the three for-eigners were staying and murdered Caldwell. It has never been satisfactorily explained exactly who the killers were, but evidence suggests that they could have been either renegade Khmer Rouge, seeking to embarrass Pol Pot whom the group had met on the previous day, or people working on behalf of Viet-nam for a similar purpose.

By this time it appears that a large Cambodian Communist armed force had already entered Vietnam, where it had been destroyed. Certainly when Viet-nam struck back on December 25, 1978, the Khmer Rouge army was already a spent force. With the Vietnamese government having a treaty of friendship and cooperation with the Soviet Union, signed on November 3, 1978, it was clear that Vietnam, backed by the Soviet Union, and Cambodia, backed by China, would go to war. On December 25, 1978, a group of pro-Vietnamese Cambodian Communist exiles who had sought refuge in Vietnam, proclaimed the invasion of Cambodia, and 200,000 Vietnamese soldiers attacked into Cambodia from Vietnam and Laos.

The Vietnamese army, previously trained in guerilla war, acted well in Cambodia. In one of the fastest moving campaigns in history, on January 6, 1979, it had captured Phnom Penh, the Cambodian capital, which was largely deserted, having been forcibly evacuated by the Khmer Rouge in April 1975. Three days later, with the vast majority of Cambodia in their hands, the pro-Vietnamese former exiles and their Vietnamese backers proclaimed the formation of the People's Republic of Kampuchea and declared themselves allies of Vietnam.

The international community was shocked by the Vietnamese action, and by the fall of the Cambodian Communists who had lost control of their entire country in a fortnight. At the United Nations, the Chinese government led the condemnation of the Vietnamese actions and was supported by the United States and its allies. On February 17, 1979, the Chinese launched their invasion of Vietnam, forcing the Vietnamese to pull out their crack soldiers from Cambodia to defend their home territory. The Chinese were able to capture the northern border region of Vietnam, but because of the mountainous terrain and the dogged fighting of the Vietnamese, as well as some ineptness in some in the Chinese command, on March 5, the Chinese started withdrawing. They had certainly not managed to defeat the Vietnamese, but the Vietnamese realized that China was prepared to strike to protect its allies in Cambodia who managed to regroup and re-form along the Cambodian-Thai border. The Chinese government later claimed that 20,000 Chinese and 50,000 Vietnamese soldiers were killed or wounded in the fighting.

## THE VIETNAMESE OCCUPATION OF CAMBODIA

The initial Vietnamese plans in Cambodia had been to send commandoes ahead of their soldiers to try to capture Prince Norodom Sihanouk, Cambodia's former king, who was being held under house arrest by the Khmer Rouge. The Khmer Rouge were able to whisk Sihanouk out of Phnom Penh just before its fall, and also evacuate their leadership. They left behind a wrecked country and clear evidence that they had been involved in the systematic mass murder of their political opponents. At Tuol Sleng in Phnom Penh, the Vietnamese came across an interrogation and execution center operated by the Khmer Rouge for the killing of people who were regarded as a serious threat to their regime. Internal dissent in the countryside was enough for people to be executed, but those suspected of treason, especially party leaders and their collaborators, were questioned at Tuol Sleng before their inevitable execution.

The Vietnamese pointed to the atrocities committed by the Khmer Rouge in Cambodia as justification of their actions in invading the country. Certainly most people around the world were horrified by the photographs and television footage of the Khmer Rouge rule. The Vietnamese and their client government in Phnom Penh, however, soon had to deal with more than just military problems. As soon as the Vietnamese had defeated the Khmer Rouge, many people in Cambodia tried to flee the country as refugees, heading for Thailand. The Thai government was worried that the Vietnamese might use this as an excuse to invade Thailand itself; furthermore other people remaining in Cambodia tried to track down members of their families from whom they had been separated during the three and a half years of Khmer Rouge rule. This quickly led to a failure to ensure that the rice crop had been planted and cultivated, and it was not long before Cambodia was hit by a massive famine.

World relief agencies quickly collected millions of dollars in food aid, and refugee groups and humanitarian organizations started to supply the refugee camps along the Thai-Cambodian border with food aid. Because of the Western blockade with Vietnam, however, relatively little food aid was provided for the starving people within Cambodia. The eastern bloc countries sent Vietnam considerable food supplies but never enough to cope with the humanitarian crisis that led to the deaths of tens of thousands of people. Even at the height of the famine, some of the aid from Eastern Europe continued to consist of textbooks on Marxist-Leninist theory, which arrived in Phnom Penh in large quantities.

From 1979 to 1989, the Vietnamese maintained between 140,000 and 200,000 soldiers in Cambodia, supporting the government led initially by Heng Samrin and then, from 1985, by Hun Sen. For the Vietnamese it was a difficult time, which led to major repercussions in their country. The cost of the fighting in Cambodia continued to cripple the Vietnamese economy. Many in Vietnam were elated when the fighting ended in 1975, but there was gradually growing dissent about the casualties suffered by the Vietnamese in Cambodia. The Vietnamese Communists had been excellent at waging a guerilla war against the French and then the South Vietnamese and the Americans. Now, in Cambodia, they had to garrison Cambodian cities, towns, and villages against attacks by guerillas who were becoming increasingly well armed.

In November 1981, one of the leading figures in the pro-Vietnamese government in Cambodia, Prime Minister Pen Sovan, began to criticize the continued Vietnamese presence in Cambodia. On December 5 of that year he was removed and "disappeared" from public view, being taken to Hanoi where he was held under house arrest for the next 10 years. For many people it was evident that the Vietnamese wanted to exercise absolute control over the country, with Hun Sen, a pro-Vietnamese politician, rising to become prime minister in January 1985.

By the mid-1980s, the West started supporting a number of anticommunist resistance groups along the Thai-Cambodian border who waged a guerilla war against the Vietnamese, with clear support from Thailand. It also saw the five (and later six) countries of the Association of Southeast Asian Nations leading the international opposition to Vietnam's actions in Cambodia, with Thailand still worried about being invaded. With Cambodian resistance groups attacking the Vietnamese and then retreating back into Thai territory when the Vietnamese counterattacked, every time the Vietnamese crossed the Thai-Cambodian border there were howls of protest in the West.

Large numbers of Vietnamese were also killed or injured in the war, with others moving to Cambodia, which engendered a further wave of Cambodian xenophobia in the 1990s. The Vietnamese pointed out that they had overthrown the Pol Pot government in Cambodia, which had presided over the death of about a million people, in a population of seven or eight million. Anti-Vietnamese rhetoric in the West, partially as a result of the war, however, ensured the continued international isolation of Vietnam. India was the only noncommunist country that recognized the pro-Vietnamese People's Republic of Kampuchea. Most of the West, and also the United Nations, supported the anti-Vietnamese Coalition Government of Democratic Kampuchea, which controlled most of the refugee camps on the Thai-Cambodian border, and increasing amounts of territory in Cambodia itself.

## THE VIETNAMESE GOVERNMENT

Rather than trying to increase engagement with the rest of the world, in 1980, the Vietnamese National Assembly adopted the country's third constitution. It was largely based on the Constitution of the Soviet Union and stated that the SRV would remain a one-party state and that the Communist Party had the role of representing the people and running the country.

During the early 1980s, the Vietnamese remained reliant on economic aid from the Soviet Union, receiving as much as $3 billion a year in Soviet subsidies. The Soviet Union was also generous in its friendship ties, and on July 23, 1980, Pham Tuan, a former North Vietnamese pilot during the Vietnam War, was launched into space on the Soyuz 37, along with a Soviet cosmonaut. He was not only the first Vietnamese to go into space, but also the first Asian; he spent 7 days, 20 hours, and 42 minutes in space. During his time there he was able to help with the servicing of the Salyut 6 space station, carry out experiments with plant cultivation, and photograph Vietnam for mapping. After his return to Vietnam, he entered politics and won a seat in the National Assembly.

While the Vietnamese government was facing international opprobrium for its actions in Cambodia, Nguyen Co Thach, the new Vietnamese foreign minister, appointed in 1980, embarked on a policy of engagement with the West. From a peasant family, Thach had fought at the battle of Dien Bien Phu and had been appointed as ambassador to India in 1956, later returning to work at the foreign ministry in Hanoi. He supported the overthrow of the Pol Pot government in Cambodia, but he recognized that the only way that Vietnam could prosper was by getting Western foreign aid, investment, and expertise. This would limit Vietnam's almost total dependence on financial aide from the Soviet Union, and a settlement to the Cambodian conflict—the Vietnamese government maintained that their invasion in 1978–1979 was "irreversible"—would help the Vietnamese economy.

When Nguyen Co Thach and other Vietnamese government officials visited a number of overseas countries, they often ran into protests organized by Vietnamese exiles and their supporters. By the 1980s, there were a number of organizations established by these exiles with the aim of overthrowing the Vietnamese Communist government. Many wanted to pressure the governments in the countries in which they had settled, but a number were keen to launch an armed struggle against the Vietnamese government. Hoang Co Minh in the United States, a mathematician originally from Hanoi, had served as a vice admiral in the South Vietnamese navy. He returned to Vietnam in August 1987 to carry out attacks on the Vietnamese Communists and was killed during an ambush in Laos. Another anticommunist fighter, Vo Dai Ton, from Australia, was captured but later released after diplomatic pressure from overseas; and Le Quoc Tuy, from his exile in France, was arrested and died in a French prison. Because of their numbers, the Vietnamese community represents a strong voting bloc in parts of the United States, in some of Canada (especially Quebec), in several constituencies in France, and also in Australia. In many of these countries, discussion groups on the Vietnam War often led to fights between supporters and opponents of rival factions; and on Vietnamese festivals, many Vietnamese restaurants and other shops in the West still flew the South Vietnamese flag.

Vietnam joined the Soviet-led boycott of the Los Angeles Olympic Games, in response to the American boycott of the previous Moscow Olympics. In 1988, Vietnam sent a team to the Seoul Olympics, and Quoc Cuong Nguyen placed 13th of 32 shooters in the rapid-fire pistol event, the best result that any Vietnamese athlete had received up to that point.

## *DO MOI* AND THE LIBERALIZATION OF VIETNAM

On July 9, 1986, the Le Duan, who had been general secretary of the Communist Party of Vietnam (CPV) for 10 years, died and was succeeded by Truong Chinh. Chinh was only a temporary replacement while the Vietnamese

Communist hierarchy sought out a new leader. From December 15–19, 1986, the Sixth Party Congress of the CPV was held in Hanoi; and at the congress, Nguyen Van Linh was elected as the general secretary. At 73, he was only six years younger than the man he replaced, so it was not the generational change that many younger Vietnamese had expected.

Although Linh had been born in Hanoi, he grew up in South Vietnam and was first arrested by the French in 1930, when he was 16 years old. He served six years in prison for political offences, was released in the amnesty of 1936, and then moved to Haiphong where he took part in Communist operations, working alongside Le Duan. Arrested in 1941, he was held at Poulo Condore prison until his release in 1945, when he started work under Le Duan again organizing the Communist movement in Cochinchina. In 1961, he was appointed director of the Central Office for South Vietnam (COSVN) and then served under General Nguyen Chi Thanh and then Pham Hung in the National Front for the Liberation of South Vietnam (NFL) and then the Provisional Revolutionary Government of the Republic of Vietnam (PRG) until 1975. Raised to the politburo in 1976, Linh was head of the Communist Party of Vietnam (CPV) Committee for Ho Chi Minh City until he was sacked in 1978 for opposing and then refusing to carry out the socialization of the economy. In 1982, he had been removed from the politburo but managed to rebuild his support in Ho Chi Minh City, the socialization schemes having collapsed, and was reinstated to the politburo in 1985. Linh was an avid supporter of greater liberalization of the economy, hoping to transform the country into a market economy. With Nguyen Co Thach as foreign minister, Vietnam was set to change.

This change in thinking among the leadership of the Communist Party of Vietnam coincided with the rise to power of Mikhail Gorbachev who became general secretary of the Communist Party of the Soviet Union in March 1985. Gorbachev introduced his policies of *Glasnost* (openness) and *Perestroika* (restructuring). The Communist Party of Vietnam was wary of the former but thought that the latter would help regenerate an otherwise stagnant economy. Some also possibly saw a time when Vietnam would no longer receive large subsidies from the Soviet Union.

The policy of greater liberalization of the economy, introduced in 1986, was named *Doi Moi* (Renovation) by the Sixth National Congress. It was similar to perestroika, but the CPV was anxious to show that it was distinctly Vietnamese. The main aim was to revitalize the economy of the country and build up its prosperity to help all the people of Vietnam. To achieve this goal, it had to restore levels of private ownership and let the farming sector sell excess production. This strategy had the immediate effect, as had a similar policy in China, of encouraging farmers to grow more food, the amount above the government quota being able to be sold at markets that quickly appeared throughout the country. It reinvigorated the capitalist spirit in the Vietnamese people and helped end any shortages of food that had existed during the late 1970s. Some outside observers claimed that the selling of excess food had been taking place on a large scale before the introduction of *Doi Moi,* and there is some truth in this; however legalizing the policy ensured its success.

Although the policy of *Doi Moi* did improve the economic basis of the country, the CPV was anxious to avoid any major political reforms that would erode the supremacy of the party organization. Party members were still preferred in government appointments, and there was certainly no question of allowing for the introduction of a multiparty system with free elections. As a result, overseas critics viewed *Doi Moi* as a method of entrenching communism in Vietnam, rather than any serious attempt to reform the country. The greater economic independence created by *Doi Moi* did allow for changes in the education system and also a flourishing of new literary and artistic talent, with many new songs being released and a large number of new novels being published. Some of these novelists such as Bao Ninh, Duong Thu Huong, and Nguyen Huy Thiep soon became internationally well known.

Bao Ninh, born in 1952 at Hanoi, had served during the Vietnam War as a member of the Glorious 27th Youth Brigade. When he went to war in 1969, he was one of 500 youths in the brigade; by the end of the war, he was one of only 10 who had survived. His book, *The Sorrow of War,* portrayed the bleak life of a North Vietnamese soldier during the war, coming to terms with the death of his friends, and the huge price that the nation paid for victory.

In spite of *Doi Moi,* however, the Vietnamese economy was still unable to grow, primarily because of little support from the West. As a result of the mounting cost of the war in Cambodia, as well as the continued opposition to Vietnam's actions there, Vietnam finally withdrew the last of its soldiers in September 1989, an action that helped ease tensions in the region. The Vietnamese government had also closed down all of its major reeducation camps, although some South Vietnamese officials were still being held in detention into the 1990s, up to 20 years after the war. Former internees, the Amerasians, and the families of Vietnamese living overseas were gradually allowed to emigrate under a number of refugee programs and family migration schemes. Many moved to the United States, with increasing numbers settling in Australia and other countries in the Pacific.

# 10

# Vietnam Today (1989–Present)

The gradual collapse of the Soviet Bloc between 1989 and 1991 led to a major rethinking among the leadership of the Communist Party of Vietnam. For them, the policy of *Doi Moi* had led to increasing prosperity. Furthermore, the withdrawal of their troops from Cambodia had lessened the international tensions in the region. The major aim of the Vietnamese was to try to engineer a peace settlement in Cambodia that would allow normalization of relations with the world community.

In July 1988, the first of the Jakarta Informal Meetings was held in the Indonesian capital. The Vietnamese met with the members of the Association of Southeast Asian Nations and the Cambodian factions to try to work out a power sharing system that could be arranged ahead of internationally supervised elections in Cambodia. On September 30, 1988, Truong Ching, longtime Vietnamese Communist ideologue, died; and by December of that year, border contact between Vietnamese and Chinese traders was officially resumed. In January 1989, Dinh Nho Liem, the Vietnamese deputy foreign minister, visited China, the highest-level official contact between the Vietnamese and Chinese governments. He was to return to Beijing in May, just before the arrival of Mikhail Gorbachev and the demonstrations in Tiananmen Square. This set the scene for the second Jakarta Informal Meeting in February, and two months later Vietnam announced that it would unilaterally withdraw all its forces from Cambodia by September. In late September, and after official celebrations, the Vietnamese soldiers were feted by their Cambodian supporters as they left. Even though some Cambodian nationalists claimed that several Vietnamese military units had remained in the country, few Western commentators believed that they had not been withdrawn. A year later, at a secret meeting held in Chengdu, China, the premiers and Communist Party general secretaries of the SRV and China agreed to normalize ties between the two countries.

Coinciding with Vietnam's attempts to improve its foreign relations, at home the government continued to crack down on dissent. In February 1989, the Communist Party of Vietnam (CPV) General Secretary Nguyen Van Linh claimed that the local press was being too critical of the government, and, on December 28, the National Assembly passed a much tougher series of press laws. With the fall of the Berlin Wall in November and the subsequent collapse of the East German government, and the overthrow and then shooting of Nicolae Ceaucescu of Romania on December 25, 1989, in March 1990, Tran Xuan Bach, a politburo member, claimed that if Vietnam did not allow a greater level of freedom of the press, the Vietnamese government might also be overthrown. Tran Xuan Bach was immediately removed from the government. Three months later the Soviet Union announced that it was reducing its economic aid to Vietnam, although it was to maintain soldiers at Cam Ranh Bay until October 2001. By December 1990, however, the CPV had realized that communism was losing its appeal around the world, and it drew up a draft plan for economic reform in the country, with the hope of improving economic growth rates while retaining the power of the Communist Party.

## THE PERIOD OF REFORM

In June 1991, at the Seventh Congress of the CPV, Nguyen Van Linh retired, and Do Muoi was appointed as the new general secretary of the Party. Vo Van Kiet became the new premier and took office on August 8. The appointment of Vo Van Kiet showed that the CPV remained cautious, choosing yet another longtime activist who had joined the Communists in the early 1940s. From a relatively prosperous family from Cantho, South Vietnam, Vo Van Kiet had been active in the communist movement in the south, running the Saigon Municipal Party Committee in the early 1970s and then serving as prime minister for three months in 1988. His first triumph was on October 23, when Vietnam was a signatory to the Paris Peace Agreement, which ended the civil war in Cambodia and transferred Cambodia to the United Nations. The next month relations with China were finally normalized; at the same time the first Export Processing Zone was established at Tan Thuan Dong, near Ho Chi Minh City. By the time that the Soviet Union collapsed in December, Do Muoi, the general secretary of the CPV, was able to claim that Vietnam was following the "correct course," in mixing capitalist economic thinking with communist state control. By this time tourism in Vietnam was starting to increase; the first Lonely Planet guide book to the country was published in 1991, the Vietnamese government had already begin to mint large numbers of silver commemorative coins in Havana for sale as tourist mementoes.

The reform process in Vietnam continued, with a new constitution promulgated in April 1992. It eliminated the council of state and changed the council of ministers into a cabinet position. Symbolically, it also reduced the importance of Marxism-Leninism as part of the state ideology. By June 1992, the government had legislated for the sale of state-owned enterprises to encourage the "equitization process." Without economic support from the Soviet Union, Vietnam started to gradually normalize its diplomatic relations with the United States. This was a difficult undertaking for a variety of reasons. There was still anger over the Vietnam War, and the "MIA" lobby in the United States urged their government to pressure the Vietnamese to help with the fullest possible accounting for all U.S. service personnel who were still listed as "Missing in Action" in Vietnam. Also, Vietnamese exiles in the United States were urging the U.S. government to keep up the pressure on the communists.

Although there had been a healing process of sorts in the United States, it was not until November 1982 that the Vietnam Veterans Memorial, designed by Maya Lin, an Ohio-born architect of Chinese ancestry, was erected in Washington, D.C. Consisting of two walls in a "V" shape, with one wall pointing to the Washington Monument, and the other toward the Lincoln Memorial, it was made from granite imported from India, with the cutting and fabrication done at Barre, Vermont. Dedicated in Washington, D.C., the wall contained the names of all the Americans who died during the war. They are listed on the day they died, with, initially, 58,159 names, although it now has 58,256 names, including those of eight women. The last 18 listed were the soldiers killed in the rescue of the crew of the *Mayaguez* from Cambodia on May 15, 1975.

By this time, interest in the war had increased and many films were set during this period. The most well known were *The Deer Hunter* (1978), *Apocalypse Now* (1979), *First Blood* (1982), *Platoon* (1986), *Hamburger Hill* and *Full Metal Jacket* (1987), and *Born on the Fourth of July* (1989). Vietnam also formed a major part of the story in *Kent State* (1981), *The Killing Fields* (1984), and *JFK* (1991). By 2007, it was calculated that there were 352 U.S. feature films either directly about, or referring to, the Vietnam War.

Ronald Reagan, the U.S. president from 1981–1989, had declared that the Vietnam War was "in truth a noble cause," and his successor, George H. W. Bush was also a keen supporter of veterans' groups. In the 1992 U.S. presidential election, the issue of the Vietnam War resurfaced. The Democratic Party candidate, Bill Clinton, had been a student during the Vietnam War and had opposed it. Rumors spread that while in England on his Rhodes Scholarship, he had been worried about being drafted and contemplated taking out British citizenship. He denied this allegation and a thorough search of British government archives failed to reveal any application having been lodged. George Bush's World War II record was not in dispute, nor was that of Clinton's vice presidential running mate, Al Gore, who had served in the 20th Engineer Brigade in Vietnam, despite his personal opposition to the war. By contrast, Bush's vice president, and his vice presidential running mate, Dan Quayle, had avoided serving in Vietnam by joining the Indiana National Guard.

On June 25, 1992, the overseas Vietnamese community cheered the astronaut Eugene Huu-Chau "Gene" Trinh, an American of Vietnamese ancestry who became the second Vietnamese to go into space. Born in 1950 in Saigon, he spent his childhood in Paris, moving with his family to the United States in 1968, and later rising to the position of director of the physical sciences research division at NASA. He was aboard the U.S. Space Shuttle working as a Payload Specialist on the STS-50/United States Microgravity Lab-1. Altogether he spent nearly 14 days in space.

The election of Bill Clinton in November 1992 was to dramatically change relations between Vietnam and the United States. In July 1993, the United States ended its veto on a Vietnamese government plan to pay its arrears to the International Monetary Fund and join the world economic system. In February 1994, the United States finally lifted its economic embargo on the country, with full diplomatic relations established in July 1995, although no ambassadors were exchanged for another two years. Immediately thereafter, Vietnam was able to join the Association of Southeast Asian Nations, the regional group that had led the opposition to Vietnam's occupation of Cambodia throughout the 1980s. Vietnam also signed a treaty of cooperation with the European Union.

On March 6, 1998, the U.S. Army formally recognized helicopter pilot Warrant Officer Hugh Thompson, his former gunner Lawrence Colburn, and the crew chief Glenn U. Andreotta (who had been killed in April 1968), awarding all three the Soldier's Medal for Gallantry for their actions at My Lai in March 1968 when then had protected escaping Vietnamese villagers. The role of the three was also recognized by the Vietnamese government.

## THE DEFEAT OF THE CONSERVATIVES

Conservatives in the CPV were worried that the moves to reform had gone too fast and too far. On September 23, 1992, Le Duc Anh had become president of the country. Originally from Hue, he had been a member of the Communist Party since 1938 and had helped plan the Vietnamese invasion of Cambodia in 1978, commanding the Vietnamese soldiers there until 1985. With a strong military background—he was subsequently minister of defense—some conservatives hoped that they might be able to temper the level of reform and ensure the continued role of the Communist Party. In January 1993, the Fourth Plenum of the Seventh Central Committee of the CPV passed resolutions to try to retain the cultural identity of Vietnam, and, in June 1994, the National Assembly passed labor laws to protect workers as the economy slowly became more capitalist and newspaper accounts of managerial abuses started to be published. In October 1995, these laws were reinforced by a Civil Code enacted by the National Assembly to develop a greater respect for the country's laws.

The conservatives in the Communist Party had been looking for somebody to champion their views, and Dao Duy Tung emerged in early 1996. Dao Duy Tung had long been the editor-in-chief of the monthly journal *Tap Chi Cong San* (Communist Review), the political and theoretical organ of the Communist Party, which had been founded in 1956 as *Hoc Top*, and by this time had a circulation of 55,000. Dao Duy Tung was also director of the Institute for Research on Marxism-Leninism and Ho Chi Minh Thought. He had also been in charge of the Propaganda and Training Department of the CPV, and from 1986 had also been in the politburo. The conservatives thought that he could replace Do Muoi who was possibly retiring, and as preparations began for the Eighth Party Congress, they rallied behind him. To serve as a manifesto for the conservatives, a political report was drawn up by Dao Duy Tung and was made public in April. Instead of endorsing it, or even seriously considering it, however, the Party Congress rejected the report and sacked Dao Duy Tung from the Politburo. The Congress also decided not to change the party leadership, the whole occasion being overshadowed by the death of Le Mai, a senior Vietnamese diplomat who had engineered normalization of relations with the United States. Dao Duy Tung also died soon after the end of the Congress.

Change finally came in the Vietnamese leadership when President Le Duc Anh suffered a stroke in November 1996. At that time, the CPV decided on a wholesale change in the leadership of the country the next year. By then Douglas "Pete" Peterson was appointed the first U.S. ambassador to the Socialist Republic of Vietnam. In June 1997, a plenum of the Central Committee of the CPV chose Tran Duc Luong as the country's new president, and Phan Van Khai as the prime minister. These appointments represented a generational change, as both were born in the 1930s, and both relied heavily on the support of the government rather than the Communist Party or the army.

Tran Duc Luong was from Quang Ngai in central Vietnam and was 17 years old at the partition of Vietnam in 1954. He moved north rather than remain in South Vietnam. Four years later he actually joined the Vietnam Workers' Party and then trained as a geologist. He then held several minor posts before becoming a member of the National Assembly and was one of the technocrats who rose to important positions during the reform period of *Doi Moi*. In 1992, he was appointed a deputy prime minister, and in 1996 was appointed to the politburo, and then later became president. The new prime minister, Phan Van Khai, was also a southerner. He was born in Saigon and, according to his official biography, was 13 when he became involved in revolutionary activities, also going to North Vietnam with the Partition of Vietnam in 1954. After studying economics in Moscow, he then worked in the State Planning Committee, and with the signing of the Paris Peace Accord of January 1973, he started working in the Communist-controlled part of South Vietnam as an economic researcher. From 1975–1989, he worked in local government in his native Ho Chi Minh City and then moved to Hanoi where he was also a deputy prime minister before becoming prime minister.

The process of change in the leadership continued with the appointment, in December 1997, of Le Kha Phieu as the new general secretary of the CPV. By contrast to the other two leaders, Le Kha Phieu was from the north. He was born in Thanh Hoa Province and then served in the military, eventually heading the army's political department. A protégé of Le Duc Anh, he had been elected to the Central Committee of the CPV in 1991, and to the politburo three years later. The army had clearly helped in his appointment as general secretary, wanting a conservative to hold that position to counterbalance the influence of the reformists.

## RAPPROCHEMENT WITH CHINA

After the fighting along the Vietnamese-Chinese border in February 1979, and the war in Cambodia, the Vietnamese government was eager to normalize its relationship with China. The dismissal of Nguyen Co Thach in 1991 had certainly helped in that goal, and in November 1991, Do Muoi and Vo Van Kiet made an official visit to China. From November 30 to December 4, 1992, the Chinese Premier Li Peng made an official goodwill visit to Vietnam. This visit was followed by the Vietnamese Vice Foreign Minister Vu Khoan and his Chinese counterpart Tang Jiaxuan signing an agreement in Hanoi to resolve outstanding border problems.

Much of this concerned the dispute between Vietnam and China over the Spratly Islands, and the hope, by both countries, that there was offshore oil near these islands. This dispute centered on about a hundred small islands and reefs in the South China Sea. Vietnam, China, and Taiwan (Republic of China) each claimed a right to these islands in their entirety; Malaysia and the Philippines each claimed a right to parts of these islands. Vietnam's claims were historical, with the islands appearing in Vietnamese territorial charts from the seventeenth century, as well as the fact that the French, in governing

Indochina, exercised sovereignty over them. Furthermore at the San Francisco Conference on July 7, 1951, the peace treaty with Japan included reference to two of the archipelagos as belonging to Vietnam. China's claim was that ancient Chinese pottery was found on these islands and there had also been Chinese fishermen living there when the French mapped them during the 1930s. After a naval clash between the Vietnamese and Chinese navies in 1988, Chinese forces were able to take physical possession of some of the islands and China's navy has controlled them ever since. With Vietnam risking the ire of the Chinese by continuing its claim, it quickly backed down, although some Vietnamese nationalists were opposed to giving in.

With better relations between the two countries, Le Duc Anh visited China in November 1993, marking the first visit by a Vietnamese head of state since Ho Chi Minh visited in 1959. It was even more significant given Le Duc Anh's role in the occupation of Cambodia during the 1980s. Chinese President Jiang Zemin then visited Vietnam in November 1994. After these visits there was a large increase in bilateral ties between the two countries and an influx of Chinese tourists to Vietnam.

## THE REFORM PROGRAM CONTINUES

In spite of Le Kha Pheu's appointment, however, reform continued with the opening ceremonies held in August 1997 for the first Vietnamese stock exchange, although it did not start trading until 2000. The steady devaluation of the currency, the *dong,* from February 1998 helped increase the number of tourists visiting Vietnam. The lifting of currency restrictions also led to many overseas Vietnamese sending money to relatives in Vietnam, with as much as $3 billion arriving in the country annually.

With increasing wealth for many people in the country, it was not long before the local press started to detail allegations of corruption, often by party officials. In August 1998, with Phan Van Khai under criticism for alleged corruption by senior communists in Thai Binh Province, the Vietnamese government announced that all government officials must declare their assets.

On October 1998, Phan Van Khai made an official visit to Beijing, the first since the Chinese invasion of the country in 1979. Two months later, Vietnam hosted its first Association of Southeast Asian Nations (ASEAN) summit conference; and in February 1999, Le Kha Phieu visited China to try to improve relations between the two countries. On December 31, 1999, Vietnam signed a border agreement with China and conceded a significant amount of territory The details of the agreement were kept secret until August 2002, but leaks about them led people to accuse Le Kha Phieu of giving in to Chinese demands, leading eventually to Le Kha Phieu himself losing the general secretaryship of the CPV in 2001. The treaty delineating the maritime border between China and Vietnam was not signed until December 2000, with final ratification finally taking place in 2004.

Vietnam's growing relationship with the United States led to the Vietnamese and U.S. governments agreeing, in July 1999, to the text of the Bilateral Trade Agreement, but two months later the Vietnamese decided not to sign. It was finally signed in July 2000 and became the law on December 10, 2001. In November 2000, Bill Clinton became the first sitting U.S. president to visit Vietnam. Richard Nixon and Lyndon Johnson had both visited the country as vice presidents. During this landmark visit, which lasted from November 16 until November 19, Clinton was feted by many people in Vietnam. Two years later, in November 2003, a U.S. frigate visited Vietnam, the first U.S. warship since 1975 to do so. On February 28, 2001, Vladimir Putin became the first Russian leader since the collapse of the Soviet Union to visit Vietnam.

When the Ninth Party Congress met in April 2001, Le Kha Phieu was replaced as general secretary by Nong Duc Manh, a member of the Tay ethnic minority from Bac Can province in the far north of Vietnam. He had trained as a forester in the Soviet Union and then held low-level Communist Party posts until 1986, when he was elected to the Party's Central Committee. Six years later he was appointed chairman of the National Assembly. Nong Duc Manh was born in 1940, and his appointment was symbolic in two ways. Not only was he the first person from an ethnic minority to hold a senior position in the Vietnamese government, but he was also the first who had not begun his political career fighting the French. The Ninth Party Congress also abolished the position of senior advisers held by Do Muoi, Le Duc Anh, and Vo Van Kiet. In March 2002, Phan Van Khai symbolically stated that private enterprise had led to a "glorious victory" for the country in a speech that received widespread attention around the world, although it was slightly overshadowed by the Nam Cam scandal, which led to a highly publicized trial of corrupt public officials.

## RELIGIOUS TENSIONS AND CONTINUED REFORM

Since 1975, the Communists in Vietnam had dealt carefully with religious groups. The Buddhists had ceased to be a major political force since their role in the overthrow of Ngo Dinh Diem in 1963, and his overthrow obviously greatly reduced the influence of the Roman Catholics. Roman Catholicism had been important in the lives of many overseas Vietnamese, especially those in Australia. Diem's sister had moved to Sydney and her son, Cardinal François Xavier Nguyen Van Thuan, continued to lead Vietnam's Roman Catholic exiles.

For the Vietnamese government, however, the greater openness and the encouragement of tourism were to lead to proselytizing by missionaries and a resurgence in the Roman Catholic Church, especially in Saigon. A dissident Vietnamese Catholic priest Father Nguyen Van Ly was jailed in 1977–1978 and again from May 1983 until July 1992 for "opposing the Revolution and destroying the people's unity." In December 1983, Amnesty International adopted him as a prisoner of conscience, and on his release he continued to campaign against religious persecution, going so far as to send testimony to a U.S. Congressional committee that was investigating allegations of religious persecution in Vietnam. He was arrested soon afterward and, in October 2001, was sentenced to 15 years in jail. This led to protests in the United States, and, in 2004, he was released from prison and held under house arrest in Hue. Undaunted, on September 8, 2006, he took part in the establishment of the Vietnam Progressive Party.

In Vietnam, the government enacted stronger laws in January 2003 to try to prevent religious groups using meetings as a place to voice dissent against the government. In February 2005, Nguyen Van Ly and other dissidents were released from prison after receiving amnesties. A month earlier, Thich Nhat Hanh, a longtime peace activist, had been able to return to Vietnam for the first time since 1967. In that year he was nominated by the U.S. Civil Rights leader Martin Luther King Jr. for the Nobel Peace Prize for preaching against the Vietnam War from his monastery in the Dordogne, in southern France.

There were also increasing tensions with minority groups who felt left out of the economic prosperity in the country. The Montagnards of the central highlands and the Khmer Krom around Tay Ninh, near Ho Chi Minh City, both faced repression as they started to form political organizations to press for an increasing role in governing the areas where they formed a majority.

In spite of the religious and ethnic problems, the reform program continued, and from December 5–13, 2003, Vietnam hosted the South East Asian Games at the newly constructed My Dinh National Stadium in Hanoi. In March 2004, the Vietnamese government introduced plans to raise the tax base of the country by levying a tax on income, but the next month, the International Monetary Fund terminated its main aid program to Vietnam after it was not allowed to audit the foreign exchange reserves of the state bank. In June, however, for the first time, the Vietnamese government allowed foreign-owned banks to operate in the country. In July Vietnam also agreed to the Berne Convention on copyright protection, which was largely aimed at preventing Vietnamese factories from pirating Western products for export and it even had an immediate effect on the local industry, which had been selling pirated goods to locals and tourists for years.

The major trade problem with the United States centered on the Vietnamese exports of shrimp, which U.S. producers claimed were wrecking the U.S. shrimp industry. With Chinese exporters paying between 55 and 112 percent tariffs, the Vietnamese were able to negotiate a tariff rate of less than 5 percent on most of their exports, although some companies did incur a tariff rate of 26 percent, still far lower than their Chinese competitors.

In March 2005, a Stock Exchange opened in Hanoi, the second in the country. This helped local firms raise share capital more easily and increased the embrace of capitalism by the north. In June, Prime Minister Phan Van Khai visited the United States, the first visit by a Communist Vietnamese premier. From November 18–19, 2006, Vietnam hosted the Annual Summit of the Asia Pacific Economic Cooperation organization at Hanoi and was also admitted to the World Trade Organization. By this time the economic reforms had begun to affect the whole economy; published data showed that the poverty rate in the country had fallen from 58 percent in 1993 to 29 percent in 2002. It was also shown, however, that Vietnam's position in the Human Development Index had improved only slightly, from 120th in 1995 to 108th in 2005 (of 177 countries). There was also a large number of Vietnamese who managed to find work overseas with the emergence of overseas communities in the Middle East, Taiwan, and South Korea, as well as in Thailand, Malaysia, and Vietnam where Vietnamese found work as guest workers.

## THE GROWTH OF TOURISM

One of the major changes affecting the Vietnamese economy was not just annual increases of 20 percent in exports, but also the great wealth brought about by tourists visiting Vietnam in ever increasing numbers. This was evident by the number of flights into the country, the large number of new hotels and guest houses appearing throughout the country, and the proliferation of guide books available in the West.

Initially most of the tourists to Vietnam were visiting either Hanoi, Ho Chi Minh City, or Hue. In Hanoi, the initial attractions included the old quarter of the city, parts still largely unchanged since the nineteenth century, and other more modern sites such as the Ho Chi Minh Mausoleum. Gradually some more intrepid tourists started to visit more remote parts of northern Vietnam, with trips to Dien Bien Phu taking up to three days, owing to the poor state of the roads.

Hue's attractions were largely the imperial palace, which was restored after having been badly damaged during the Tet Offensive of 1968. It was not long before tours started to include the tombs of the Nguyen Emperors along the Pearl River, and also Danang and Hoi An, where the Japanese bridge became a much-photographed attraction. Gradually as tourism increased in the late 1990s, day trips were offered to the demilitarized zone and Khe Sanh, as well as the massive Vietnamese Communist Cemetery at Truong Son, on the south bank of the Ben Hai River, and the Vinh Moc tunnels where locals just north of the demilitarized zone hid during U.S. shelling. It would certainly be incomplete to mention Hue without some reference to the success of the Lac Thanh Restaurant, run by a deaf couple and endorsed heavily by the Australian-produced Lonely Planet Guide. Providing some of the best meals in Vietnam, the restaurant fills up so quickly that a group of deaf people have taken over the premises next door, catering for people who have been unable to get a place at the other restaurant, calling theirs the Lac Thien Restaurant.

Ho Chi Minh City was the place most transformed by the tourists. Hotels started to appear in Nguyen Thi Minh Khai Street, and the Gia Long Palace, the site of the fighting in 1963, became the Revolutionary Museum, with plans being drawn up to enlarge it as a tourist attraction, possibly by opening up the tunnel through which Ngo Dinh Diem and his brother escaped. The tank that crashed through the gates of the presidential palace in 1975 was mounted at the entrance to what is now the Reunification Palace, one of the major tourist sites in the city, the U.S. Embassy having been flattened many years earlier. Indeed in the late 1980s, the main Saigon cemetery, the Mac Dinh Chi Cemetery, was also cleared and turned into a public park, with "the land which once belonged to the wealthy being returned to the people" as guides politely tell visitors.

One of the major tourist attractions remains the Museum of Chinese and American War Crimes, which was politely renamed the War Remnants Museum. The museum has countless exhibits showing many of the atrocities that took place in the war, along with a guillotine used by the French to execute criminals, as well as those convicted of political offenses. Many of the photographs are horrific, including those of deformed babies born in areas where defoliants such as Agent Orange were used. Critics point out obvious omissions such as photographs of people murdered in Hue in 1968, or even any mention of Thich Quang Duc's self-immolation in 1963, one of the most famous events in recent Vietnamese history. As tourism to Vietnam increased, tours from Saigon also started taking in the Cu Chi tunnels, the Cao Dai temples at Tay Ninh, and, away from the Vietnam War sites, boat trips down the Mekong Delta.

After the start of the War on Terror, the number of Western tourists visiting Indonesia declined markedly, with a large increase in tourism to Vietnam. There were 2.3 million tourists visiting the country in 2001, nearly a third of whom were from China; more than 200,000 come annually from three more countries: Japan, Taiwan, and the United States. The population of Vietnam is approximately 85 million, making it the 13th most populous country in the world. The average annual per capita income is now about U.S.$3,025, although 63 percent of the population still gain most of their income from agriculture. Although there has been a proliferation of Western ideas, and many newspapers are published in Vietnam, as well as easy availability of foreign papers, social problems, including drugs and prostitution, and environmental problems from pollution have started to tarnish Vietnam's image.

On June 27, 2006, Nguyen Minh Triet, born in South Vietnam, was elected president of the country by the National Assembly, receiving 464 votes (94.12 percent). He had been a student in Saigon at the time of the overthrow of Diem in 1963. Triet assumed office immediately, and on the same day, Nguyen Tan Dung, from Ca Mau, the most southern province in Vietnam, became prime minister. As the first Communist leader in Vietnam to have been born after the August Revolution of 1945, he has been eager to promote Vietnam around the world and he became the first Communist Vietnamese leader to visit the Vatican and meet with the pope. In November 2006, President Nguyen Minh Triet and his wife Tran Thu Kim Chi entertained George W. Bush and Laura Bush when the U.S. President and his wife visited Hanoi, and Bush was involved in amicable talks with Nguyen Tan Dung. Vietnam remains one of the few countries in the world where the Communist Party has remained in charge of the government, with the current constitution, promulgated in 1992, stating that it remains the "leading force of state and society," a change from the 1980 constitution where it was the "sole force."

# Notable People in Vietnam since 1945

**Bao Dai** (1913–1997). Emperor of Vietnam from 1926 until 1945; chief of state of the Associated State of Vietnam from 1949 until 1955. Born on October 22, 1913 at Hue as Prince Nguyen Vinh Khai; his father became Emperor Khai Dinh in 1916. His father died when he was 12, and he was chosen to succeed him as emperor. After studying in the Paris Lycée Condorcet and the École des Sciences Politiques, he returned to Vietnam in September 1932 and was crowned emperor. Initially he tried to introduce reforms but was blocked by the French, and he then spent much of the rest of his reign as a playboy. On March 11, 1945, the Japanese persuaded him to declare independence, and he ruled as emperor until August 25, when he abdicated at the urging of Ho Chi Minh to become the "Supreme Counsellor" to the new Communist government. Bao Dai then moved to Hong Kong and lived there until the French offered him the status as titular head of the Associated State of Vietnam, and on June 30, 1949, he returned to Vietnam where he headed a new government. For most of that period, Bao Dai lived in Dalat, which he tried to build into a gambling center. After the Geneva Peace Accords, Bao Dai, who was already living in France, remained in Europe and was deposed after the 1955 referendum that established the Republic of Vietnam. Bao Dai lived in his chateau at Cannes and maintained an apartment in Paris, a fleet of sports cars, and a 500-tonne steam yacht. He ended up living in Paris and died on July 31, 1997, at a military hospital in Paris. His eldest son, Prince Bao Long, was anointed as his successor if the Vietnamese royal family were restored.

**Do Muoi** (b. 1917). General secretary of the Communist Party of Vietnam from 1991 until 1997. Do Muoi was born on February 2, 1917, at Dong My, to a family of artisans. In the late 1930s, he joined the Indochina Communist Party and was arrested by the French in 1941. In 1945, he took part in the proclamation of the Democratic Republic of Vietnam. After the Geneva Peace Accord he was appointed minister of domestic trade and a member of the Central Committee of the Communist Party of Vietnam. From 1988 until 1991, Do Muoi was prime minister of the SRV, and on June 27, 1991, he was elected to replace Nguyen Van Linh as general secretary of the Communist Party of Vietnam. He was a supporter of reform and presided over a period when the Vietnamese economy was transformed. In 1997, he was succeeded by Le Kha Phieu and retired from politics the next year. Two years later he was involved in delaying the signing of the U.S.-Vietnam Bilateral Trade Agreement.

**Duong Van Minh** (1916–2001). Chairman of the Revolutionary Committee and president of the Republic of (South) Vietnam from 1963 until 1964, in 1964 (twice), and in April 1975. Born on February 16, 1916, at My Tho, he was educated at Lycee Chasseloup Laubat in Saigon, and then joined the military, gaining the nickname "Big Minh." During the French colonial period, he was one of only 50 Vietnamese officers to be commissioned and in 1954 became an important figure in the new South Vietnamese Armed Forces. Soon afterwards he led successful campaigns against the Hoa Hao sect and the Binh Xuyen gangsters, and then trained at the U.S. Command and General Staff College at Fort Leavenworth, Kansas. Serving as military adviser to Ngo Dinh Diem from 1962, he became the leader of the group known as the "Buddhist Generals" who staged the coup in 1963 that overthrew Diem. Minh seems to have been the person who ordered the murder of Diem and Nhu and then headed the military junta that took power. Overthrown by General Nguyen Khanh on January 30, 1964, he went into exile in Bangkok, but he returned to power from February 8 until August 16, 1964. Eleven days later he was a member of the Provisional Leadership Committee, serving until September 8, when he was appointed chairman of the committee and thus titular head of state until October 26, 1964. Remaining active in the military, he considered standing in the 1971 presidential elections and was regarded by many, especially the French, as the possible leader of a coalition government, as his brother Duong Van Nhut was a leading North Vietnamese general. He was president of South Vietnam from April 28–30, 1975, surrendering to the Communists. Living in seclusion in Saigon for eight years, in 1983 he migrated to France, living near Paris and then moving to Pasadena, California, where he died on August 6, 2001.

**Ho Chi Minh** (1890–1969). Chairman of the Indochina Communist Party from 1930 until 1951 and chairman of the Vietnam Workers' Party from 1951 until 1969; president of the Democratic Republic of Vietnam from 1945 until 1969. The major figure in Vietnam's history during the twentieth century, Ho Chi Minh was born on May 19, 1890, in Nghe An province, central Vietnam, the son of a minor official, and was educated at the Quoc Hoc in Hue. From an early age he came to dislike French rule in Vietnam. He found work as a cook's apprentice on a French ocean liner and using the name Nguyen Ai Quoc (Nguyen "The Patriot"), he traveled throughout much of the world. He lived in London and then in France where, in 1920, he became a founding member of the French Communist Party. He moved to Moscow in 1923, and then went to China and established links with the Chinese Communist movement. In 1930, he founded the Indochina Communist Party and the next year was arrested in Hong Kong, held in prison by the British, and then released, returning to the Soviet Union for recuperation and further training. In 1938, he started running the Vietnamese Communist movement and in 1941 formed the League for the Independence of Vietnam, working for the end of French colonial rule. In 1945, now known as Ho Chi Minh ("He who enlightens"), he worked against the French and established links with U.S. agents in China. Proclaiming Vietnam's independence in September 1945, he was involved in negotiations with the French, and when they failed, from 1946 until 1954, he led the Viet Minh in the Indochina War. In 1954, he moved to Hanoi to run the Democratic Republic of Vietnam and led the country from then until his death in 1969. A devoted Communist, he sought the reunification of Vietnam by military means and wanted the Communist Party of Vietnam to maintain a stance independent of the Soviet Union and China. He died on September 3, 1969, and was embalmed, and his body placed in a mausoleum in Hanoi. After the defeat of South Vietnam in 1975, Saigon was renamed Ho Chi Minh City in his honor.

**Huynh Tan Phat** (1913–1989). Leader of the Provisional Revolutionary Government of South Vietnam from 1969 until 1975, and president of the Republic of (South) Vietnam from 1975 until 1976. Born in 1913 at Mytho, Huynh Tan Phat studied architecture and joined the Communist movement as a young man and was placed in charge of the Information Service of the Southern Revolutionary Region. In 1960, he became one of the leaders of the National Front for the Liberation of South Vietnam and in 1964 was placed in charge of the organization, becoming leader of the Provisional Revolutionary Government of South Vietnam five years later. In this capacity he visited many other countries, and at the fall of the Saigon South Vietnamese government in 1975, he became the titular head of state of South Vietnam, a position he held for a year.

**Le Duan** (1908–1986). First secretary of the Vietnam Workers' Party from 1960 until 1976, and general secretary of the Communist Party of Vietnam from 1976 until 1986. Born on April 7, 1908, in Quang Tri province (now Binh Tri Thien province) in central Vietnam, he was the son of a railway clerk. He joined the Revolutionary Youth League of Ho Chi Minh in 1928 and became a founding member of the Indochina Communist Party in 1930. From 1931 until 1936, he was jailed by the French and in 1939 was appointed as a member of the Communist Party's Central Committee. From 1940 until March 1945, he was again held in jail by the French. Le Duan opposed the Geneva Agreements because he saw it as a betrayal of the southern Communists whom he had been appointed to organize. He became secretary of the party's main bureau in the south, the central office for South Vietnam. In 1957, Le Duan was recalled to Hanoi to become a member of the politburo, after having become reconciled with rival Truong Chinh. He became a major player in the creation of the People's Revolutionary Party, which led to the proclamation of the National Front for the Liberation of South Vietnam in 1960. With the formal reunification of North Vietnam and South Vietnam in 1976, Le Duan became general-secretary of the Communist Party and led the country through the confrontation with the Khmer Rouge in Cambodia, the Vietnamese occupation of Cambodia, and the Chinese invasion of Vietnam. In 1979, Le Duan was awarded the Lenin Peace Prize and tried to promote economic reforms. He died on July 10, 1986, in Hanoi.

**Le Duc Anh** (b. 1920). President of Vietnam from 1992 until 1997. Born on December 1, 1920, near Hue, he spent his youth working as a laborer and joined the Indochina Communist Party in 1938. He was in charge of militia operations in the First Indochina War and then was put in charge of soldiers along the Cambodian border during the Vietnam War. With the invasion of Cambodia in December 1978, Le Duc Anh took charge of the Vietnamese forces during the invasion and remained in command of the troops during the occupation of Cambodia. In 1985, he returned to Vietnam after having been promoted to full general; he was also given a seat in the politburo. In 1987, he was appointed minister of defense and helped to extricate the Vietnamese soldiers from Cambodia two years later. In 1992, he was appointed president of the SRV, a position he held for five years. During that time he ensured that the military had a significant role in the running of the country. He suffered a major stroke in 1996.

**Le Kha Phieu** (b. 1931). General secretary of the Communist Party of Vietnam from 1997 until 2001. Born on December 27, 1931, at Dong Khe commune, Thanh Hoa, Le Kha Phieu served in the People's Army of Vietnam and was put in charge of the army's political department. In 1991, he was elected to the Central Committee of the Communist Party of Vietnam, and three years later was given a seat in the politburo. A protégé of Le Duc Anh, Le Kha

Phieu was able to use his influence in the military to ensure that he took over as president at the retirement of his mentor. Le Kha Phieu was heavily criticized for his land border agreement with China, which was signed in 1999. He also had many enemies who saw him as an opponent of reform and may have used it as an excuse to ease him from office and replace him with Nong Duc Manh.

**Ngo Dinh Diem** (1901–1963). Prime minister of the Associated State of Vietnam from 1954 until 1955; president of the Republic of (South) Vietnam from 1955 until 1963. From a strong Roman Catholic family, Ngo Dinh Diem was born on January 3, 1901, in Hue. His father was a palace official who became headmaster of the Quoc Hoc, the school Diem was later to attend. Graduating in law from the University of Hanoi, Diem was appointed minister of the interior in 1933, but soon resigned when he realized that he had no real power. Removing himself from active politics for the next 12 years, he lived with his aged mother in Hue, and in 1945 he refused to join with Ho Chi Minh after his (Diem's) eldest brother was murdered by the Vietminh. Diem then went to the United States, considering life as a monk, and in 1954 was appointed prime minister of the State of Vietnam during the last stages of the Geneva Conference. Returning to Saigon, Diem established the Republic of Vietnam in the following year and became its president. Although he tried to introduce land reforms and establish a democratic government, he was too conservative for many of the ideas he initially supported. Gradually managing to erode communist support in South Vietnam, he started to become unpopular with Buddhist generals who resented the influence of Diem's younger brother Ngo Dinh Nhu. The generals, with U.S. support, staged a coup d'état on November 1, 1963, killing Diem and his brother on November 2.

**Ngo Dinh Nhu** (1910–1963). Minister of the interior of the Republic of (South) Vietnam from 1955 until 1963, and chief adviser of President Ngo Dinh Diem. Nhu was born in 1910 at Hue, the son of a palace official and the fourth of the six Ngo Dinh brothers. He attended university in France where he became interested in the French philosopher Emmanuel Mounier (1905–1950). Mounier had developed his own political concept of personalism, which would later become the state ideology of South Vietnam. On his return to Saigon, Nhu was active as an organizer of the Vietnamese Federation of Christian Workers, the Catholic labor union movement. He soon became the major power behind his brother Ngo Dinh Diem and engineered the sacking of General Nguyen Van Hinh as commander of the South Vietnamese Army in 1954. As minister of the interior, he helped establish the Personalist Labor Party, the Can Lao Nhan Vi, and became the man most associated with the Strategic Hamlets program, designed to isolate villagers from the Communist guerillas. In 1963, when he suspected that the U.S. government might be trying to undercut his power, he opened some lines of communication with the Communists and hinted that he might be prepared to negotiate with them. He was overthrown in a coup d'état on November 1, 1963, and assassinated, along with his brother, on the next day.

**Nguyen Cao Ky** (b. 1930). Vice president of the Republic of (South) Vietnam from 1967 until 1971. Born on September 8, 1930, at Son Tay, he left high school and joined the armed forces, training in France and French Morocco. He later transferred to the air force and became a colonel under Ngo Dinh Diem. In January 1964, Ky took part in the coup d'état that put Nguyen Khanh into power. He then took an active part in the political machinations over the next few years, joining up with Nguyen Van Thieu and taking power in June 1965. When Thieu was formally elected president in 1967, Ky was his vice presidential running mate. Ky's relations with Thieu deteriorated, however, and a number of Ky's prominent supporters were killed during the Tet Offensive in 1968. Ky remained popular with war veterans and planned to stand in the 1971 presidential elections, but he was disqualified. Although he was later allowed to stand, he decided to retire from politics. In 1975, he was critical of Thieu's abandonment of the central highlands. Just before Saigon fell to the Communists, Ky fled to the United States and opened a liquor store in California. In 2004, he returned to Vietnam for a visit, his first since 1975.

**Nguyen Co Thach** (1923–1998). Foreign minister of Vietnam from 1980 until 1991. Born on May 15, 1923, to a peasant family in northern Vietnam, Nguyen Co Thach entered the Communist movement in the late 1930s. He was arrested and jailed by the French from 1941 until 1945. In 1954, he was a staff officer at Dien Bien Phu and then changed from a soldier to a diplomat. After 1954, he was a member of the North Vietnamese foreign ministry and became ambassador to India from 1956 until 1960. The protégé of Le Duc Tho, he had been involved in the secret talks with the United States that led to the Paris Peace Accord in 1973. In 1980, he was appointed minister of foreign affairs, becoming the first career diplomat in the politburo after he joined in 1982. Nguyen Co Thach wanted greater engagement with the West and had to deal with the diplomatic fallout from the continued Vietnamese occupation of Cambodia. He opposed restoring full ties with China, which led to his dismissal in 1991, as the Vietnamese government was eager to rebuild relations with their northern neighbor, which improved with the end of the Cambodian Civil War. He died on April 10, 1998.

**Nguyen Khanh** (b. 1927). President of the Republic of (South) Vietnam in 1964 (twice). Nguyen Khanh was born on November 8, 1927, in Tra Vinh Province; his father ran a nightclub in Dalat. During the early 1940s, Khanh joined the Viet Minh but soon ended up joining the French forces, studying at the Vietnamese military academy, and then in France and in the United States. He served in Vietnam as a parachutist, and when the French left in 1954, he became the first commander of the Vietnamese Armed Forces. Rising in the military, he was appointed as secretary general of the defense ministry in 1959 and in the next year was promoted to the rank of major general. Taking part in the military coup that overthrew Ngo Dinh Diem in 1963, he was given command of the army in the north of South Vietnam and, on January 30, 1964, led a bloodless coup that overthrew the government of Duong Van Minh. Khanh's government lasted only a little more than a week, however, and on February 8, he was forced from office, although he returned as president from August 16 until August 27, 1964, and then became a member of the Provisional Leadership Committee, which ruled until September 8. Remaining commander-in-chief of the armed forces, in 1965 he was appointed as ambassador to France and was there during the collapse of South Vietnam. He then started working for a French company and, in 1977, migrated to the United States where he became active among the Vietnamese exile communities. On January 2, 2005, Nguyen Khanh was chosen as the chief of state of the government of Free Vietnam, an anticommunist government-in-exile operating from Westminster, California.

**Nguyen Minh Triet** (b. 1942). President of Vietnam from 2006. Born on October 8, 1942, at Ben Cat district, Binh Duong province, he studied mathematics at the University of Saigon, and, in the early 1960s, became associated with the Communist movement around Saigon. From 1963 until 1973, he was active in the South Vietnamese Communist organizations, and from 1974 until 1979, he was deputy director of the General Affairs Department of the Youth Union. After studying at Nguyen Ai Quoc Party School in Hanoi, he continued to be involved in youth groups and organizations, and in January 1997, he was appointed to the Central Committee of the Communist Party of Vietnam. He was elected to the politburo in 1997 and president by the National Assembly on June 27, 2006.

**Nguyen Tan Dung** (b. 1949). Prime minister of Vietnam from 2006. Born on November 17, 1949, at Ca Mau, he studied law and joined the Communist Party of Vietnam on June 10, 1967. He served in the army and was the first deputy prime minister from September 29, 1997. On June 27, 2006, his nomination as prime minister was confirmed by the National Assembly.

**Nguyen Van Linh** (1915–1998). General secretary of the Communist Party of Vietnam from 1986 until 1991. Born on July 1, 1915 near Hanoi, as "Nguyen Van Cuc," he was a teenager when he joined the Communist movement and was arrested in 1930; he was released with the amnesty of 1936. He then worked in Haiphong and in Cochinchina for the Indochina Communist Party. He was arrested again by the French and spent the rest of the war in the Poulo Condore prison. He then worked under Le Duan, using the pseudonym "Muoi Cuc." From 1961 until 1964, he was director of the Central

Office for South Vietnam and was deputy director from 1964 until the end of the war. In 1976, Nguyen Van Linh was given a seat in the politburo and put in charge of the Party Committee for Ho Chi Minh City. He failed to implement the drastic economic plans drawn up for the South and was dismissed in 1978, but as the government wanted to reform in 1978, he was reinstated to the politburo. In December 1986, he was named to succeed Truong Chinh as general secretary of the Communist Party of Vietnam, remaining in office for five years and presiding over a period of great economic reform. He died on April 27, 1998.

**Nguyen Van Thieu** (1923–2001). President of the Republic of (South) Vietnam from 1967–1975. Born on April 5, 1923 in Ninh Thuan province, Annam, Thieu spent World War II working on the family farm and then served briefly with the Viet Minh forces before joining the Vietnamese National Army of the Associated State of Vietnam. Commissioned as a second lieutenant in 1949, he was appointed the commandant of the National Military Academy with the establishment of the Republic of Vietnam in 1955. After military training in the United States, he took part in the 1963 coup d'état that overthrew Ngo Dinh Diem, leading the attack on the Gia Long Palace. Emerging as one of the "Young Turks," he took part in the military coup of December 1964, and in 1965 he became deputy prime minister and minister of national defense. Promoted to major-general, he replaced Nguyen Khanh as chairman of the Armed Forces Council and then led the military coup of June 1965, heading the military junta, and becoming president. He promulgated the new constitution in April 1967 and in September won the presidential election and was sworn into office on October 31, 1967. From 1969, Thieu formed a close alliance with U.S. President Richard M. Nixon and became the focus for the U.S. involvement in South Vietnam. In October 1971, Thieu was reelected and opposed the U.S. negotiations with the Communists. He was against the Paris Peace Agreement of January 1973 but eventually signed under immense pressure. In January 1975, he was shocked by the Communist attacks and was angered by the U.S. refusal to become involved in the fighting. On April 21, 1975, Thieu fled Saigon, taking with him a large personal fortune. After a short period in Thailand, he moved to England, his house just outside London having been named "The White House" by a previous owner. He later moved to the United States and died on September 29, 2001, at his home in Newton, Massachusetts.

**Nong Duc Manh** (b. 1940). General secretary of the Communist Party of Vietnam from 2001. Born in 1940, at Bac Can, northern Vietnam, from the Tay ethnic minority, he trained in forestry in the Soviet Union and then held a variety of Communist Party positions until 1986 when he was appointed to the Party's Central Committee. In 1992, Nong Duc Manh was appointed chairman of the National Assembly and six years later to the politburo. In 2001, he was elected general secretary of the Communist Party and was the first person from an ethnic minority to hold such a position in Vietnam. He was also the first communist leader who was not involved in the Communist movement during World War II.

**Pham Hung** (1912–1988). Chairman of the Council of Ministers of Vietnam from 1987 until 1988. Bon on June 11, 1912, at Vinh Long, as Pham Van Thien, from a wealthy middle class family, Pham Hung was a founding member of the Indochina Communist Party in 1930. The next year he was arrested and jailed at Poulo Condore Island until he was released by the Japanese in 1945. He worked under Le Duan in the First Indochina War and in 1955 moved to Hanoi, becoming a member of the politburo two years later. Using the name "Bay Cuong," he took charge of the Central Office for South Vietnam in 1967, running the Communist movement in South Vietnam. By the end of the war, he was the fourth-ranking member of the politburo, and in 1979, he was appointed minister of the interior. Replaced in 1987, in June he was appointed chairman of the Council of Ministers, replacing Pham Van Dong; however, he died soon after, on March 10, 1998.

**Pham Van Dong** (1906–2000). Prime minister of the Democratic Republic of Vietnam from 1955 until 1976. Born on March 1, 1906, in Duc Tan village, Quang Ngai province, central Vietnam, Pham Van Dong was from a mandarin family, and his father was chief secretary to the Vietnamese Emperor Duy Tan. He was educated in Hue and at the University of Hanoi. In 1926, he traveled to Guangzhou, China, and trained at the Whampoa Military Academy. He was jailed by the French from 1931–1936. Using the alias Lam Ba Kiet (Lin Pai-chieh), he served under Ho Chi Minh during World War II. In 1946, he was named minister of finance of the newly formed Democratic Republic of Vietnam and became a member of the politburo of the Communist Party of Vietnam five years later. As minister of foreign affairs and vice premier in 1954, he led the Vietnamese Communist delegation to the Geneva Peace Talks in 1954, and became prime minister the next year. An effective administrator, he also became involved in the peace talks with Lyndon B. Johnson and Richard M. Nixon. On July 2, 1976, after the formal reunification of North Vietnam and South Vietnam, Pham Van Dong was appointed chairman of the Council of Ministers, a position he held until June 18, 1987, when Pham Hung was appointed to that position. He resigned from the politburo in December 1986, and died on April 29, 2000, the day before the 25th anniversary of the end of the Vietnam War, at the age of 94.

**Phan Van Khai** (b. 1933). Prime minister of the Socialist Republic of Vietnam from 1997 until 2006. Born on December 25, 1933, near Saigon, he was a teenager when he joined the Communist movement, and moved to North

Vietnam at the time of the partition in 1954. After studying economics in the Soviet Union, he returned to Hanoi to take up a position in the State Planning Committee. Working on the economic structure of the country after reunification, he was back in his native Ho Chi Minh City from 1975 until 1989 when he moved back to Hanoi, becoming deputy prime minister. On September 24, 1997, he was elected prime minister of Vietnam. He was reelected in August 2002, and was a keen supporter of reform. He announced his resignation on June 24, 2006.

**Ton Duc Thang** (1888–1980). President of the Democratic Republic of Vietnam 1969 until 1976. Born on August 19, 1888, at Long Xuyen, he became sympathetic with the communist cause as a teenager. In World War I he served in the French navy and was involved in the mutiny on the *Waldeck-Rousseau* in 1919. Returning to Vietnam he started working for the Communists and in 1929 was arrested and jailed at Poulo Condore prison, where he remained until 1945. A member of the first National Assembly, elected in 1945, he took an active part in the war against the French. After the Geneva Peace Agreement he led the Fatherland Front to unite Communists in South Vietnam, and in July 1960, he was appointed vice-president to Ho Chi Minh. Awarded the Lenin Peace Prize in 1967, at the death of Ho Chi Minh, Ton Duc Thang became president of North Vietnam on September 2, 1969, retaining that position until reunification in 1976, at which point he became president of the SRV, a position he held until his death on March 30, 1980.

**Tran Duc Luong** (b. 1937). President of Vietnam from 1997 until 2006. Born on May 5, 1937, in Quang Ngai Province, he went to school in Hanoi and then became a geologist and a cartographer. Joining the Communist Party of Vietnam in 1959, he continued to work as a geologist and during the 1970s was able to win a seat in the National Assembly. In 1987, he was appointed deputy prime minister and in June 1996, was given a seat in the politburo. Elected president on September 24, 1997, he was reelected in 2002. On June 24, 2006, he announced his resignation as president.

**Tran Le Xuan ("Mme Nhu")** (b. 1924). The first lady of the Republic of (South) Vietnam from 1955 until 1963. Born as Tran Le Xuan, her father was Tran Van Chuong, and her mother was a member of the Vietnamese royal family. She was educated in Hanoi and Saigon and married Ngo Dinh Nhu, younger brother of Ngo Dinh Diem, in 1943. A devout Roman Catholic, she was a dedicated anticommunist. When Diem became prime minister of the Republic of Vietnam in 1954, her husband became his chief adviser, and when Diem became president, as he was unmarried, Mme Nhu, as she became known, assumed the role of "first lady" of the Republic. She established the Women's Solidarity Movement and was active with Catholic and anticommunist groups in Saigon and Hue. Narrowly surviving the bombing of the presidential palace in 1960, she gained a reputation as a major influence on the policies adopted by the Diem government. In 1963, when she referred to the semi-immolation of Buddhist monks as "barbecues," she received wide international press coverage and quickly became known as the "Dragon Lady." She was in Los Angeles when Diem and her husband were assassinated and since then has lived in exile in Rome, Italy.

**Tran Van Huong** (1903–1982). Vice president of the Republic of (South) Vietnam from 1971 until 1975, and president in 1975. Born on December 1, 1903, at Vinh Long Province, Tran Van Huong was a school teacher who joined the Viet Minh and then served as mayor of Saigon. He was appointed prime minister of South Vietnam by General Nguyen Khanh on November 4, 1964. He quickly earned respect for his appointment of people to positions because of their capability rather than because they belonged to one or another faction. Deposed by the military in January 28, 1965, he was reappointed after the Tet Offensive, holding the premiership from May 28, 1968, until September 1, 1969. In the 1971 presidential elections, he was the vice presidential running mate of Nguyen Van Thieu, and he held the position until April 21, 1975, when Thieu resigned and Tran Van Huong became president. Tran Van Huong held office until April 28 and then allowed Duong Van Minh to take power. and Tran Van Huong remained in Saigon, refusing to have anything to do with the new Communist government. He died in 1982.

**Truong Chinh** (1907–1988). First secretary of the Indochina Communist Party from 1941 until 1951; the Vietnam Workers' Party from 1951 until 1956; chairman of the State Council of Vietnam from 1981 until 1987; and general secretary of the Communist Party of Vietnam in 1986. The leading theoretician of the Vietnamese Communists, he was born Dang Xuan Khu on February 9, 1907, into a scholar-gentry family in Ha Nam Ninh Province, Vietnam. Educated in Hanoi, he took part in demonstrations against the French in 1928, which led to his expulsion from school. He then worked for the Communists, editing their newspaper in Hanoi. He was jailed from 1930 until 1936 and was active in the Communist leadership from 1941, taking the name Truong Chinh ("Long March"). He became the leading ideologue of the Communists but lost office in 1956 when he was held responsible for the failures of the land reform programs. In 1958, however, he became vice premier of the Democratic Republic of Vietnam, retaining his seat on the politburo. He headed the party faction that opposed the liberalization of the economy, which he thought would undermine the role of the Communist Party. On the death of Le Duan on July 10, 1986, Truong Chinh took over the Communist Party but resigned on December 18, 1986. He stepped down from the politburo and died on September 30, 1988 in Hanoi.

**Vo Chi Cong** (b. 1913). Chairman of the State Council of Vietnam from 1987 until 1992. A longtime Vietnamese Communist activist, he became interested in the nationalist struggle against the French after meeting Phan Boi Chau. Arrested by the French in 1942, he was released in 1945 and played a minor role in the First Indochina War. In 1961, he emerged as a founder of the NFL, and was clearly one of the leading southern Communists. In 1976, with the reunification of Vietnam, he was appointed to the politburo, serving as deputy prime minister from 1976 until 1982, and also minister of fisheries from 1976 until 1977 and minister of agriculture from 1977 until 1978. From 1987 until 1992, he was the titular head of state of Vietnam. On September 22, 1992, he retired and now lives in Ho Chi Minh City.

**Vo Nguyen Giap** (b. 1911). Leading Vietnamese Communist general. From a farming family in central Vietnam, Vo Nguyen Giap attended the Quoc Hoc in Hue and in his late teens started taking part in demonstrations against the French. As a result, he was expelled from school and became involved in the Indochina Communist Party. Arrested in 1930, after two years in custody, he was released and studied law at the University of Hanoi. After a stint teaching history, he worked as a journalist in Hue and from World War II was active in the Viet Minh. Becoming a member of the politburo, he was soon the highest ranking general in the People's Army of Vietnam. He led the Vietnamese Communists and the decisive battle of Dienbienphu in 1954, when the French were defeated. Remaining as minister of defense until 1975, he helped in the planning of the Tet Offensive, the final defeat of South Vietnam in 1975, and the invasion of Cambodia in 1978–1979. His influence waned, however, and in 1982 he was dropped from the politburo and now lives in retirement in Hanoi.

**Vo Van Kiet** (b. 1922). Chairman of the Council of Ministers of Vietnam from 1991 until 1992. Born on November 23, 1922, from a middle class family from Cantho, Vo Van Kiet joined the Communist movement in the early 1940s, and became active among the Communists in South Vietnam. He became secretary of the Saigon Municipal Party Committee in the early 1970s. At the end of the fighting in 1975, Vo Van Kiet became chairman of the People's Committee of Ho Chi Minh City. In 1976, when Nguyen Van Linh moved to Hanoi to take charge of the trade union movement, Vo Van Kiet became chairman of the Ho Chi Minh City Party Branch. A moderate who supported economic reform, in 1982 Vo Van Kiet was elected as a full member to the politburo and was also appointed vice-chairman of the Council of Ministers. At the death of Pham Hung in March 1988, he served as acting prime minister, but failed to be elected in June when the National Assembly met. A leading reformer, he served as prime minister from August 8, 1991, until September 25, 1997.

# Selected Bibliography

## GENERAL WORKS

Buttinger, Joseph. *Vietnam: A Political History*. New York: Praeger Publishers, 1972.
Hall, D.G.E. *A History of Southeast Asia*. New York: St. Martin's Press, 1968.
Karnow, Stanley. *Vietnam: A History*. Harmondsworth, U.K.: Penguin Books, 1984.
Kien Truc. *Saigon 1698–1998*. Ho Chi Minh City: Nha Xuat Ban Thanh, 1997.
Lockhart, Bruce and William J. Duiker. *Historical Dictionary of Vietnam*. Lanham, MD: The Scarecrow Press, 2006.
Logan, William S. *Hanoi: Biography of a City*. Sydney: University of New South Wales Press, 2000.
Nguyen Khac Vien. *Vietnam: A Long History*. Hanoi: The Gioi Publishers, 2002.
Smith, Ralph B. *Vietnam and the West*. London: Heinemann, 1968.
Thai Van Kiem. *Vietnam: Past and Present*. Saigon: Commercial Transworld Editions, 1957.

## VIETNAM TO 1945

Augustin, Andreas. *Sofitel Metropole, Hanoi*. London: The Most Famous Hotels in the World, 1998.
Board, Lucien. *The Quicksand War: Prelude to Vietnam*. Boston: Little, Brown, 1967.
Coedès, Georges. *The Making of Southeast Asia*. Berkeley: University of California Press, 1966.

Doyle, Edward, and Samuel Lipsman. *Setting the Stage.* Boston: Boston Publishing Company, 1981.

Duiker, William J. *The Rise of Nationalism in Vietnam 1900–1941.* Ithaca, NY: Cornell University Press, 1976.

Foster, Harry L. *A Beachcomber in the Orient.* London: John Lane, The Bodley Head, 1923.

Great Britain. *Indo-China.* London: Naval Intelligence, 1943.

Hammer, Ellen J. *The Struggle for Indochina 1940–1955.* Stanford, CA: Stanford University Press, 1955.

Hickey, Gerald Cannon. *Kingdom in the Morning Mist: Mayrena in the Highlands of Vietnam.* Philadelphia: University of Pennsylvania Press, 1988.

Huu Ngoc. *Dictionary of Traditional Vietnam.* Hanoi: The Gioi, 1992.

Irving, R.E.M. *The First Indochina War: French and American Policy 1945–1954.* London: Cdroom Helm, 1975.

Lamb, Alistair. *The Mandarin Road to Old Hue.* London: Chatto & Windus, 1970.

Langlois, Walter G. *Andre Malraux: The Indochina Adventure.* New York: Praeger, 1965.

Lockhart, Bruce M. *The End of the Vietnamese Monarchy.* New Haven, CT: Yale University Press, 1993.

Marr, David G. *Vietnamese Anticolonialism 1885–1925.* Berkeley, CA: University of California Press, 1985.

McLeod, Mark W. *The Vietnamese Response to French Intervention 1862–1874.* New York: Praeger, 1991.

O'Ballance, Edgar. *The Indo-China War 1945–1954: A Study in Guerilla Warfare.* London: Faber & Faber, 1964.

Osborne, Roger. *The Deprat Affair: Ambition, Revenge and Deceit in French Indo-China.* London: Jonathan Cape, 1999.

Quinn-Judge, Sophie. *Ho Chi Minh: The Missing Years, 1919–1941.* Berkeley: University of California Press, 2002.

Sherry, Norman. *The Life of Graham Greene—Volume 2: 1939–1955.* London: Jonathan Cape, 1994.

Short, Anthony. *The Origins of the Vietnam War.* London: Longmans, 1989.

Taylor, Keith W. *The Birth of Vietnam.* Berkeley: University of California Press, 1983.

Thompson, Virginia. *French Indochina.* New York: Octagon, 1968.

Tuck, Patrick J. N. *French Catholic Missionaries and the Politics of Imperialism in Vietnam 1857–1914.* Liverpool: Liverpool University Press, 1987.

## VIETNAM 1945–1975

Blair, Anne. *Lodge in Vietnam: A Patriot Abroad.* New Haven, CT: Yale University Press, 1995.

Bouscaren, Anthony T. *The Last of the Mandarins: Diem of Vietnam.* Pittsburgh: Duquesne University Press, 1965.

Bowman, John S., ed. *The World Almanac of the Vietnam War.* New York: World Almanac, 1985.

Bui Tin. *Following Ho Chi Minh: Memoirs of a North Vietnamese Colonel.* Honolulu: University of Hawaii Press, 1995.

Cooper, Chester. *The Lost Crusade.* New York: Dodd, Mead, 1970.

Critchfield, Richard. *The Long Charade: Political Subversion in the Vietnam War.* New York: Harcourt, Brace & World, 1968.

Davidson, Phillip B. *Vietnam at War: The History 1946–1975.* Oxford: Oxford University Press, 1988.

Dommen, Arthur J. *The Indochinese Experience of the French and the Americans: Nationalism and Communism in Cambodia, Laos and Vietnam.* Bloomington: Indiana University Press, 2001.

Duiker, William J. *Ho Chi Minh.* New York: Hyperion, 2000.

———. *The Communist Road to Power in Vietnam.* Boulder, CO: Westview Press, 1981.

Fall, Bernard. *Hell in a very Small Place: The Siege of Dien Bien Phu.* London: Pall Mall Press, 1967.

———. *The Two Vietnams.* New York: Praeger, 1967.

———. *Vietnam Witness 1953–1966.* New York: Praeger, 1966.

Fitzgerald, Frances. *Fire in the Lake.* New York: Vintage, 1972.

Gettleman, Marvin E., ed. *Vietnam: History, Documents and Opinions.* New York: Fawcett, 1965.

Havens, Thomas R. H. *Fire across the Sea: The Vietnam War and Japan 1965–1975.* Princeton: Princeton University Press, 1987.

Herr, Michael. *Dispatches.* New York: Knopf, 1977.

Hilsman, Roger. *To Move a Nation.* New York: Doubleday, 1969.

Isaacs, Arnold R. *Without Honor: Defeat in Vietnam and Cambodia.* Baltimore: John Hopkins University Press, 1983.

Kahin, George M. and John W. Lewis. *The United States in Vietnam.* New York: Delta, 1967.

Kolko, Gabriel, *Anatomy of a War: Vietnam, the United States and the Modern Historical Experience.* New York: Pantheon, 1985.

Kosut, Hal. *Cambodia and the Vietnam War.* New York: Facts on File, 1971.

Lacouture, Jean. *Ho Chi Minh: A Political Biography.* New York: Random House, 1968.

Leepson, Marc. *Dictionary of the Vietnam War.* New York: Webster's New World, 1999.

Marr, David G. *Vietnam 1945: The Quest for Power.* Berkeley: University of California Press, 1995.

McNamara, Robert S. *In Retrospect: The Tragedy and Lessons of Vietnam.* New York: Vintage Books, 1996.

McNeill, Ian G. *To Long Tan: The Australian Army and the Vietnam War 1950–1966.* Crows Nest, N.S.W., Australia: Allen & Unwin in association with the Australian War Memorial, 1993.

McNeill, Ian and Ashley Ekins. *On the Offensive: The Australian Army in the Vietnam War 1967–1968.* Crows Nest, N.S.W., Australia: Allen & Unwin in association with the Australian War Memorial, 2003.

Nguyen Cao Ky with Marvin J. Wolf. *Buddha's Child: My Fight to Save Vietnam.* New York: St. Martin's Press, 2002.

Nguyen Tien Hung and Jerrold L. Schecter. *The Palace File.* New York: Harper & Row, 1986.

Pike, Douglas. *Viet Cong: The Organization and Techniques of the National Liberation Front of South Vietnam.* Cambridge, MA: The M.I.T. Press, 1966.

Pike, Douglas. *War, Peace and the Viet Cong.* Cambridge, MA: The M.I.T. Press, 1969.

———. *A History of Vietnamese Communism 1925–1978.* Stanford, CA: Hoover Institution Press, 1978.

Salisbury, Harrison E. *Behind the Lines—Hanoi.* New York: Harper & Row, 1967.

Schlesinger, Arthur M. Jr. *The Bitter Heritage: Vietnam and American Democracy 1941–1966.* Boston: Houghton Mifflin, 1967.

Shaplen, Robert. *The Lost Revolution: The U.S. in Vietnam 1946–1966.* New York: Harper & Row, 1966.

Smith, Harvey H. et al. *Area Handbook for South Vietnam.* Washington, D.C.: Government Printing Office, 1967.

Snepp, Frank. *Decent Interval.* New York: Random House, 1977.

Thompson, Robert. *No Exit from Vietnam.* New York: McKay, 1969.

Tucker, Spencer C., ed. *Encyclopedia of the Vietnam War: A Political, Social & Military History.* Oxford, UK: ABC Clio, 1998.

Warner, Denis. *The Last Confucian.* New York: Macmillan, 1963.

———. *Not with Guns Alone.* London: Hutchinson, 1977.

Windrow, Martin. *The French Indochina War 1945–54.* London: Osprey Publishing, 1998.

## VIETNAM 1975 TO THE PRESENT DAY

Brown, Frederick Z. *Second Chance: The United States and Indochina in the 1990s.* New York: Council on Foreign Relations Press, 1989.

Burchett, Wilfred. *The China Cambodia Vietnam Triangle.* New York: Vanguard, 1979.

Chang, Pao-Min. *Kampuchea between China and Vietnam.* Singapore: Singapore University Press, 1985.

Duiker, William J. *Vietnam since the Fall of Saigon.* Athens: Ohio University, 1989.

Elliott, David W. P., ed. *The Third Indochina Conflict.* Boulder, CO: Westview Press, 1981.

Evans, Grant and Kelvin Rowley. *Red Brotherhood at War.* London: Verso, 1990.

Gough, Kathleen. *Political Economy in Vietnam.* Meerut, India: Archana, 1990.

Klintworth, Gary. *Vietnam's Intervention in Cambodia in International Law.* Canberra: Australian Government Publishing Service, 1989.

Morris, Stephen J. *Why Vietnam Invaded Cambodia: Political Culture and the Causes of the War.* Stanford: Stanford University Press 1999.

Nguyen Van Canh. *Vietnam under Communism 1975–1982.* Stanford, CA: Hoover Institution Press, 1983.

Sheehan, Neil. *After the War Was Over: Hanoi and Saigon.* New York: Vintage Books, 1992.

## BIBLIOGRAPHIES

Burns, R. D. and Milton Leitenberg. *The Wars in Vietnam, Cambodia and Laos, 1945–1982.* Santa Barbara, CA: Clio, 1984.

Marr, David G., with Kristine Alilunas-Rodgers. *Vietnam.* Oxford: Clio, 1992.

# Index

Adams, Eddie (1933–2004; war photographer), 84–85

Agent Orange, 89, 105

Ainley, Henry (b. 1918; foreign legionnaire), 49

Alexander of Rhodes (1591–1660; missionary), 15

Alvarez, Santiago (1919–1998; Cuban filmmaker), 90

*The Ambassador*, novel, 70

"Amerasians," 113

Amnesty International, 123

Andreotta, Glenn U. (1947–1968; U.S. soldier), 118

An Duong (king, 3rd century B.C.E.), 3

Ang Mei (Queen of Cambodia, 1835–1847), 17, 18

Arnett, Peter (b. 1934; war correspondent), 81

Asia Pacific Economic Cooperation, 124

Associated State of Vietnam, 46

Association for Marxist Studies, 43

Association of Southeast Asian Nations, 110, 115, 118, 121

Au Co (legendary figure), 2–3

Au Lac kingdom, 3

Auriol, Vincent (1884–1966; French president), 46

Australia, involvement in Vietnam War, 82–83, 94, 100

Au Viet kingdom, 3

Bach Dang, battle of, 6

Bac Son culture, 2

Ba Cut (d. 1956; sect leader), 59

Badcoe, Peter John (1934–1967; Australian soldier), 83

Ball, George (1909–1994; U.S. politician), 70

Bao Dai (1913–1997; emperor 1926–1945), 34–36, 40, 41, 46, 48, 59

"Bao Dai" Solution (1947), 46

Bao Ninh (b. 1952; novelist), 113

Bay Vien (d. 1972; gangster leader), 59

Bazé, William (b. 1899-c1980s; elephant hunter), 48

Beaumont, Jean, Comte de (1904–2002; French businessman), 52

Becker, Elizabeth (b. 1947; U.S. journalist), 107

Bidault, Georges (1899–1983; French politician), 44

Bigart, Homer (1907–1991; war correspondent), 81

Binh Xuyen gangsters, 43, 48, 59

Blum, Léon (1872–1950; French politician), 36

"Boat People," 106

Bokassa, Jean-Bebel (1921–1996; soldier, later politician), 49

Brinks Hotel Bombing (1964), 75

Bronze Age. See Dong Son period

Brooke, James (1803–1868; Rajah of Sarawak 1841–1868), 27

Bui Tin (b. 1927; DRV colonel), 101

Bundy, McGeorge (1919–1996; U.S. politician), 73

Bunker, Ellsworth (1894–1984; U.S. ambassador), 98

Burdick, Eugene (1918–1965; U.S. writer), 59

Bush, George H. W. (b. 1924; U.S. president), 117

Bush, George W. (b. 1946; U.S. president), 126

Caldwell, Malcolm (1931–1978; academic), 107

Calley, William L. (b. 1943; U.S. soldier), 85–86

Cambodia, relations with, 12, 17, 18, 20, 79, 81, 90, 93–94, 106–10, 113, 115–16

Canh Thinh (ruler, 1792–1802), 13

Can Lao (Personalist Labor Party), 63, 67

Can Vuong Movement (1886–1888), 23–24

Cao Dai sect, 42, 61

Carter, Jimmy (b. 1924; U.S. president), 104

Castries, Christian de (1902–1991; French general), 52–53, 54

Catroux, Georges (1877–1969; governor-general), 36

Cédile, Jean (1908–1984; French army officer), 42

Champa, kingdom of, 5–6, 7, 8, 10, 12

Charner, Léonard Victor Joseph (1797–1869; French admiral), 20

Chasseloup-Laubat, Justin de (1805–1873; French politician), 20

Chennault, Claire L. (1890–1958; U.S. pilot), 37

Chinese influences and rule, 2–6, 11; civilians, 106; invasion of Vietnam (1979), 108; relations, 115–16, 120–21

Chin Shih Huang Ti (Chinese emperor 221–210 B.C.E.), 3

Christian missionaries, 15–16, 20

Churchill, Winston S. (1874–1965; British prime minister), 54

Cline, Ray S. (1918–1996; U.S. official), 74

Clinton, Bill (b. 1946; U.S. president), 117–18, 122
Coa Loa (ancient capital), 3
Cochinchina, Autonomous Republic of, 44
Colburn, Lawrence (fl. 1968; U.S. soldier), 118
Communist Party of Vietnam, 41, 111–13
Conein, Lucien E. (1919–1998; U.S. agent), 59, 70, 71–72
Confucian ideas, 4–5, 8, 17
Conway, Thomas de (1733–1800; French governor), 16
Cu Chi Tunnels, 81, 125
Cuong De (1882–1951; Marquess), 32, 40

Danang (Tourane), 16, 19, 20, 99, 124
Dao Duy Tung (1922–1998; SRV politician), 119
D'Argenlieu, Georges-Thierry (1889–1964; French administrator), 44, 45
Decoux, Jean (1884–1963; governor-general), 36
Dellinger, David (1915–2004; U.S. protest leader), 87
De Min (legendary ruler), 2
Denard, Bob (1929–2007; French soldier), 49
Deprat, Jacques (1880–1935; French geologist), 34
Dewey, Peter A. (1917–1945; U.S. army officer), 43
Dien Bien Phu, Battle of (1954), 50, 52–54, 111
Dinh Bo Linh (ruler, 966–979), 6
Dinh Nho Liem (SRV politician), 115
*Doi Muoi*, 112–13, 115

Do Muoi (b. 1917; SRV politician), 116–17, 119, 120, 122
Dong Khanh (1864–1889; emperor, 1885–1889), 27
Dong Son period, 2
Doumer, Paul (1857–1932; French colonial administrator), 25, 27
Downes, Alan C. (1928–1996; war correspondent), 95
Duc Duc (1852–1883; emperor, 1883), 21–22
Dudman, Richard (b. 1918; U.S. journalist), 107
Dulles, John Foster (1888–1959; U.S. politician), 53
Duong Dinh Nghe (governor, 10th century C.E.), 6
Duong Tam Kha (king, 945–951), 6
Duong Thu Huong (b. 1947; novelist), 113
Duong Van Minh (1916–2001; RVN president, 1963–1964, 1964, 1975), 71, 74, 94,-95, 100–01, 102
Dupuis, Jean (1829–1912; French merchant), 21
Durbrow, Elbridge (1903–1997; U.S. ambassador), 66
Duy Tan (1900–1945; emperor, 1907–1916), 29–30, 36–37
Dynasties: Early Le dynasty, 7; Earlier Ly dynasty, 5; Ho dynasty, 10–11; Later Ly dynasty, 7–9; Le dynasty, 11; Mac dynasty, 12–13; Ngo dynasty, 6–7; Nguyen dynasty, 13–41; Tay Son dynasty, 13; Tran dynasty, 9–10

Eden, Anthony (1897–1977; British politician), 54

Eisenhower, Dwight D. (1890–
  1969; U.S. president), 54, 55,
  66
Elford, George Robert (author),
  49
Escoffier, G. Auguste (1846–1935;
  London chef), 33

Far Eastern Conference (Geneva,
  1954), 54–55
Fenwick, Millicent (1910–1992;
  U.S. politician), 98
Ferry, Jules (1832–1893; French
  prime minister), 21
Fonda, Jane (b. 1937; actress), 96
Ford, Gerald (1913–2007; U.S.
  president), 98, 104
Foster, Harry L. (1894–1932; U.S.
  traveler), 34
France, relations with, 16, 18, 19–
  24, 25–37, 39–55, 100, 104–5
Free School of Tonkin, 32
French Colonial Rule, 25–55;
  colonial administration, 25–27

Garnier, Francis (1839–1873;
  French explorer), 21
Garvey, Marcus (1887–1940; Black
  nationalist), 33
Gaulle, Charles de (1890–1970;
  French politician), 36, 39, 41,
  42
Geneva Agreement (1954), 54–55,
  60
Giac Chia Voi Rebellion (1866),
  19
Gia Long (1762–1820; Nguyen
  Anh, emperor 1802–1820), 13,
  15–17
Gilpatric, Roswell L. (1906–1996;
  U.S. politician), 70
Goldwater, Barry M. (1909–1998;
  U.S. politician), 74

Gorbachev, Mikhail (b. 1931;
  Soviet politician), 115
Gore, Al (b. 1948; U.S.
  vice-president), 118
Gracey, Douglas (1894–1964;
  British army officer), 42, 43
Grandière, Pierre Paul Marie
  Benoît de la(1807–1876;
  French admiral), 21
Great Depression, 30–31, 36
Greene, Graham (1904–1991;
  British writer), 59
Grey, Anthony (b. 1938; British
  author), 30
Gulf of Tonkin Incident, 74

Haiphong Incident (1946), 45
Halberstam, David (1934–2007;
  war correspondent), 81
Ha Long Bay Agreements (1946,
  1947), 46
Ham Nghi (1871–1943; emperor,
  1884–1885), 23–24, 27, 60
Hang Lang (prince, 10th
  century), 6
Hang Lien (prince, d. 979), 6–7
Hang Toan (ruler, 979–980), 7
Hanoi, 7, 9, 12, 21, 25, 27, 31, 33,
  34, 39, 40, 41–43, 45–46, 48,
  51, 55, 61, 64, 66, 88
Hanoi Hilton. *See* Hoa Lo prison
Hanoi Medical School, 31
Harmand Treaty (1883), 22
Heng Samrin (b. 1934;
  Cambodian leader), 107, 109
Hersh, Seymour (b. 1937; war
  correspondent), 81
Hiep Hoa (1847–1883; emperor,
  1883), 22–23
Hilsman, Roger (b. 1919; U.S.
  politician), 70, 73
Hoa Binh culture, 2
Hoa Hao sect, 42, 59

Hoa Lo prison, 89
Hoang Co Minh (1935–1987; RVN admiral), 111
Ho Chi Minh (1930–1969; nationalist and communist), 33, 37, 41–42, 43–45, 47, 48, 61–62, 64, 90–91
Ho Chi Minh City, 103, 120. *See also* Saigon, prior to 1976
Ho Chi Minh Trail, 79–80, 88, 93–94, 104
Hoffman, Abbie (1936–1989; U.S. anarchist), 87
Ho Han Thuong (ruler, 1400–1407), 11
Hoi An, 15, 124
Hong Bao (1825–1854; prince), 19
Ho Quy Ly (ruler, 1400), 10–11
Ho Tan Quyen (d. 1963; RVN navy captain), 71–72
Hotels: Brinks Hotel, 81; Caravelle Hotel, 81; Continental Palace Hotel, 81; Hotel Métropole (Hanoi), 34; Majestic Hotel, 81; Rex Hotel, 81
Ho Van Minh (b. 1936; RVN politician), 94
Hue, 13, 16, 84; Imperial Palace, 16; as a tourist site, 124–25
Humphrey, Hubert H. (1911–1978; U.S. politician), 86–87
Hung Bang dynasty, 3
Hun Sen (b. 1951; Cambodian leader), 107, 109
Huynh Tan Phat (1913–1989; NFL politician), 90, 101, 102

Indochina Communist Party, 33, 43
*Indochine*, film, 30
Indrapura, 7
International Monetary Fund, 118, 123

*Jaunissement*, 50
Jiang Zemin (b. 1926; Chinese president), 121
John, Colin (fl. 1952; foreign legionnaire), 49
Johnson, Lyndon B. (1908–1973; U.S. president), 74–75, 81, 83, 86–87, 122

Karnow, Stanley (b. 1925; U.S. journalist and writer), 43, 45, 74
Kennedy, John F. (1917–1963; U.S. president), 58, 66, 69, 73
Kennedy, Robert F. (1925–1968; U.S. politician), 86–87
Kent State University, 94
Khai Dinh (1885–1925; emperor, 1916–1925), 30, 34
Khe Sanh, Siege of, 79, 83; as tourist site, 124
Khmer Krom, 13, 17, 123
Khmer Rouge, 107
Khrushchev, Nikita (1894–1971; Soviet leader), 73
Kien Phuc (1869–1884; emperor 1883–1884), 23
King, Martin Luther (1929–1968; civil rights leader), 86–87
Kissinger, Henry A. (b. 1923; U.S. politician), 88, 96–97, 100
Kitt, Eartha (b. 1927; actress), 87
Korea, South, involvement in Vietnam War, 82, 100
Kublai Khan (Chinese emperor, 1260–1294), 9

Lac Long Quang (legendary figure), 2–3
Lansdale, Edward (1908–1987; U.S. agent), 59
Lattre de Tassigny, Jean de (1889–1952; French commander), 47, 60

Le Chien Tong (prince, fl, 1786), 13

Lederer, William (b. 1912; U.S. writer), 59

Le Duan (1908–1986; SRV politician), 36, 98, 111, 112

Le Duc Anh (b. 1920; SRV politician), 118–19, 120, 121, 122

Le Duc Tho (1911–1990; DRV politician), 96–97

Lefebvre, Dominique (1810–1865; missionary), 18–19

Legal codes: Hong Duc Code, 12; Gia Long Code, 17

Le Hien Tong (ruler, 1740–1786), 13

Le Hoan (ruler, 980–1005), 7

Lehrer, Tom (b. 1928; U.S. singer and satirist), 97

Le Kha Phieu (b. 1931; SRV politician), 120, 121, 122

Le Loi (ruler, 1428–1433), 11

Le Long Binh (ruler, 1005–1009), 7

Le Mai (1940–1996; SRV politician), 119

LeMay, Curtis E. (1906–1990; U.S. general), 86

Le Minh Dao (b. 1933; RVN general), 99–100

Le Quang Tung (1923–1963; RVN soldier), 71

Le Quoc Tuy (former RVN soldier), 111

Le Thai To (ruler, 1433–1442), 11

Le Thanh Ton (ruler, 1460–1497), 12

Le Van Duyet (1763–1832; official), 18, 79

Le Van Khoi (d. 1834; official), 18

Liddell Hart, Adrian J. (1922–1991; foreign legionnaire), 49

Lin, Maya (b. 1959; architect), 117

Loc Duc (legendary figure), 2

Lodge, Henry Cabot (1902–1985; U.S. ambassador), 69, 71–72

Long Tan, Battle of (1966), 82

Lon Nol (1913–1985; Cambodian leader), 93

Lu Han (1896–1974; Chinese general), 43

Ly Anh Tong (ruler, 1137–1174), 8

Ly Bi (anti-Chinese rebel, 6th century C.E.), 5

Ly Cao Tong (ruler, 1174–1210), 8–9

Ly Chieu Hoang (Phat Kim, ruler, 1224–1225), 9

Ly Dao Thanh (mandarin, 11th century), 8

Ly Hue Tong (ruler, 1210–1224), 9

Ly Nhan Tong (ruler, 1072–1127), 8

Ly Thai Thong (Ly Phat Ma, ruler, 1028–1054), 7–8

Ly Thai To (Ly Cong Uan, ruler, 1009–1028), 7

Ly Than Tong (ruler, 1127–1137), 8

Ly Thanh Tong (ruler, 1054–1072), 8

Ly Thuong Kiet (1030–1105; mandarin), 8

Mac Dang Dung (ruler, 1527–1530), 12

Macdonald, Malcolm (1901–1981; British writer and official), 34

Mac Mao Hop (ruler, 1562–1592), 12

Mai Huu Xuan (RVN general, fl. 1963), 72–73

Malenkov, Georgy M. (1902–1988; Soviet leader), 62

Malraux, André (1901–1976; French socialist and writer), 34

Mao Zedong (1893–1976; Chinese leader), 62

Marie I of Sedang. *See* Mayréna, Charles

Martin, Graham A (1912–1990; U.S. ambassador), 98

Ma Tuyen (Chinese merchant, fl. 1963), 72

Maugham, W. Somerset (1874–1965; British writer), 34

Mayréna, Charles (born Charles David, 1842–1890; "Emperor Marie I of Sedang"), 27–28

Ma Yuan (Chinese general, 1st century C.E.), 5

McCain, John (b. 1936; U.S. soldier), 89

McCarthy, Eugene J. (1916–2005; U.S. politician), 83, 86–87

McCarthy, Mary (1912–1989; U.S. writer), 96

McGovern, George S. (b. 1922; U.S. politician), 95–96

McNamara, Robert S. (b. 1916; U.S. Secretary of State), 66

Mears, Walter R. (b. 1935; U.S. journalist), 87

Mekong River Expedition (1866), 21

Mendès-France, Pierre (1907–1982; French politician), 51, 54–55

Menzies, Robert G. (1894–1978; Australian prime minister), 82

Messmer, Pierre (1916–2007; French politician), 42

Minh Mang (1791–1841; emperor, 1820–1841), 17–18

"Missing in Action" (MIAs), 117

Mongol invasions of Vietnam (1279 and 1287), 9–10

Montagnards, 123

Montmorin, Comte Armand de (1744–1792 French foreign minister), 16

Mordant, Eugène (1885–1959; French general), 40

Mounier, Emmaniel (1905–1950; French philosopher), 67

Muong tribesmen, 13

My Lai massacre, 85

Nam Cam scandal (2002), 122

Nam Viet ("Southern Viet") kingdom, 3

Napalm, use of, 95

Napoleon III of France, 19–21

National Front for the Liberation of South Vietnam (NFL), 64, 65–67

Navarre Plan, 47–48

Navarre, Henri (1898–1983; French commander), 47–48, 52

New Zealand, involvement in Vietnam War, 82, 100

Nghe An Uprising (1956), 62

Ngo Dinh Can (1911–1963; politician), 58, 68

Ngo Dinh Diem (1901–1963; RVN president 1955–1963), 35, 57–59, 62–64, 65–73, 125

Ngo Dinh Kha (headmaster, father of Ngo Dinh Diem), 31–32

Ngo Dinh Khoi (d. 1945; politician), 48, 58, 60

Ngo Dinh Luyen (1914–1990; diplomat), 58–59, 68

Ngo Dinh Nhu (1910–1963; RVN politician), 58, 67, 68, 70–73

Ngo Dinh Thuc (1897–1984; Bishop of Hue), 58, 68

Ngo Quyen (king 939–945), 6

Ngo Van Chieu (1878–?; sect leader), 61

Nguyen Ai Quoc. *See* Ho Chi Minh

Nguyen Cao Ky (b. 1930; RVN vice-president 1967–1971), 76, 78, 84, 94–95, 100

Nguyen Chi Thanh (1914–1967; PLAF soldier), 112

Nguyen Co Thach (1923–1998; SRV politician), 111–12, 120

Nguyen Dy (1765–1820; writer), 104

Nguyen Hue (Quang Trung, ruler, 1788–1792), 13, 79

Nguyen Huu Tho (1910–1996; SRV politician), 65, 90

Nguyen Huy Thiep (b. 1950; novelist), 113

Nguyen Khanh (b. 1927; president 1964), 74

Nguyen Kim (d. 1545; official), 12

Nguyen Minh Triet (b. 1942; SRV president 2006–), 126

Nguyen Ngoc Loan (1932–1998; RVN general), 84–85

Nguyen Phan Long (1889–1960; SVN politician), 47

Nguyen Sinh Sac (b. 1929; father of Ho Chi Minh), 32–33

Nguyen Tan Dung (b. 1949; SRV prime minister 2006–), 126

Nguyen Thai Hoc (1904–1930; nationalist), 35, 60

Nguyen Tuong Tam (1906–1963; politician), 44

Nguyen Van Hinh (fl. 1955; army commander), 47, 59

Nguyen Van Lem (d. 1968; PLAF soldier), 84

Nguyen Van Linh (1915–1998; politician), 112

Nguyen Van Ly (b. 1946; priest), 123

Nguyen Van Tam (1895–?; SVN politician), 47

Nguyen Van Thieu (1923–2001; RVN president 1968–1975), 72, 76, 77–78, 89, 94–95, 97, 100

Nguyen Van Thinh (1884–1946; politician), 45

Nguyen Van Thuan, François Xavier (1928–2002; Cardinal), 122

Nguyen Van Tuong (Regent, fl. 1884), 23

Nguyen Van Xuan (1892–1989; politician), 47

Nhu, Madame. *See* Tran Le Xuan

Nixon, Richard M. (1913–1994; U.S. president), 83, 86–88, 89–90, 94, 96–98, 122

Nixon Doctrine (Guam Doctrine), 89–90

Nolting, Frederick (1911–1989; U.S. ambassador), 66, 69

Nong Duc Manh (b. 1940; SRV politician), 122

Nung tribal people, 8

Olympic Games, 111

Ono, Eisuke (banker, father of Yoko Ono), 36

Operation Bravo I and II (1963), 71

Operation Castor (1954), 50

Operation Frequent Wind (1975), 101

Operation Rolling Thunder, 75

Oufkir, Mohammed (1920–1972; soldier, later politician), 49

Paleolithic era, 1

Paris Peace Accord (1973), 96–97, 120

Partition of Vietnam (1954), 55, 57

Patenotre Treaty (1884), 23

Pathet Lao, 106
Patti, Archimedes L. A. (1913–1998; U.S. soldier), 42
Payne, Keith (b. 1933; Australian soldier), 83
Pen Sovan (b. 1936; Cambodian leader), 109
People's Liberation Armed Forces (PLAF), 66, 68, 69, 73, 79, 81, 84, 101
Percival, John (1779–1862; U.S. naval captain), 19
Personalism, 67
Peterson, Douglas (b. 1935; U.S. ambassador), 119
Pham Du (rebel, fl. 1208–10), 9
Pham Hung (1912–1988; politician), 112
Pham Tuan (b. 1947; cosmonaut), 110
Pham Van Dong (1908–2000; DRV/SRV prime minister), 48–49, 102
Phan Boi Chau (1867–1940; nationalist), 32
Phan Chu Trinh (1872–1926; nationalist), 32, 51
Phan Dinh Phung (1847–1895; nationalist), 24
Phan Huy Quat (1909–1979; RVN politician), 82
Phan Khac Suu (1905–1970; RVN president), 78
Phan Thi Kim Phuc (b. 1963; civilian), 95
Phan Van Khai (b. 1933; SRV prime minister 1997–2006), 119–20, 121–22, 124
Philippines, involvement in Vietnam War, 82
Phomvihan, Kaysone (1920–1992; Laotian leader), 107
Phung Nguyen culture, 2

Pigneau de Béhaine, Pierre-Joseph (1741–1799; missionary), 15–16
Piroth, Charles (1906–1954; French officer), 52
Pol Pot (1925–1998; Cambodian leader), 106
Portuguese influences, 15
Potsdam Agreement (1945), 41
Poulo Condore, 20; prison, 35, 112
Proclamation of Independence (1945), 41–42
Provisional Revolutionary Government of the Republic of Vietnam, 90
Putin, Vladimir (b. 1952; Russian leader), 122

Quayle, Dan (b. 1947; U.S. vice-president), 118
*The Quiet American* (novel), 59
Quoc Cuong Nguyen (Olympian, fl. 1988), 111
Quoc Hoc (National Academy, Hue), 31, 32
Quoc Tu Giam (Imperial Academy), 31

Radford, Arthur (1896–1973; U.S. admiral), 53–54
Reagan, Ronald (1911–2004; U.S. president), 104, 117
Republic of Vietnam, proclamation, 60
Revolutionary Youth League of Vietnam, 33
Rigault de Genouilly, Charles (1807–1873; French admiral), 20
Rivière, Henri (1827–1883; French captain), 21
Roman Catholicism, 31–32

Rousseau, Armand (1835–1896; French governor-general 1895–1896), 60

Roussel de Courcy, Philippe Marie Henri (1827–1887; French general), 23

Rubin, Jerry (1938–1994; U.S. protest leader), 87

Rusk, Dean (1909–1994; U.S. politician), 70

Saigon, 12, 20, 84

Sainteny, Jean (1907–1978; French representative), 44

Salan, Raoul (1899–1984; French commander), 47

Sarraut, Albert (1872–1962; French colonial administrator), 25, 27, 36

Sheehan, Neil (b. 1936; war correspondent), 81

Sihanouk, Norodom (b. 1922; Cambodian leader), 79, 89–90, 93, 108

Simpson, Rayene Stewart (1926–1978; Australian soldier), 83

Snepp, Frank W. (b. 1943; U.S. agent), 88

Soc Trang province, 12

Soglo, Christophe (1909–1983; soldier, later politician), 49

Souphanouvong, Prince (1909–1995; Laotian leader), 107

South East Asia Games, 123

Southeast Asia Treaty Organization, 58, 82

Soviet Union, relations with, 33, 46, 50, 61, 73, 104, 108

Spain, involvement in Vietnam War, 82

Spellman, Francis (1889–1967; U.S. Cardinal), 58

Spratly Islands, 120–21, 122

Strategic Hamlets Program, 67–68

Sun Yat-sen (1886–1925; Chinese nationalist), 32

Su Ting (Chinese administrator, 1st century C.E.), 5

Tam Assoa, François Xavier (d. 1934; Vicar Apostolic), 72

Tang Jiaxuan (b. 1938; Chinese politician), 120

Tay Ninh, 61, 123

Tay Son Rebellion (1771–1802), 13

Temple of Literature (Hanoi), 8

Tet Offensive, 83

Thailand, involvement in Vietnam War, 82, 100; relations with, 109, 110

Thai Nguyen Rebellion (1917), 35

Thanh Thai (1879–1959; emperor, 1889–1907), 27, 29

Thich Nhat Hanh (b. 1926; Buddhist activist), 123

Thich Quang Duc (1897/1907–1963; monk), 69, 125

Thien Mu Pagoda (Hue), 30

Thien Tu Binh (Imperial Guard), 8

Thieu Tri (1807–1847; emperor, 1841–1847), 18–19

Thi Sach (nobleman, 1st century C.E.), 5

Thompson, Hugh C. (1943–2006; U.S. soldier), 85, 118

Thuc Phan, 3

Thu Van (PLAF camerawomen, fl. 1975), 99

Tiira, Ensio (fl. 1953; foreign legionnaire), 49

Ton Duc Thang (1888–1980; DRV president 1969–1976), 36, 91, 102, 104

Tonkin Gulf Resolution, 74
Ton That Dinh (b. 1926; RVN general), 71–72
Ton That Thuyet (1835–1913; official), 22–24
Tourism, 117, 121, 122, 124–25
Tran Anh Tong (ruler, 1293–1314), 10
Tran Duc Luong (b. 1937; SRV president 1997–2006), 119–20
Tran Du Tong (ruler, 1341–1369), 10
Tran Hien Tong (ruler, 1329–1341), 10
Tran Hung Dao (1226–1300; general), 79
Tran Le Xuan, "Mme Nhu," (b. 1924; RVN politician), 67, 68
Tran Ming Tong (ruler, 1314–1329), 10
Tran Nghe Tong (ruler, 1370–1372), 10
Tran Ngoc Chau (RVN politician), 89
Tran Nhan Tong (ruler, 1278–1293), 9–10
Tran Thai Tong (ruler, 1225–1258), 9
Tran Thanh Tong (ruler, 1258–1278), 9
Tran Thu Kim Chi (SRV first lady, fl. 2006), 126
Tran Thien Khiem (b. 1925; RVN prime minister), 78
Tran Thu Do (courtier, fl. 1225), 9
Tran Thuan Tong (ruler, 1388–1398), 10
Tran Truong Kim (1882–1953; SVN politician), 40
Tran Van Chuong (1898–1986; diplomat), 59
Tran Van Do (1904–1990; foreign minister), 59

Tran Van Don (b. 1917; general), 59, 71, 100
Tran Van Huong (1903–1982; RVN president 1975), 82, 101, 102
Tran Van Huu (1896–1984; SVN politician), 47
Tran Xuan Bach (1924–2006; SRV politician), 116
Trieu Da (Chinese commander, 3rd century B.C.E.), 3
Trieu Quang Phuc (rebel commander, 6th century C.E.), 5
Trinh, Eugene Huu-Chau (b. 1950; cosmonaut), 118
Truman, Harry S. (1884–1972; U.S. president), 46–47
Trung sisters (Trung Trac and Trung Nghi), 5, 63
Truong Chinh (1907–1988; SRV politician), 36, 62, 111–12, 115
Truong Vinh Le (b. 1914; RVN politician), 94
Tu Duc (1829–1883; emperor, 1847–1883), 19–21

*The Ugly American* (novel), 59
United Kingdom, 100
United States involvement in Vietnam War, 47, 53–54; deployment of ground troops, 75–76

Van Tien Dung (1917–2002; DRV general), 98–100
Vèrges, Jacques (b. 1925; French lawyer), 51
Viet Nam Quoc Dan Dang, 35, 43, 60
Vietnam Liberation Army, 41
Vietnam Veterans Memorial (Washington, D.C.), 117
Vietnam Workers' Party, 73

Vijaya, 7, 11–12
Vo Chi Cong (b. 1913; SRV politician)
Vo Dai Ton (former RVN soldier), 111
Vo Nguyen Giap (b. 1912; SRV general), 50–51, 53
Vo Suu (war correspondent, fl. 1968), 84
Vo Van Kiet (b. 1922; SRV politician), 116, 120, 122
Vu Khoan (b. 1936; SRV politician), 120
Vuong Quang Nhuong (SVN politician), 37
Vuong Van Dong (soldier, fl. 1960), 63

Walewski, Comte Alexander (1810–1868; French foreign minister), 20
Wallace, George C. (1919–1998; U.S. politician), 86, 87, 95
Watergate incident, 95, 98

West, Morris (1916–1999; Australian novelist), 70
Westmoreland, William (1914–2005; U.S. commander), 83
Wheatley, Kevin Arthur (1937–1965; Australian soldier), 83
White, John (U.S. shipping captain, fl. 1820), 18
World War I, 29, 33, 34
World War II, 36–42
Wu Ti (Chinese emperor 141–87 B.C.E.), 3

Xuan Loc, Battle of (1975), 99–100

Yen Bay Mutiny (1930), 35
Yung Lo (Chinese emperor 1402–1424), 11

Zerbo, Saye (b. 1932; soldier, later politician), 49
Zhou Enlai (1898–1976; Chinese politician), 54

## About the Author

JUSTIN CORFIELD is a teacher of history and international studies at Geelong Grammar School. He is the author of *Encyclopedia of Singapore* (2006).

## Other Titles in the Greenwood Histories of the Modern Nations
*Frank W. Thackeray and John E. Findling, Series Editors*

The History of Afghanistan
*Meredith L. Runion*

The History of Argentina
*Daniel K. Lewis*

The History of Australia
*Frank G. Clarke*

The History of the Baltic States
*Kevin O'Connor*

The History of Brazil
*Robert M. Levine*

The History of Canada
*Scott W. See*

The History of Central America
*Thomas Pearcy*

The History of Chile
*John L. Rector*

The History of China
*David C. Wright*

The History of Congo
*Didier Gondola*

The History of Cuba
*Clifford L. Staten*

The History of Egypt
*Glenn E. Perry*

The History of Ethiopia
*Saheed Adejumobi*

The History of Finland
*Jason Lavery*

The History of France
*W. Scott Haine*

The History of Germany
*Eleanor L. Turk*

The History of Ghana
*Roger S. Gocking*

The History of Great Britain
*Anne Baltz Rodrick*

The History of Haiti
*Steeve Coupeau*

The History of Holland
*Mark T. Hooker*

The History of India
*John McLeod*

The History of Indonesia
*Steven Drakeley*

The History of Iran
*Elton L. Daniel*

The History of Iraq
*Courtney Hunt*

The History of Ireland
*Daniel Webster Hollis III*

The History of Israel
*Arnold Blumberg*

The History of Italy
*Charles L. Killinger*

The History of Japan
*Louis G. Perez*

The History of Korea
*Djun Kil Kim*

The History of Kuwait
*Michael S. Casey*

The History of Mexico
*Burton Kirkwood*

The History of New Zealand
*Tom Brooking*

The History of Nigeria
*Toyin Falola*

The History of Panama
*Robert C. Harding*

The History of Poland
*M.B. Biskupski*

The History of Portugal
*James M. Anderson*

The History of Russia
*Charles E. Ziegler*

The History of Saudi Arabia
*Wayne H. Bowen*

The History of Serbia
*John K. Cox*

The History of South Africa
*Roger B. Beck*

The History of Spain
*Peter Pierson*

The History of Sri Lanka
*Patrick Peebles*

The History of Sweden
*Byron J. Nordstrom*

The History of Turkey
*Douglas A. Howard*

The History of Venezuela
*H. Micheal Tarver and Julia C. Frederick*